Children at Risk

An Interdisciplinary Approach to Child Abuse and Neglect

Children at Risk

An Interdisciplinary Approach to Child Abuse and Neglect

Edited by

Renitta L. Goldman

and

Richard M. Gargiulo

pro·ed

8700 Shoal Creek Boulevard
Austin, Texas 78758

Printed in the United States of America

Library of Congress Cataloging-in-Publication Data

Children at risk: an interdisciplinary approach to child abuse and
   neglect / edited by Renitta L. Goldman and Richard M. Gargiulo.
        p.   cm.
     ISBN 0-89079-220-8
     1. Child abuse – United States.   2. Child molesting – United States.
   I. Goldman, Renitta L.   II. Gargiulo, Richard M.
   HV6626.5.C53   1990
   362.7'6'0973 – dc20   89-10984
                                                                CIP

pro·ed

8700 Shoal Creek Boulevard
Austin, Texas 78758

10 9 8 7 6 5 4 3 2 1   90 91 92 93 94

Contents

Contents

This book is dedicated to my husband,
Jay Goldman.

RLG

It is also dedicated to my daughters, Christina and Cara,
and to the memory of my father, Michael J. Gargiulo.

RMG

Preface

Child abuse, whether physical, mental, and/or sexual, persists in frightening numbers. The news media give almost daily account of victims and perpetrators throughout the United States. Explanations offered to account for this epidemic are often too simplistic to comprehend this multifaceted scourge on our society. Drugs, divorce, stress, and poor parenting are a few of the numerous variables commonly cited in dialogue about the causes of abuse. How do these variables interact to initiate and perpetuate abuse? How should we, in the caring professions, intervene? How can we stop abuse and prevent it in the future? The answers to these complex questions constitute our mission, one that is both awesome and crucial.

Chapters 1 and 2 orient the reader to the nature of abuse. How should it be properly defined, recognized, and reported? Educators occupy a unique role because they have an ongoing relationship in their work with children. Very young and special needs children are particularly at risk for abuse. Federal mandates are providing opportunities for educators to interact with children from birth onward.

Chapters 3, 4, and 5 address the role of helping professionals who are often involved *after* abuse has been disclosed. A practicing attorney presents the strengths and weaknesses of the legal system in chapter 3. The medical role is described in chapter 4 by an obstetrician/gynecologist who has worked with sexually abused victims for several years. The management of child abuse through the eyes of a social worker is also portrayed. Such relevant issues as family dynamics, treatment, and prevention are discussed in chapter 5.

The final two chapters, 6 and 7, reflect on the past and anticipate the future. They review previous community efforts and scientific research on preventing child abuse. Chapter 6 suggests what is needed to effectively activate people and resources. Chapter 7 concludes this important topic by showing how to conduct research that is sound and, therefore, truly meaningful.

In this book an interdisciplinary group of experienced professionals has come together to inform the practicing professional and the lay public about child abuse and neglect so as *to protect the child*.

Chapter 1

Child Abuse and Neglect: An Overview

Richard M. Gargiulo

Child abuse thrives in the shadows of privacy and secrecy. It lives by inattention.

David Bakan
Slaughter of the Innocents

In recent years child abuse and neglect has shocked the collective consciousness of our country. From our comfortable homes, we see abuse and neglect portrayed and characterized in made-for-television movies, hear about it on the evening news, read about it in our morning newspapers, and listen to the lyrics of popular songs on car radios about children who are beaten, starved, sexually exploited, and, in some instances, killed by adult caregivers. Unfortunately, most citizens do not know enough about child abuse and neglect and may not recognize it when they see it. How much do you know? Could you detect abuse and neglect when exposed to it? What would you do if you knew or suspected that:

- A father poured lighter fluid on his child's arm and lit it?
- A 42-month-old child had been beaten and sexually abused by a babysitter?
- A small child was kicked in the face for simply making a noise?
- A child was left alone in a locked car on a 90° summer day?
- A parent failed to regularly send her child to school?
- A mother refused to seek medical care for her children?

The preceding incidents are actual episodes of reported child abuse and neglect taken from the files of the Ohio Department of Public Welfare. Many of these victims were either infants or toddlers who could not talk or children too young or scared to seek help. Thus, as concerned professionals, it is our responsibility to help and protect these children.

Quiz Yourself

Q. *Many abused and neglected children become abusive and neglectful parents themselves.* True or False?

A. True. Parents frequently treat their children as they themselves were treated. Abuse and neglect tend to occur in successive generations often as a result of inappropriate parental role models and the absence of parenting skills and knowledge.

Q. *Perpetrators who sexually abused children are usually of low intelligence.* True or False?

A. False. According to Goldman and Wheeler (1986), few abusers manifest inferior intelligence. In fact, most perpetrators have average or above-average intelligence quotients.

Q. *If there is more than one child in the family, only one youngster is likely to be the target of abuse.* True or False?

A. True. Often a child who is perceived to be "special," "hard to manage," or "different," such as a handicapped child, is singled out for abuse. The child who is most vulnerable in the family is generally the victim. Many children, however, are abused for no apparent reason.

Q. *Sexual abuse and exploitation are indigenous to lower income and social status groups.* True or False?

A. False. This is a very common misconception. Sexually abusive families come from all social and income levels. Statistics gathered by the Federal Bureau of Investigation (Barry, 1984) suggest that incest, for example, more commonly occurs in middle-class families.

Q. *Professionals must possess hard data or evidence before contacting child protective service agencies.* True or False?

A. False. Certain professionals such as teachers, psychologists, and health care providers are mandated by law to report their suspicions of abuse and neglect. State reporting laws usually contain language such as "reason to believe" or "reasonably suspects" that abuse and neglect has occurred. Information will be held in confidence and reporters, according to statute, are immune from civil or criminal liability if they acted in good faith.

Q. *Emotional abuse is the easiest form of abuse to detect.* True or False?

A. False. Identifying a victim of emotional abuse is very difficult. Psychological maltreatment is subtle, cumulative, and illusive. The consequences of emotional abuse may not manifest themselves for several years. Actually emotional injury to a child may be more damaging than physical assault. The child's behavior is frequently the best indicator of emotional mistreatment.

Child Abuse — Personal Perspectives

The following three vignettes portray adult recollections of the trauma of child abuse. Hopefully, these accounts will help the reader appreciate the terrible consequences of abuse — not only for the victim but also the perpetrator.[1]

Verbal Abuse

"I used to think it was better than hitting them, but now I'm not so sure. Every day of my life I was beaten, sometimes by my mother, sometimes by my father, sometimes by both. I've said to myself, *At least I'm not doing that to my kids*. But more and more lately I've been thinking about what really hurt me the most. You know, for all those beatings, I don't have one broken bone left, not one bruise, maybe a few scars (actually quite a few scars), but they don't show much. The problem I have now is that I know I'm no good. I know that because my folks told me I was no good so often that I believed them. You don't hear that all the time and not grow up believing it. That's my problem now. And that's exactly what I'm doing to my kids. I'm making them think they're no good.

"So I think maybe verbal abuse is worse than physical abuse. At least the physical stops; the verbal just goes on and on in my head. It never stops. When I get uptight at my kids, or just uptight in general, when I lose control, the first thing I know I'm screaming at them. And I'm screaming every awful thing my parents ever said to me. Honest to God, the one thing I said I would never say is that they are whores, and every day I scream that at them. I open my mouth and out comes my mother. It's like I'm not even there. I don't even mean the stuff I say, I really don't even mean it. And sometimes afterwards I can't even remember what I was yelling about. I forget whatever it was, and I just yell and yell and yell. I'm so out of control then. Some days I can't even talk afterwards; I'm so hoarse I have to whisper. That's abuse, I know it is. It's abuse" (Herbruck, 1979, p. 21).

Emotional Abuse

"It's not fair, it's not fair, it's not fair! I washed that floor all morning; it took me three hours. I washed it on my knees. I always do it that way. And I waxed it the same way. Now he's gone and thrown his cracker on the floor. He's out to drive me crazy. I know he is. I don't even like him to eat between meals, but he kept saying he was hungry. I gave him a cracker and look what happened. He has no respect for me. He doesn't care what I go through. He only thinks of himself. He has got to learn some respect.

"His father says I don't love the boy. I take care of him, what more does he want? His clothes are clean and neat; at least I try to keep them that way. He's a very malicious child, though; he rips his clothes just to make it harder for me.

"Right now he's sitting on the couch in the other room. He'll sit there until bedtime and that might teach him something. He had no business being so clumsy

[1] From *Breaking the Cycle of Child Abuse* (pp. 21, 22–24, 29–30) by C. Herbruck, 1979, New York: Harper & Row. Copyright 1979 by Harper & Row. Reprinted by permission.

with that cracker. I've told him over and over again not to spill things and not to make messes. His father says I'm too hard on him, that what he does is just an accident. How long am I suppose to put up with accidents? He'll stop having them when I teach him not to. He's four years old and that's old enough to learn. Actually, he's not quite four, but he will be. I'm not going to have him messing up the house for the next ten years. He's going to learn better.

"He's in there crying again. I told him not to cry, and he was pretty good for the first two hours, but now he's up to his old tricks. He's going to drive me crazy, which is exactly what he wants. He says he wants a toy. Well, if I let him have a toy, he'll just throw that around, too. I told him until he learns to be more careful, he's not getting any toys. I put them all away a week ago, when he didn't pick them up.

"When his father gets home, he'll spoil him and let him off the couch. He's always working against me. Whatever I do or say, he does the opposite. He says I don't love the boy. I take care of him. He's been with us ever since one month after we were married. I thought we wouldn't have to have him for at least two years. He isn't even my child; he's his!

"It's been bad for us since day one, and it's gone downhill from there. I thought that when I got married I'd finally be happy. My parents were both alcoholics. They never had any time to take care of me. They weren't even home. I did everything in our house, not only for myself but also for my kid brother. They had him, and that was it. Even when he first came home from the hospital, I was the one who had to get up and feed him in the middle of the night. I kept him in my room. I had to dress him and feed him. I stayed home from school at least once a week to clean the house. It could have been a pigsty as far as they were concerned.

"My brother had terrible asthma, and sometimes I'd have to take him to the hospital. Then when we got home, I would get beaten for taking him. But he had to be taken care of, and they weren't going to do it. It was bad when they beat me, but then it was worse because they would beat him, too. That would make his asthma even worse, and then I'd have to hold him in my bed all night long. I won't have this kid in my bed, not ever.

"Yesterday morning he was eating his cereal with his fingers. It was disgusting. I won't waste money on milk for him to leave in his bowl any more, but still you wouldn't think he'd have to eat like an animal. So I said, 'Okay, you want to act like an animal, I'll treat you like an animal.' I gave him the cat dish on the floor and now he has to eat his meals out of it on the floor. If he's going to act like an animal, he'll get treated like an animal.

"But his father will say I'm to hard on him. His father would give in to him all the time. He never does anything to correct him. He says it's because he feels so bad that the boy was beaten by his real mother. It's more than that, though. He's afraid to correct him, afraid to tell him to do anything. He won't even tell him to go to bed. I have to do it all. I always have to do it all.

"And it's such a bother; the boy is a bother. I make him stay in bed in the mornings until I have his father off to work. It's hard enough in the morning. Sometimes I have to wake his father up five times before he gets up. I get so upset, I throw up just trying to get him out of here on time. And the boy makes it so much worse, always calling on his father or me, anything to get an answer. I tell him, 'Just ignore the boy. He has to learn sometime. If you keep answering him, he'll just keep calling.' But he answers him anyway. He makes it so much harder for me. I have to teach that boy better. I have to be stricter with him" (Herbruck, 1979, pp. 22–24).

Sexual Abuse

"Well, the big thing was that communication between my wife and myself was really gone. I mean it just wasn't there. That sounds simple, really simple, but that's where it was at. We never talked. I knew I was needing something, but I didn't know what it was. I couldn't tell that, I just knew I was hurting.

"One night I went into my daughter's room to rub her back. She was thirteen. She was wearing a brace at the time, and she had taken it off, and I went in to massage her. That's okay, I'm her dad. Well, when I touched her, I found out through my hand that that was what I had been wanting. It was the touch, the feel of the closeness of her. The only time I ever touched my wife was when we were having sex, and we didn't do that very often. There's more to touching than sex. I could go to a prostitute if sex was what I wanted, but I'm not that kind of a guy. That wasn't what I wanted. Screwing isn't the answer to being close. It's part of it; it's very special; but it isn't the answer. It was the closeness I wanted – the closeness I was feeling with my daughter. My daughter and I have always been very close.

"Well, I started to rub her, and then I kind of lost control, and I was rubbing her all over, and then I was having oral sex with her. Once I found out what I was doing, I couldn't stop. I went to a priest to talk about it and try to figure out a way to stop. I knew it was wrong. He told me to say ten 'Hail Mary's,' ten 'Our Father's,' and to stay out of her room. Well, that didn't do it for me, if you know what I mean. It was with her that I felt the only love and closeness that I ever felt in my life. That was hard to want to give up. I guess I was kind of getting back at my wife, too, at least after it started. I knew there was some of that there, too.

"I started laying all kinds of trips on my daughter. I told her it was our secret, that if she told, they'd call the police and I'd have to go to jail, that we'd have to sell the house and get a divorce and our family would be broken up and it would be her fault. I also told her I loved her and I'd take care of her. I said I'd be the man around the house, and I'd be the one in charge, and I'd have all the answers for her. It felt good to her, too, so she wasn't going to tell anyone. What finally happened was that she wrote about it in her diary, and someone found it and read it and turned it in to the school. That happened about a year after we got started.

"It was really earth-shattering for me then, I'll tell you. I lost my job, we had to sell our house, and I did get a divorce. It was really painful. I mean, we hadn't had much of a marriage, but I did love my wife" (Herbruck, 1979, pp. 29–30).

Definitions

What do the terms *abuse* and *neglect* mean? The answer is generally unclear, as both abuse and neglect are generic terms. Similar to many phrases or expressions, a universally accepted understanding of the construct is difficult to achieve. The enormity of the different types of abuse and injury endured and inflicted on children is certainly a contributing factor to the absence of agreement about what these terms mean. Perhaps more importantly, the definition of abuse and neglect, according to Meier and Sloan (1984), varies over time, across cultures, and between dissimilar cultural and social groups. Maher (1985) noted that "different societies accept, and condone, different levels of violence towards its members, including the children" (p. 54). Gil (1970), in particular, believes that a cultural predisposition toward physical violence in childrearing is at the heart of all physical abuse in America. In contrast, since 1979 any form of physical punishment, such as a slap, is illegal in Sweden. Thus, one finds that cultural expectations and standards tolerate and even condone acts such as the African custom of stretching necks, piercing lips and ears, and tattooing or the Indian tradition of flattening heads. As further illustration, in the United States, humiliating, potentially dangerous, and absurd rites that frequently accompany fraternity and sorority initiations are viewed as normal by young adults on many college campuses (Meier & Sloan, 1984).

Despite the problems of offering a definition that is acceptable to various professionals and satisfies differing community standards, one must be put forth if for no other reason than to facilitate and establish a language of understanding. Therefore, for the purposes of this book, the following descriptions are used.

One simple way of distinguishing between abuse and neglect is to consider abuse as an act of *commission* and neglect an act of *omission*. Abuse implies an active, participatory relationship between an adult caregiver (i.e., parent, child care worker, residential aide) and child victim. Neglect, on the other hand, is characterized by adult withdrawal, indifference, and the nonrecognition of the child's physical, intellectual, or emotional needs.

The four major types of child maltreatment are physical abuse, neglect, emotional abuse, and sexual abuse. These areas will first be described in broad, general terms followed by statutory definitions. The physical, behavioral, and environmental indicators of child abuse and neglect will be presented later in this chapter.

Physical Abuse.   According to the National Center on Child Abuse and Neglect (1986), physical abuse includes violent assault with an instrument such as a knife or strap, burns, fractures, or other nonaccidental inflictions or actions that lead to possible injury or harm of the child.

Neglect.   Most definitions of neglect identify, among other behaviors, abandonment; inadequate physical supervision; refusal to seek, allow, or provide medical treatment; poor nutrition; disregard of health hazards in the home; inadequate or inappropriate clothing; and chronic school truancy as constituting neglect (National Center on Child Abuse and Neglect, 1986).

Neglect can occur in many forms and may vary from mild to severe episodes. It can also be chronic, periodic, or episodic (Jenkins, Salus, & Schultze, 1979). With chronic neglect, caregivers are continually indifferent to the child's welfare. In the second instance, adults neglect children at fairly regular intervals such as on weekends, holiday periods, or special events like birthdays. Finally, neglect may be considered episodic when it occurs in reaction to precipitating stressful events occurring in the caretaker's life.

Emotional Abuse.   Emotional abuse is difficult to define. Brenner (1984) suggests that "emotional maltreatment occurs when adults attempt to shape children's behavior through the use of severe disparagement, humiliation, rejection, guilt, and fear" (pp. 97, 100). The National Center on Child Abuse and Neglect (1986) believes that emotional abuse is distinguished by verbal or emotional assaults, close confinement as illustrated by locking a child in a closet, inadequate nurturance, and knowingly permitting antisocial behavior, such as delinquency or substance abuse. In the vast majority of instances, psychological injury is a consequence of physical abuse, neglect, and sexual abuse.

Sexual Abuse.   "Sexual abuse is the most denied, concealed, distressing, and controversial form of child abuse" (Summit & Kryso, 1978, p. 250). It can occur anywhere along a continuum, from exposure to obscene telephone calls, to forcible rape, to incestuous relationships. The sexual maltreatment of children is generally described as occurring in two forms — sexual abuse and sexual exploitation. Kempe (1978) defined *sexual abuse* as "the involvement of dependent, developmentally immature children and adolescents in sexual activities that they do not fully comprehend, to which they are unable to give informed consent or that violate the social taboos of families" (p. 382). A more concise, yet parallel interpretation was developed by Sgroi, Blick, and Porter (1982) who said "Child sexual abuse is a sexual act imposed on a child who lacks emotional, maturational, and cognitive development" (p. 9). An even simpler characterization is offered by the National Committee for the Prevention of Child Abuse (1982) wherein sexual abuse is the exploitation of a child (under age 18) for the sexual gratification of an adult. In the barest of terms, the youngster is used.

Children are victims of sexual exploitation when they serve as prostitutes, pose for pornographic pictures, engage in pornographic performances, or become part of a club that meets for the express purpose of providing sexual gratification for one or more adults (Brenner, 1984).

Sexual abuse is shrouded in a "conspiracy of silence" and is viewed as the most underreported form of child abuse.

Legislative and statutory definitions.   Definitions portrayed in broad terms, although beneficial, have limited usefulness for the professional seeking a detailed description or understanding of child abuse and neglect. A perusal of federal and state statutes reveals, unfortunately, varying degrees of specificity in the interpretation of the terms. This absence of clarity and agreement at both the national and state level complicates attempts to clearly articulate an acceptable explanation of what constitutes abuse and neglect of children.

A significant day in securing rights for children occurred in January 1974 when President Ford signed Public Law 93-247 into law. The Child Abuse Prevention Act (as amended by PL 95-266 and PL 98-457) defines child abuse and neglect as:

> physical or mental injury, sexual abuse or exploitation, negligent treatment, or mal-treatment of a child under the age of 18, or the age specified by the child protection laws of the state in question, by a person, including any employee of a residential facility or any staff person providing out-of-home care, who is responsible for the child's welfare under circumstances which indicate that the child's health or welfare is harmed or threatened thereby, as determined in accordance with regulations prescribed by the Secretary of Health and Human Services (Section 3).

Although serving as the federal definition, the preceding formulation fails to describe in precise terminology the meaning of many key terms. This ambiguity is reflected in some state statutes. As an example, in Arizona child abuse is:

> the infliction of physical injury, impairment of bodily function or disfigurement or the infliction of serious emotional damage as evidenced by severe anxiety, depres-sion, withdrawal or untoward aggressive behavior and which emotional damage is diagnosed by a medical doctor or psychologist . . . (Arizona Revised Statutes, Chapter 5, Article 3, Title 8, Section 8-546.A.2).

Likewise, the 1975 Michigan Child Protection Law (Act 238, Michigan Compiled Laws) considers child abuse as:

> harm or threatened harm to a child's health or welfare by a person responsible for the child's health or welfare which occurs through non-accidental physical or mental injury; sexual abuse; sexual exploitation or maltreatment (Section 2-C).

Other states have chosen to be more specific in their description of child abuse and neglect. The 1973 New York Child Protective Services Act and the Family Court Act defined an abused child as follows:

> (e) "Abused child" means a child less than 18 years whose parent or other person legally responsible for his care
>
> (i) inflicts or allows to be inflicted upon such child physical injury by other than accidental means which causes or creates a substantial risk of death, or serious or protracted disfigurement, or protracted impairment of physical or emotional health or protracted loss or impairment of the function of any bodily organ; or
>
> (ii) creates or allows to be created a substantial risk of physical injury to such child by other than accidental means which would be likely to cause death or serious or protracted impairment of physical or emotional health or pro-tracted loss or impairment of the function of any bodily organ or;
>
> (iii) commits, or allows to be committed, a sex offense against such child, as defined in the penal law, provided, however, that the corroboration require-ments contained therein shall not apply to proceedings under this article.

Section 1012 of the Family Court Act defined a neglected child as follows:

(f) "Neglected child" means a child less than 18 years of age

    (i) whose physical, mental, or emotional condition has been impaired or is in imminent danger of becoming impaired as a result of the failure of his parent or other person legally responsible for his care to exercise a minimum degree of care

        (A) in supplying the child with adequate food, clothing, shelter or education in accordance with provisions of part one of article sixty five of the education law, or medical, dental, optometrical or surgical care though financially able to do so or offered financial or other reasonable means to do so; or

        (B) in providing the child with proper supervision or guardianship, by unreasonably inflicting or allowing to be inflicted harm, or a substantial risk thereof, including the infliction of excessive corporal punishment; or by using a drug or drugs; or by misusing alcoholic beverages to the extent that he loses self-control of his actions; or by any other acts of a similarly serious nature requiring the aid of the court; provided, however, that where the respondent is voluntarily and regularly participating in a rehabilitative program, evidence that the respondent has repeatedly misused a drug or drugs or alcoholic beverages to the extent that he loses self-control of his actions shall not establish that the child is a neglected child in the absence of evidence establishing that the child's physical, mental or emotional condition has been impaired or is in imminent danger of becoming impaired as set forth in paragraph (i) of this subdivision; or

    (ii) who has been abandoned, in accordance with the definition and other criteria set forth in subdivision five of section three hundred eighty-four-b of the social services law, by his parents or other person legally responsible for his care.

Similarly, the 1975 Alabama Child Abuse and Neglect Reporting Law (Act 1124), and earlier legislation, provides definitions of key terms. Codified within Alabama law are the following interpretations:

Abuse has been defined as harm or threatened harm to a child's health or welfare, which can occur through nonaccidental physical or mental injury, sexual abuse, or attempted sexual abuse, sexual exploitation or attempted sexual exploitation. Sexual abuse includes rape, incest, and sexual molestation as those acts are defined by Alabama law. Sexual exploitation includes allowing, permitting, or encouraging a child to engage in prostitution or allowing, permitting, encouraging, or engaging in the obscene or pornographic photographing, filming, or depicting of a child for commercial purposes. Neglect has been defined as negligent treatment or maltreatment of a child, including the failure to provide adequate food, medical treatment, clothing, or shelter. However, a special exception has been made for a parent or guardian legitimately practicing his religious belief in the provision of medical treatment for a child. A child has been defined as a person under the age of 18 years (see sections 26-14-1 through 26-14-13).

Finally, the Ohio Revised Code (Section 2151.03) identifies a neglected child as any child:

(A) Who is abandoned by his parents, guardian, or custodian;
(B) Who lacks parental care because of the faults or habits of his parents, guardian, or custodian;
(C) Whose parents, guardian, or custodian neglects or refuses to provide him with proper or necessary subsistence, education, medical or surgical care, or other care necessary for his health, morals, or well being;
(D) Whose parents, guardian, or custodian neglects or refuses to provide the special care made necessary by his mental condition;
(E) Whose parents, legal guardian, or custodian have placed or attempted to place such child in violation of sections 5103.16 and 5103.17 of the Revised Code. A child who, in lieu of medical or surgical care or treatment for a wound, injury, disability, or physical or mental condition, is under spiritual treatment through prayer in accordance with the tenets and practices of a well-recognized religion, is not a neglected child for this reason alone.

It is not the intent to debate the merits and demerits of particular state laws or the advantages and disadvantages of general versus specific interpretations of maltreatment of children. Rather, this review should bring to the reader's attention the diversity inherent in legal perspectives of abuse and neglect and the need for professionals to keep abreast of current definitions in their community.

An Historical Overview

Child abuse has a long and tragic history. Children have been abused for centuries. Segal (1978), citing the child historian, De Mause, noted that "the history of childhood is a panorama of incredible cruelty and exploitation" (p. 171). As an example of this indictment, Segal, who considers children as an endangered species, described two cases of abuse.

> "The two-year-old child lies frail and immobile in her crib. Only her eyes move, as if fearfully searching the world for the next violent blow. Her body – shoulders, back, arms, legs, chin, cheekbones – is a mosaic of angry bruises and scars, her sunken buttocks are laced with cigarette burns. The child cannot or will not speak, and her response to a gesture of open-armed tenderness is panic – an empty, tearless, and agonizing scream.
> Another child, only seven, but appearing ancient, has become a grotesque satire of youth – the product of chronic abuse and mutilation by his elders. His feet are crushed, his shoulders bent out of shape, his head held at a tilt, the result of repeated insult to the brain. As he walks alone in the busy market, he excites the curious gaze and revulsion of passersby" (p. 171).[2]

---

[2] From *A Child's Journey* (p. 171) by J. Segal, 1978, New York: McGraw-Hill. Copyright 1978 by McGraw-Hill. Reprinted by permission.

The latter description is chronicled in the archives of ancient Rome, whereas the former is an accounting of a patient in a Washington, D.C., hospital. Although these episodes are separated by more than 2,000 years, they poignantly depict the brutality and cruelty inflicted frequently on innocent children. This violence has led Segal (1978) to comment that children are "a yielding target for the frustrations, conflicts, projections, unresolved hates, and smoldering anger of the adults who so often tyrannically bestride their lives" (p. 171). The youth of our country may truly be an endangered species.

Ancient Civilization.   One of the earliest recorded descriptions of child abuse occurred more than 5,000 years ago in ancient Sumer where a clay tablet tells of a young girl who was sexually abused (Goldman & Wheeler, 1986) and boys who were whipped at school for the slightest provocation (Kramer, 1956). Religious beliefs and practices frequently contributed to maltreatment. Boys were flogged by their parents before altars erected to the goddess Diana (Ryan, 1862). Isaac accompanied his father, Abraham, to the mountain top where he was to be slaughtered as a test of his father's obedience to his lord. In ancient Palestine, the sacrifice of first-born sons was ordinary. Children were also burned as offerings to various gods (Segal, 1978). In the days of the Roman empire, the doctrine of *Patria Potestas* gave a father absolute authority over his children and allowed him, should he desire, to sell, kill, eat, or otherwise dispose of his offspring in any manner he desired (Steele, 1976).

Children were subjected not only to physical abuse, but also sexual deviancy — a common practice. The sexual exploitation of children was frequently noted in Greek mythology. Male youths were worshipped, and pederasty (sexual contact between adult males and children) was a prevalent practice. According to Goldman and Wheeler's historical review (1986) of sexual abuse, incest was considered a model of godly behavior and upheld. The pharaohs of ancient Egypt, for example, among other civilizations, practiced incestuous marriages.

Thus, since time immemorial, children have been victimized by their elders. Even as society became enlightened, abuse did not diminish.

Modern Society.   Throughout history, up to and including present day society, adults have assumed that they had the right to treat children in any way they desired. This belief held true regardless if you were rich or poor, famous or unknown. Physical punishment, for example, was considered a key component of the educational process. Henry VI was regularly beaten by his tutor as was Charles I, although Charles I was fortunate to have a whipping boy accept punishment meant for him (Radbill, 1974). In the typical English and American schoolhouse, the hickory stick was a common instructional tool. Segal (1978) related that the poet Milton beat his nephews, and Beethoven was known to have abused his pupils with a knitting needle and, on occasion, of biting them.

The physical mistreatment of children has its roots in western Judeo-Christian culture wherein youngsters are perceived as easily spoiled, stubborn, or, in some instances, "born with original sin." Physical punishment was seen as the most expedient way of combatting this behavior (Steele, 1976). John Calvin reportedly preached that it was the parent's duty to God to "break the will" of the child at the earliest possible age (Segal, 1978). The Bible was frequently used to justify physical abuse. For example, Proverbs 23: 13–14, "Withhold not correction from the child: for if thou beatest him with the rod, he shall not die. Thou shalt beat him with the rod, and shalt deliver his soul from hell."

Physical punishment is very common. It is often the first line of behavior control, rather than the last, exhibited by parents who are unaware of alternative child management strategies. Consider, if you will, the popular nursery rhyme:

> There was an old woman who lived in a shoe;
> She had so many children she didn't know what to do;
> She gave them some broth without any bread;
> She whipped them all soundly and put them to bed.

Likewise, children are frequently abused for simply displaying age-appropriate behavior. A typical parental response is captured in the following nursery rhyme.

> Little Polly Flinders;
> Sat among the cinders;
> Warming her pretty little toes.;
> Her mother came and caught her;
> And whipped her little daughter;
> For spoiling her nice new clothes.

In some instances, children were only beaten for presenting inappropriate behaviors. In 1646, however, Massachusetts adopted a law whereby unruly children encountered the death penalty. Connecticut soon followed the lead of their neighboring state. Luckily, for many young persons, public whippings were frequently substituted for the death penalty (Radbill, 1974).

Yet, in some segments of society, little progress has been made regarding the rights of children. As an illustration, only four states (California, Maine, New Jersey, and Massachusetts) have abolished corporal punishment in the schools. In many jurisdictions, children may be paddled legally. The U.S. Supreme Court has upheld the right of schools to utilize corporal punishment. In a 1977 decision (*Ingraham v. Wright*) the Court ruled, by a 5 to 4 margin, that corporal punishment administered by public school teachers and administrators was not a violation of the cruel and unusual punishment clause of the Eighth Amendment.

Goldman and Wheeler (1986) remind us that progress is also lacking when examining the sexual abuse and exploitation of children. The "cult of the little girl" fascinated many men of letters. Charles Dickens and Edgar Allan Poe among others lauded the virtues of young girls. The 17th-century English poet, John Dryden, wrote of the sexual desires of a young female. The lust of an elderly pedophile for seductive little girls was told in *Crime and Punishment*, Dostoyevsky's masterpiece. One of the more renowned 19th-century child pornographers was Charles Dodgson, a deacon at Oxford's Christ Church College. Dodgson kept detailed descriptions of his photographs in a diary. His writing, however, was not restricted to personal reflections. He is perhaps best remembered for his story about a young, innocent girl, Alice, which he wrote using a *nom de plume*, Lewis Carroll (Tyler & Stone, 1985).

In the mid-19th century, prostitution was rampant in London, while in America, indentured girls, as well as slaves, were sexually exploited by their masters. Today, many runaways, both male and female, find that a life of prostitution is their only avenue for survival.

The sexual exploitation of children continues. The *femme fatale* image is increasingly popularized in films (e.g., *Taxi Driver*) and advertising. Adolescent girls, in seductive poses, urge us to buy jeans, perfumes, and cosmetics. Dolls with adultlike figures are thrust on prepubescent children (Goldman & Wheeler, 1986). One could sadly conclude that the attitudes of many toward females has not changed for centuries.

Incidence of Child Abuse and Neglect

Obtaining reliable and accurate figures on child abuse and neglect is a difficult task. One of the reasons that estimates fluctuate significantly is that definitions tend to vary from community to community. In addition, researchers believe that there is a significant problem of underreporting. Many experts are of the opinion that the figures represent only the "tip of the iceberg." There are several explanations why there is a serious problem of underestimating abuse and neglect. Many times parents fail to seek medical attention for their injured or battered child. If attention is sought, caregivers do not routinely use the same physician or hospital for fear of being detected. Some types of injuries are difficult to detect; also, mandated reporters may fail to inform child protective service agencies of their suspicions. Likewise, family members do not report for fear of legal action against the perpetrator and apprehension about the destruction of their family (Goldman & Gargiulo, 1987; Park & Collmer, 1975).

The first national survey that attempted to gauge the incidence of child abuse was reported by Gil in 1970. He estimated that approximately 6,000 children were abused in the United States in 1967. Other surveys of that time period reported abuse and neglect figures that ranged from 60,000 to 665,000 children (Light, 1973). In an effort to gain reliable estimates, the National Center on Child Abuse and Neglect funded the American Humane Association (Child Protection Division) to conduct annual national surveys of child abuse and neglect reporting. Their investigations endeavored to accurately portray documented reports of child abuse and neglect in all states, the District of Columbia, and the U.S. territories. The most recently available statistics show that 1,928,000 cases of abuse and neglect were reported in 1985 (American Humane Association, personal communication, April 13, 1988).

Perhaps a better way to grasp the magnitude of abuse and neglect in the United States is to review figures for the preceding 10-year, data-gathering period (Table 1.1).

The number of reports filed for 1984 versus 1985 demonstrate a 12% increase. In contrast, a 1976 versus 1985 comparison reveals a 212% increase in cases reported. The latest data from the American Humane Association suggest a rate of 30.6 children for every 1,000 children in the United States who are reported to be abused (personal communication, April 13, 1988).

Utilizing a national perspective, the National Center on Child Abuse and Neglect was able to generate a demographic profile of abused/ neglected children and their families.

Age

- The average age of children reported as abused and/or neglected in 1984 was 7.2 years versus 8.6 years for all U.S. children.
- Preschool children, from birth to 5 years of age, represented 34% of the overall child population in 1984, but accounted for 43% of maltreated children.
- Children ages 12–17 show the highest rate of sexual maltreatment and the lowest for neglect.

Table 1.1 Child Abuse and Neglect by Reporting Year

Year	Number of children reported
1976	669,000
1977	838,000
1978	836,000
1979	988,000
1980	1,154,000
1981	1,225,000
1982	1,262,000
1983	1,477,000
1984	1,727,000
1985	1,928,000

Note. National Center on Child Abuse and Neglect, 1986.

- In general, neglect affects the youngest age groups, declining as children get older; conversely, sexual maltreatment increases with age. The highest risk of physical injury is found among the youngest children.
- The incidence rate of sexual abuse is highest among adolescent females, but half the female victims of sexual abuse are under 11 years of age.

Sex
- The percentages and incidence rates for males and females differ only slightly when all forms of maltreatment and all age groups are considered. Adolescent females, however, are more likely to experience the range of maltreatments compared with their male counterparts.
- Teenage boys, on the other hand, are more likely to experience educational neglect and emotional abuse than are teenage girls, but are slightly less likely to experience physical neglect than are girls.

Family Characteristics
- Maltreated children can be found in all income groups.
- More than four times as many reported families were receiving public assistance as compared with all U.S. families with children.
- Families involved in child maltreatment are more likely to be headed by a female.
- Reported families tend to have more children than do U.S. families in general.

Race
- 67% of perpetrators reported for maltreatment in 1984 were white, close to 21% were black, about 10% were Hispanic, and almost 3% were classified as "other."
- Minorities are disproportionately represented; 81% of all U.S. children are white, yet only 67% of involved children are white.

Geographic Location
- No geographic setting is free of child abuse and neglect. The incidence rates are similar for urban, suburban, and rural communities.
- In rural counties, the incidence rate for sexual abuse is higher than elsewhere.
- In suburban locations, the incidence rate for emotional abuse and neglect is higher than elsewhere (National Center on Child Abuse and Neglect, 1986, pp. 4–5).

Although national figures give a broad overview of the incidence of child abuse and neglect, sometimes focusing on a particular state provides insight into the crisis of maltreatment of children and youth. Alabama, similar to many states, has witnessed an alarming increase in the reported cases of child abuse and neglect.

Table 1.2 Number of Cases of Child Abuse and Neglect Reported in Alabama

Year	Number of cases
1975	878
1976	3,347
1977	11,011
1978	13,887
1979	16,835
1980	17,315
1981	18,654
1982	20,213
1983	23,574
1984	28,403
1985	31,385
1986	29,693
1987	30,908
1988	35,641

Note. From Alabama Department of Human Resources.

Data compiled by the Alabama Department of Human Resources found that in 1986 there were 7,926 reports of physical abuse, 2,879 reports of sexual abuse, 16,409 reports of neglect, and 2,482 reports of abuse and neglect combined (Table 1.2). Even though this represents a 5% decrease when compared with reports filed in 1985, the 1986 statistics show a 146% increase when compared to 1975 data. It should be noted, however, that these figures depict reported rather than confirmed instances of maltreatment. Approximately 49% or 14,550 cases were actually verified in 1986.

What most discussions concerning the incidence of abuse and neglect fail to capture are the children who die each year at the hands of their parents or caregivers. In 1979 the National Center on Child Abuse and Neglect (1981) estimated that 1,000 children were killed by their parents or, on the average, three children a day. Three out of every four victims were five years old or younger. Seventy-two percent died from physical injuries whereas 28% expired as a result of serious neglect. Current estimates suggest that between 2,000 and

5,000 children die each year as a consequence of abuse and neglect. This figure is considered inaccurate, however, because, frequently, childrens' deaths are sometimes labeled as "accidental" or by "natural causes" rather than as homicide. In addition, variability of definition and ineffective documentation and data reporting procedures cloud the true incidence of children who are killed by adult caregivers (Zirpoli, 1986).

As disturbing as national and state incidence figures are, they do not reveal the incredible degree of torment children suffer. In his aptly entitled book, the *Slaughter of the Innocents*, psychologist David Baken characterizes this abuse.

> Children have been brought into hospitals with skulls fractured and bodies covered with lacerations. One parent disciplined a child for presumptive misbehavior with the buckle end of a belt, perforating an intestine and killing the child. Children have been whipped, beaten, starved, drowned, smashed against walls and floors, held in ice water baths, exposed to extreme outdoor temperatures, burned with hot irons and steam pipes. Children have been tied and kept in upright positions for long periods. They have been systematically exposed to electric shock; forced to swallow pepper, soil, feces, urine, vinegar, alcohol, and other odious materials; buried alive; had scalding water poured over their genitals; had their limbs held in open fire; placed in roadways where automobiles would run over them; placed on roofs and fire escapes in such a manner as to fall off; bitten, knifed, and shot; had their eyes gouged out (1971, p. 4).[3]

Sexual Abuse.   As noted earlier, the stigma and taboo surrounding sexual abuse has created a "conspiracy of silence" involving, obviously, the perpetrator but also the victim, and, in some instances, even professionals (Pettis & Hughes, 1985). Thus, exact data on the incidence of sexual abuse is difficult to achieve. Compounding this difficulty are differing reporting standards and definitions of what constitutes sexual abuse. As an illustration, some reports include only female victims disregarding abuse directed toward males; other reports include both boys and girls. Additionally, the age that identifies children as victims varies, according to state statute, from incorporating children 12 years of age or younger, to youngsters less than 14, 16, or 18 years of age. As noted by the National Committee for the Prevention of Child Abuse (1982), most estimates of the incidence of child sexual abuse fail to include child prostitutes and those youngsters who are involved in pornographic exploitation. A final contributing factor to the underreporting of sexual abuse is the absence, in some circumstances, of identifying sexual abuse as a separate child offense.

These problems notwithstanding, statistics are generated from three major areas: clinical records, empirical studies, and retrospective investigations.

A major drawback of utilizing pediatric or psychiatric records are reporting biases and selective results frequently extrapolated from small samples (Chan-

---

[3] From *Slaughter of the Innocents* by D. Bakan, 1971, San Francisco: Jossey-Bass. Copyright 1971 by Jossey-Bass. Reprinted by permission.

dler, 1982). Empirical investigations frequently use larger sample sizes in an attempt to generalize their results. However, this data is usually gathered from social service agencies, police files, or hospital emergency room records, which may be overrepresentative of minority and lower socioeconomic groups (Pettis & Hughes, 1985).

Two widely quoted empirical studies offer some insight to the problem of sexual abuse. The 1969 De Francis investigation conducted in Brooklyn, New York, for the American Humane Association, estimated a rate of 149.2 episodes of sexual crimes occur per 100,000 children. On the basis of this Brooklyn projection, De Francis conservatively estimated an annual reported incidence of 3,068 cases of sexual abuse in New York City.

Utilizing a much larger sample drawn from the cities of Washington, D.C., Minneapolis, Brooklyn, and the state of Connecticut, Sarafino's review (1979) of incidence figures suggested a rate of 122.5 cases per 100,000 children. Sarafino extended his data by projecting an unreported rate of three to four times the rate of known sexual assaults and then added estimates of reported and unreported cases to generate an estimated figure of 336,200 cases of sexual abuse nationwide.

The final strategy used to project incidence of sexual abuse is confidential retrospective investigations. This technique seeks to assess sexual abuse that occurred at an earlier time in the person's life. Finkelhor (1979), in a survey of 796 undergraduate college students at six New England schools, discovered that 19% of the women and 9% of the men in his sample reported that they were sexually victimized as children. In a retrospective study of 1200 college-age women, 28% indicated a sexual experience with an adult before age 13; yet, only 6% of the incidents were reported (Barry, 1984). Sociologist Diana Russell (1983) surveyed 930 randomly chosen women from the San Francisco area. She found that 152 of her respondents (16%) had been sexually assaulted before age 18; 42 (4.5%) were abused by their fathers. Only four of the attacks, however, were reported to the authorities. Finally, a recent investigation conducted in the Boston area by Finkelhor (reported in Pettis & Hughes, 1985) revealed that 15% of the women interviewed and 5% of the men ($n = 521$) had been sexually victimized as children.

Goldman and Wheeler (1986) reported that researchers estimate that between 100,000 and 500,000 children are sexually abused each year. It is generally agreed that one out of every four girls and approximately one out of every seven to ten boys will experience some type of sexual contact with an adult prior to age 18 (Seattle Institute for Child Advocacy, 1985). The most recent figures available from the American Humane Association indicated that in 1985 there were 113,000 confirmed cases of sexual abuse in this country as compared to only 6,000 reported episodes in 1976 (personal communication, April 13, 1988). The unreported rate of sexual abuse is at least three or four times that of the reported rate (Vander Mey & Neff, 1982). Thus, one can quickly grasp the magnitude of the problem confronting concerned professionals. Yet, it is not clear how much of the increase for all types of abuse and neglect reflect an actual increase of occurrence or is an artifact of heightened public awareness and improved data collection procedures.

Identification of Abused and Neglected Children

Some instances of abuse and neglect are readily identifiable such as a child who is seriously malnourished or a young girl with multiple facial bruises. Sadly, these represent a very small percentage of the children who are suffering and need the help of concerned professionals. Many forms of abuse occur behind closed doors or are subtle, making detection and intervention difficult. Knowing what to look for is critical. However, a degree of caution must also be exercised. When examining a composite list of physical and behavioral indicators frequently exhibited by abused and neglected children, professionals must remember that the presence of a single indicator does not prove that maltreatment exists. Anyone of the following signs may not mean anything or may be reasonably explained. Yet, if one discovers that a number of signs are present or there is the repeated occurrence of an indicator, then the professional should be alert to the possibility that child abuse exists.

The following list (Broadhurst, 1979; National Center on Child Abuse and Neglect, 1986; Ohio Department of Public Welfare,[4] undated) is neither exhaustive nor all inclusive. These indicators are only clues. Recognition is the first step toward elimination of child abuse and neglect.

Physical Indicators of Physical Abuse
Bruises
- Occurring on the posterior side of the body
- On the face, lips, or mouth
- Occurring in clusters forming regular patterns or reflective of the instrument used to inflict them (e.g., electrical cord, board, belt buckle)
- Occurring on an infant, especially on the face
- In various stages of healing
- Human bite marks

Burns
- Immersion or wet burns, such as "stocking burns" or doughnut shaped burns on the buttocks

---

[4] From *Open the Door on Child Abuse and Neglect*. Columbus, OH: Ohio Department of Human Services. Reprinted by permission.

- Cigarette or cigar burns, especially on the palms of hands, soles of feet, or genitals
- Rope burns, possibly from confinement
- Patterned or dry burns which show a clearly defined mark such as those caused by an iron

Lacerations and Abrasions

- On lips, eyes, or any portion of an infant's face
- Of gum tissue, caused by forced feeding
- On external genitals
- On back of arms, legs, torso

Missing or Loose Teeth
Skeletal Injuries (Medical Diagnosis)

- Metaphyseal or corner fractures of long bones, caused by twisting and pulling
- Epiphyseal separation – separation of the growth center at the end of the bone from the rest of the shaft, caused by twisting or pulling
- Periosteal elevation – detachment of periosteum from shaft of bone with associated hemorrhaging periosteum and shaft
- Spiral fractures
- Stiff, swollen, enlarged joints

Head Injuries

- Absence of hair
- Hemorrhaging beneath scalp, caused by pulling hair
- Subdural hematomas, caused by hitting or shaking
- Retinal hemorrhages or detachment, caused by shaking
- Nasal, skull, or jaw fracture.

Internal Injuries (Medical Diagnosis)

- Duodenal or jejunal hematoma, caused by hitting or kicking
- Rupture of inferior vena cava
- Peritonitis, which can be caused by hitting or kicking
- Constant vomiting

Behavioral Indicators of Physical Abuse

- Overly compliant, passive
- Fearful of physical contact
- Sporadic temper tantrums
- Craves attention
- Wears long sleeves or other concealing clothing even in hot weather
- Reports injury by a parent or caregiver

- Appears frightened of parent(s) or caregiver
- Demonstrates extremes in behavior — overly aggressive or very withdrawn
- Inappropriate neatness while playing or eating
- Unable to offer reasonable explanation for injury
- Lack of distress at being separated from parent(s) or caregiver
- Is often sleepy in class
- Arrives early for school, stays late
- Complains that physical activity causes pain or discomfort
- Excessive school absence and/or tardiness
- Overly cautious, lacks curiosity

According to the Ohio Department of Public Welfare (undated), physical indicators of abuse should be evaluated in light of the victim's medical history and the developmental ability of the child to injure him/herself. The behavioral clues of physical abuse are influenced by the severity and frequency of the abuse, the age of the child at onset, the child's relationship to the abuser, and his/her coping strategies.

Physical Indicators of Neglect
- Abandonment
- Poor personal hygiene
- Inappropriate or inadequate clothing
- Absence of needed medical or dental care
- Inadequate supervision for long periods of time
- Constantly tired, listless
- Complaints of being constantly hungry
- Substandard or inadequate physical environment

Behavioral Indicators of Neglect
- Falls asleep in school, lethargic
- Begs for or steals food, eats classmate's leftovers
- Irregular school attendance
- Dull, apathetic appearance
- Use of drugs or alcohol
- Engages in delinquent acts such as petty theft or vandalism
- Failure to thrive among infants
- Poor academic performance

The preceding physical and behavioral signs of neglect should be considered in terms of community standards, cultural values, and parental/caregiver ability to provide. Observers of children should ask themselves, "Is this true neglect or a different lifestyle?" The answer to this question will help professionals distinguish between instances of neglect and differing ways of life.

Physical Indicators of Emotional Abuse

Emotional maltreatment is rarely manifested in physical signs. Emotional abuse is usually related to a constellation of interactions and is cumulative. It can range in degree from mild and infrequent to pervasive and psychologically destructive (Ohio Department of Public Welfare, undated). The child's behavior is often the best indicator.

Behavioral Indicators of Emotional Abuse

- Absence of positive self-image
- Behavioral extremes: hyperactive and demanding or passive and withdrawn
- Depression
- Psychosomatic complaints
- Attempted suicide
- Impulsive, defiant, antisocial behavior
- Behavior inappropriate for chronological age: too adult-like or too infantile
- Inappropriate habits: nervous tics, rocking, sucking, head banging
- Enuresis
- Inhibited intellectual/emotional development
- Difficulty in establishing and maintaining peer relationships
- Overly fearful, vigilant
- Sleep and eating disorders
- Self-destructive
- Rigidly compulsive

Physical Indicators of Sexual Abuse

- Pregnancy at an early age
- Bruises of or bleeding from external genitalia, vagina, or anal regions
- Swollen or red cervix, vulva, or perineum
- Presence of semen
- Torn, stained, or bloody undergarments
- Hymen stretched at very young age
- Presence of sexually transmitted diseases
- Vaginal or penile discharge
- Complaints of difficulty with urination

Behavioral Indicators of Sexual Abuse

- Poor peer relationships
- Sexual promiscuity

- Reluctance to participate in physical activities
- Sexually precocious
- Prostitution
- Withdrawal from social relationships
- Comments that he/she was sexually assaulted
- Exhibits infantile behavior
- Acts in seductive fashion in the presence of peers and/or adults
- Substance abuse
- Irregular school attendance
- Engages in delinquent acts or runs away
- School work (poems, stories, art) that manifest sexual themes
- Arrives early or stays late at school
- Sleep disturbances
- Decline in academic performance
- Phobias

Sexual abuse is difficult to detect outside of the clinical setting. Victims are generally reluctant to discuss the abuse, and physical indicators are frequently unexposed. When a child tells you that he or she has been sexually assaulted in some fashion, believe them! Most children do not have a frame of reference for the events described unless it actually occurred.

The preceding descriptions of abuse and neglect are only clues. If present they should give rise to suspicion that a child is at risk. Professionals need not verify their hunches — that is the role of the child protective service agencies. Your suspicions may be wrong and not substantiated yet, if accurate, you could help end a child's fear and torment. You might even save a life.

Perpetrator and Victim Characteristics

Child abuse usually requires three elements — the perpetrator, the victim, and a precipitating crisis. Although all parents have the potential to be abusive, chronically abusive individuals exhibit particular characteristics and behavior patterns. Likewise, some children are more vulnerable than others (e.g., special needs children and adopted children). Finally, when life circumstances become too stressful for the caregiver events such as long-term illness, financial problems, divorce, or job-related difficulties can cause the parent to lose control and overreact, frequently resulting in child abuse (Ohio Department of Public Welfare, undated).

Abusive and neglectful parents are likely to share several common characteristics. These indicators may be both personal and environmental. The following composite list is not exhaustive and the presence of one or more descriptors does not mean that the parent is abusing his/her child.

- Misuse of alcohol or other drugs
- Geographic and/or social isolation of the family
- Poor emotional control
- Unaware of age appropriate behavior of children
- Emotional immaturity
- Poor self-concept
- Unrealistic behavioral expectations
- Marital disharmony
- Indifferent parental attitude
- Absence of parenting skills/knowledge
- Inappropriate or excessive discipline
- Parental history of abuse/neglect
- Overreaction or underreaction to situations
- Inability to trust others
- Low self-esteem
- Overly critical of child, views child as evil
- Unable to cope with situational stress
- Emotionally dependent, passive spouse
- Unable to offer reasonable explanation for child's injury
- Perceives child as "different" or "difficult"
- Rigidity and compulsiveness
- Expects rejection and criticism
- Unable to express emotions in socially acceptable fashion
- Loss of control or fear of losing control
- Inability to offer or accept emotional support

According to the research literature (Pettis & Hughes, 1985) and some reports (e.g., Ohio Department of Public Welfare, undated) the behavior of the parent or caregiver who engages in sexual abuse (incest) is distinguished by:

- Misuse of alcohol
- Intergenerational pattern of incest
- Prolonged absence of one parent
- Overcrowding in the home
- Dysfunctional marital relationship
- Unmet emotional needs
- Social and/or geographic isolation

- Inadequate coping skills
- Protectiveness and jealousy of the child victim
- Absence of impulse control
- Confusion concerning family roles

The question that is frequently asked by both professionals and the general public is, "Why does a parent abuse his/her own child?" There frequently is not a simple or concise answer. The author's personal view is that there is no single event or behavior that produces an abusive individual. Rather, abusive parents/caregivers are products of a complex interaction of personal psychological factors and particular environmental conditions.

The research literature provides some clues to the etiology of child abuse. Early researchers reported a high incidence of marital discord and minor criminal offenses in abusive families (Kempe, Silverman, Steele, Droegemueller, & Silver, 1962). Young (1964) and Elmer (1967) noted the factors of social isolation, unemployment, high mobility, and the absence of support systems. Yet, as these investigators and others observed, it would be wrong to conclude that economic or social stressors alone cause child abuse. Parental history and the attitude of the caregiver toward childrearing were also found to contribute to child abuse and neglect. It was frequently observed that abusing parents were themselves abused or neglected as children (Steele & Pollock, 1968). As a result of their unfortunate childhood experiences, abusive parents were characterized by Fontana (1968) as emotional cripples. In addition to their experiential history, abusive individuals were found to have high expectations for their children, place age-inappropriate and unrealistic demands on them, and interact with their children as though they were adults — often satisfying their own emotional needs while disregarding the child's needs and limitations (Galdston, 1965; Johnson & Morse, 1968; Steele & Pollock, 1968). Abusive parents are frequently unable to respond to the poignant message of the following poem.

More recent investigations appear to support the findings of earlier workers, although, a clear picture of the abusive individual does not emerge. Males were found to be abusive more often than females, yet, mothers were more likely than fathers to inflict serious injury on their child (Johnson & Showers, 1985; Solomon, 1973). Social isolation and the lack of social support systems are still recognized as contributing factors as is the parents' experiential history (Garbarino, 1982; Salzinger, Kaplan, & Artemyeff, 1983; Straus, 1980). Perception of and adaptation to environmental stressors also continues to play a role in abusive families (Rosenburg & Reppucci, 1983; Wolfe, 1985), although their impact is still unresolved (Starr, 1982).

In an investigation designed to assess family circumstances of children who sustain abuse and neglect (abandonment, physical abuse, emotional abuse, neglect, and sexual abuse), Martin and Walters' (1982) examination of 489 cases gleaned from two Southeastern cities revealed that different types of abuse are correlated

I AM YOUR CHILD
AND I NEED YOU BADLY.

Please look at me carefully the next time you see me.

Please notice that I am small and weak.

Please listen to me carefully the next time you see me.

Please notice that I don't know much.

Like you, I was born helpless. And growing up so I can
take care of myself will take me a long time, too.

I need food.

I need rest.

I need to be kept clean.

I need to be kept warm in winter and cool in summer.

I need to be taken in your arms or sat on your lap.

I need to feel your skin against my skin.

I need you to help heal my hurts.

I need you to play with just so you and I can have some good
times together.

I need you to teach me everything you can so I'll have a chance
in this world when I grow up.

I need your patience. I know I'm not very orderly. I cry out for
things like food and attention the second I need them. I can't
help it, and I know that bothers you sometimes. All I can hope is
that you will be patient with me until I can learn to be patient, too.

Above all, I need to know you love me. Even if your parents gave
you no love, try to give a little to me so I can give a little
to my children and they can give a little to their children.

I need so much from you, yet I have only one thing I can give
you in return.

That is my love.

Today and tomorrow and as long as I live.

Note. From "I am Your Child and I Need You Badly." Toledo, OH: Libbey-Owens-Ford.
Copyright 1987 by Libbey-Owens-Ford. Reprinted by permission.

with different antecedent variables. These researchers discovered, through multiple regression analysis and multivariate analysis of variance, that abandonment is associated with promiscuousness and/or alcoholism of the mother. Parent-child conflict and the biological/nonbiological relationship of the perpetrator to the child were significant indicators of physical abuse. The most important predictors of emotional abuse were emotional/psychological problems of the child along with intellectual inadequacy. Neglect appears to be predicted by knowing the intellectual ability of the parents. Finally, when considering sexual abuse, the father's promiscuousness and use of alcohol were the most important variables.

In a similar vein, Merrill (1962) an early researcher concerned with parental motivational factors, identified three distinct clusters of personality characteristics that were shared by abusive fathers and mothers. The first group of parents in his typology seemed to manifest continual and pervasive hostility and aggressiveness. The second group was distinguished by its rigidity, compulsiveness, lack of warmth, lack of reasonableness, and absence of flexibility in thinking and belief. Passiveness and dependency characterized the third group of Merrill's parents.

Segal (1978) believes that there are qualitative differences between abusive and nonabusive parents. "Three characteristics of abusive parents stand out: an acceptance of abuse as a way of parental life, a tendency to harbor grossly unrealistic expectations of children and to view them as evil, and a background of abuse in their own childhood" (pp. 188–189). It is, perhaps, this final dimension of abuse in their own childhood that distinguishes the behavior of adults who violate their own children. According to Brandt Steele, professor of psychiatry at the University of Colorado Medical Center, "Children who have been abused and neglected provide the pool from which the next generation of neglecting, abusive parents are derived" (1976, p. 19).

Can we recognize a potentially abusive parent before a child is born? According to the Ohio Department of Public Welfare, in many cases, abuse or neglect might have been prevented if high-risk families were identified early. Certain characteristics are often present in high-risk families and may be particularly noticeable before the birth of a child. The following are warning signals only. Their presence does not mean that abuse or neglect will occur, but that the potential for its occurring is high. A single characteristic or even a few characteristics displayed for a short time may be the result of the normal anxiety a new mother or father experiences; however, if many of the characteristics are present and continue, the parent should look for help. A potentially abusive parent may exhibit several of these characteristics:

- The mother denies the pregnancy, refuses to talk about it, has made no plans whatsoever.
- The mother is very depressed over the pregnancy.

- The mother is not willing to gain weight during the pregnancy.
- The mother is alone and frightened, especially frightened of the prospect of delivery.
- The mother lacks support from husband or family.
- The parent is overly concerned with what the sex of the baby will be.
- The parent is overly concerned with how the baby will perform, whether it will measure up to standards.
- The parent believes that the child is going to be one too many children.
- The mother wanted an abortion but did not go through with it or waited until it was too late.
- The parents considered giving up the child, but changed their minds.
- The parents are isolated, do not have relatives or friends close by.
- After delivery of the baby, the parent shows no active interest in it, does not want to touch or hold it, seems hostile toward it, is disappointed over the baby's sex.
- After the baby comes home, the parent is very bothered about the baby's crying; sees the baby as too demanding, yet frequently ignores the baby's needs, not comforting it when it cries; finds changing diapers distasteful.
- The parent does not have fun with the baby, doesn't talk to the baby, says mostly negative things about it.
- One parent resents the time the other spends with the baby and is jealous of any affection shown toward the baby.

Child Characteristics.   Are some children more vulnerable than others to abuse? Are there certain attributes or distinguishing features that place some youngsters at risk for abuse and/or neglect? Once again, researchers have provided answers to these questions. It appears that the child does play a role in the abuse triangle. Susceptibility to abuse seems to be related to the perception or actual requirement of additional parental attention and care (Zirpoli, 1986). Children who are viewed as different or difficult to raise are at risk for abuse (Soeffing, 1975).

Specific variables that heighten a child's vulnerability include low birth weight (Solomons, 1979), impairment in mother-infant bonding (Kaplan & Pelcovitz, 1982), mental retardation (Sandgrund, Gaines, & Green, 1974), emotional/behavioral disorders (Bousha & Twentyman, 1984), and physical impairments (Blacher & Meyers, 1983). Other risk factors include difficult temperament (Ounsted, Oppenheimer, & Lindsay, 1974), provocative behavior such as hyperactivity, and childhood problems like colic and incontinence (Meier & Sloan, 1984). A stepchild, depending on his or her age, is from two to six times more likely to be abused or neglected than if he or she were residing with both biological parents (Wilson, Daly, & Weghorst, 1980).

Of course, the intriguing question that must be answered is whether a particular child characteristic (e.g., mental retardation) is a cause or effect of the abuse. This is a difficult question to answer. Retrospective studies are unable to assess whether the abuse or handicap occurred first. As an illustration, Caffey (1974), a pediatric radiologist, described the "whiplash shaken infant syndrome" wherein an infant is lifted and vigorously shaken as a result of misbehavior. This action is so violent and the infant so vulnerable, that intraocular bleeding, permanent brain damage, and mental retardation are common consequences.

Although a conclusive answer is unavailable, it has been speculated that some children are part of a reciprocal interaction process wherein the child's characteristic(s) provokes abuse that exacerbates the condition and family dysfunction and thereby gives rise to further abuse (Meier & Sloan, 1984).

The consequences of abuse for the victim are far reaching. The research literature suggests that abused children have serious problems in their intellectual, emotional, and social functioning. Roscoe's (1985) review of the literature indicated that, in comparison to nonabused peers, victims of maltreatment are (1) intellectually disadvantaged, (2) emotionally immature, and (3) socially unable to interact with peers and adults in an appropriate manner.

One must remember, however, that a child's behavior or characteristic(s) in and of itself does not cause abuse. Particular child attributes are only one factor in the abuse equation. As noted earlier, abuse is the product of the interaction of parental/caregiver characteristics, cultural factors, environmental considerations, and a precipitating event. The etiology of abuse cannot be traced to a sole condition. The relationship among these variables is illustrated in Figure 1.1.

Child Abuse Reporting Laws

Professionals must be cognizant of child abuse reporting laws. All states, the District of Columbia, Guam, Puerto Rico, the Virgin Islands, and American Samoa have reporting legislation. The purpose of these statutes is to identify and protect abused children, and not to punish perpetrators of abuse and neglect. Generally speaking, these laws mandate that various professionals report, to the appropriate agency, suspected maltreatment of children. The Michigan Child Protection Law (Act 238) is typical in its language identifying those individuals who are required to report

Section 3. (1)

A physician, coroner, dentist, medical examiner, nurse, a person licensed to provide emergency medical care, audiologist, psychologist, family therapist, certified social worker, social worker, social work technician, school administrator, school counselor or teacher, law enforcement officer, or duly regulated child care provider who has reasonable cause to suspect child abuse and neglect immediately by telephone or otherwise, shall make an oral report, or cause an oral report to be made,

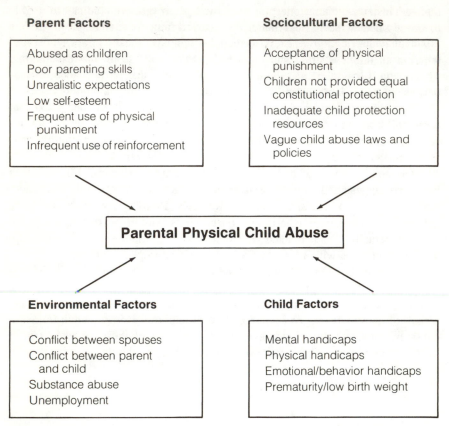

Parent Factors

Abused as children
Poor parenting skills
Unrealistic expectations
Low self-esteem
Frequent use of physical
    punishment
Infrequent use of reinforcement

Sociocultural Factors

Acceptance of physical
    punishment
Children not provided equal
    constitutional protection
Inadequate child protection
    resources
Vague child abuse laws and
    policies

Parental Physical Child Abuse

Environmental Factors

Conflict between spouses
Conflict between parent
    and child
Substance abuse
Unemployment

Child Factors

Mental handicaps
Physical handicaps
Emotional/behavior handicaps
Prematurity/low birth weight

Figure 1.1 A model of the interaction of primary factors contributing to parental child abuse. (The conditions provided under each primary factor represent only a limited number of examples.) *Note.* From "Child Abuse and Children with Handicaps" by T. Zirpoli, 1986, *Remedial and Special Education, 7,* p. 42. Copyright 1986 by PRO-ED. Reprinted by permission.

of the suspected child abuse or neglect to the department (State Department of Social Services).

All jurisdictions provide for the legal protection of reporters. Immunity from liability, civil or criminal, is granted mandated reporters who act in good faith and without malice. The good faith of an individual required to report their suspicions is, in many states, presumed. As an illustration, according to Arizona law (Chapter 5, Article 3, Title 8, of the Arizona Revised Statutes):

> Any person making a complaint, or providing information or otherwise participating in the program authorized by this article shall be immune from any civil or criminal liability by reason of such action...(Section 8-546.04.A.).

Codified in Michigan law is the following stipulation:

A person acting in good faith who makes a report or assists in any other requirement of this act shall be immune from civil or criminal liability which might otherwise be incurred thereby. A person making a report or assisting in any other requirement of this act shall be presumed to have acted in good faith (Section 5, Act 238).

Instances of suspected cases of abuse and neglect are reported to public social service departments and/or local law enforcement agencies (see Appendix). In New York State, if a person has reasonable cause to suspect maltreatment, he or she is to telephone the New York State Central Register via a toll-free number. In Ohio, reports are directed to the local Children Services Board, the county Department of Welfare or to a municipal or county law enforcement agency. Likewise, Alabama requires that the police or sheriffs department be notified or the Department of Human Resources be informed of suspected abuse or neglect. In each of these representative states, reports may be oral with follow-up written documentation usually required within a prescribed time, generally 48 to 72 hours. Ohio statutes require that the written report contain: (1) the names and addresses of the child and his or her parents or person or persons having custody of such child, if known; (2) the child's age and the nature and extent of the child's injuries, abuse, or neglect, including any evidence of previous injuries, abuse, or neglect; (3) any other information that might be helpful in establishing the cause of the injury, abuse, or neglect. The Alabama Child Abuse and Neglect Reporting Form parallels the information sought by many child protective service agencies (Figure 1.2).

Failure to report suspicions of abuse and neglect can frequently result in legal problems for the professional. Many states attempt to ensure the cooperation of mandated reporters through immunity provisions, anonymity, and the enactment of penalties for those individuals who fail to report instances of suspected abuse and neglect. In the states of New York and Michigan, for example, professionals who willfully fail to make a report are guilty of a misdemeanor and subject to civil damages. Teachers in Virginia who are remiss in their reporting responsibility are susceptible to fines. Named reporters are obligated legally, and in the author's opinion, morally, to report suspected episodes of abuse and neglect. Failure to act may lead to fines, jail terms, and in some instances, charges of negligence. Perhaps the greatest tragedy, however, is the child who suffers and possibly dies as a result of the inaction of a professional.

Intervention Opportunities

Professionals and concerned citizens can intervene and assist in breaking the cycle of child abuse and neglect in many ways. In addition to recognizing children who are victims of abuse/neglect and knowing what their reporting respon-

FORMERLY PSD-159

**STATE OF ALABAMA
DEPARTMENT OF PENSIONS AND SECURITY
REPORT OF SUSPECTED CASE OF CHILD ABUSE/NEGLECT**

☐ ABUSE ☐ NEGLECT

County Name

Co. No.   Rec'd in State Office

PSD Case Number

SECTION I — AUTHORITY

ACCORDING TO ACT NO. 563, ACTS OF ALABAMA 1965 AS AMENDED BY ACT NO. 725, REGULAR SESSION 1967 AND ACT NO. 1124, REGULAR SESSION 1975, NOW CODIFIED AS CODE OF ALABAMA, 1975, SECTION 26-14-1 THROUGH 26-14-13. A WRITTEN REPORT IS REQUIRED BY STATUTE, PERSONS REPORTING ARE REQUESTED TO FILL OUT IN TRIPLICATE AS MUCH INFORMATION AS IS KNOWN TO THEM.

SECTION II — VICTIMS

First Name	MI	Last Name	Sex	Race	Date of Birth

SECTION III - PARENT(S)/CUSTODIAN

(Father's) First Name	MI	Last Name		Race	Date of Birth
Street Address	City	State	Zip Code	Marital Status	Telephone No.
(Mother's) First Name	MI	Last Name		Race	Date of Birth
Street Address	City	State	Zip Code	Marital Status	Telephone No.
(Custodian's) First Name	MI	Last Name		Race	Date of Birth
Street Address	City	State	Zip Code	Relationship to Victim	Telephone No.

SECTION IV — OTHER CHILDREN

First Name	MI	Last Name	Sex	Race	Date of Birth

SECTION V — ALLEGED PERPETRATOR(S)

First Name	MI	Last Name	Sex	Race	Date of Birth
Address	City	State	Zip Code	Relationship to Victim	

SECTION VI — INCIDENT

Time	Place	Date	Name of person reporting	Relationship to Victim

Case Reported To: ☐ Police ☐ Sheriff ☐ DPS ☐ Other (specify)

Description of Incident:

Result:

Previous incident(s) of abuse/neglect involving child(ren) or perpetrator(s). Describe:

Signature of person completing form	Title, Agency, or Relationship to Victim(s)

SECTION VII — DPS DISPOSITION

Summary Removal Required ☐ Yes ☐ No	Where placed if removed: ☐ Shelter ☐ Relative ☐ Foster Home	Date Rec'd in County DPS	Date investigation started
☐ Founded ☐ Undetermined ☐ Unfounded	Other Services (specify)	Worker's Signature	

PSD-BFC-959
05/81 Supersedes all previous editions of PSD-159

DISTRIBUTION: White Copy — State Office
Yellow Copy — County Office
Pink Copy — State Office

Figure 1.2 Alabama child abuse form. *Note.* From Alabama Report of Suspected Case of Child Abuse/Neglect (Form 959). Montgomery, AL: Alabama Department of Human Resources. Reprinted by permission.

sibilities are, professionals can become active in local community efforts aimed at providing services to families and children who need assistance. There is no one solution for combatting the rising tide of child abuse. The following suggestions represent only a few of the available strategies. Many more will be developed when communities mobilize their resources.

- Work with local government and school officials to establish child abuse and neglect as a community priority.

- Organize telephone "hot line" services wherein parents or other caregivers can call for support in a crisis situation or seek a referral for assistance.

- Offer parent education programs, through the public schools, which focus on parenting skills, behavior management techniques, child care suggestions, parent-child communication strategies, etc.

- Establish a local chapter of Parents Anonymous (PA), a volunteer self-help group for individuals who have abused their children. Parents Anonymous affords participants an opportunity for group discussion, emotional support, and social contact.

- Develop workshops on child abuse and neglect for concerned individuals, distribute literature, establish a speaker's bureau — all of which are intended to heighten public awareness of child abuse and neglect.

- Arrange visits by public health nurses to help at risk families after the birth of their first child.

- Provide short-term respite day care through Mother's Day-Out programs, which are frequently sponsored by local churches.

- Apply to be a foster parent. Your home may be certified to provide foster care for children who are victims of abuse and neglect.

- Volunteer to be a Big Brother or Big Sister.

- Institute a parent aide program whereby parent volunteers enter single-parent households or the homes of young and/or first-time mothers and provide assistance and support as well as model effective parenting techniques.

Conclusion

The abuse and neglect of children is a frightening phenomenon that, unfortunately, is on the increase. Although the eradication of child abuse is not completely possible, informed and concerned professionals are key ingredients in attempts to bring this crisis under control. The purpose of this chapter was to present an overview of the many issues and dimensions basic to a person's understanding of child abuse and neglect. Some of these topics will be expanded and addressed in subsequent chapters. The editors are hopeful that, as a result of this information, child abuse and neglect will emerge from behind the veil of secrecy.

References

Bakan, D. (1971). *Slaughter of the innocents*. San Francisco: Jossey-Bass.

Barry, R. (1984). Incest: The last taboo. *FBI Law Enforcement Bulletin, 53*, 2–9.

Blacher, J., & Meyers, C. (1983). A review of attachment formation and disorders of handicapped children. *American Journal of Mental Deficiency, 84*, 359–371.

Bousha, D., & Twentyman, C. (1984). Mother-child interactional style in abuse, neglect, and control groups: Naturalistic observations in the home. *Journal of Abnormal Psychology, 93*, 106–114.

Brenner, A. (1984). *Helping children cope with stress*. Lexington, MA: Lexington Books.

Broadhurst, D. (1979). *The educator's role in the prevention and treatment of child abuse and neglect*. (OHDS 79-30172). Washington, DC: National Center on Child Abuse and Neglect.

Caffey, J. (1974). The whiplash shaken infant syndrome: Manual shaking of the extremities with whiplash-induced intracranial and intraocular bleedings, linked with residual permanent brain damage and mental retardation. *Pediatrics, 54*, 396–403.

Chandler, S. (1982). Knowns and unknowns in sexual abuse of children. *Journal of Social Work and Human Sexuality, 1*, 51–68.

De Francis, V. (1969). *Protecting the child victims of sex crimes committed by adults*. Denver: American Humane Association.

Elmer, E. (1967). *Children in jeopardy: A study of abused minors and their families*. Pittsburgh: University of Pittsburgh Press.

Finkelhor, D. (1979). *Sexually victimized children*. New York: Free Press.

Fontana, V. (1968). Further reflections on maltreatment of children. *New York State Journal of Medicine, 68*, 2214–2215.

Galdston, R. (1965). Observations on children who have been physically abused and their parents. *American Journal of Psychiatry, 122*, 440–443.

Garbarino, J. (1982). *Children and families in the social environment*. New York: Aldine.

Gil, D. (1970). *Violence against children: Physical abuse in the United States*. Cambridge, MA: Harvard University Press.

Goldman, R., & Gargiulo, R. (1987). Special needs of children: A population at risk for sexual abuse. *Reading Improvement, 24*, 84–88.

Goldman, R., & Wheeler, V. (1986). *Silent shame*. Danville, IL: Interstate.

Herbruck, C. (1979). *Breaking the cycle of child abuse*. Minneapolis: Winston Press.

Ingraham v. Wright, 430 U.S. 651 (1977).

Jenkins, J., Salus, M., & Schultze, G. (1979). *Child protective services: A guide for workers*. (OHDS 79-30203). Washington, DC: National Center on Child Abuse and Neglect.

Johnson, B., & Morse, H. (1968). Injured children and their parents. *Children, 15*, 147–152.

Johnson, C., & Showers, J. (1985). Injury variables in child abuse. *Child Abuse and Neglect, 9*, 207–215.

Kaplan, S., & Pelcovitz, D. (1982). Child abuse and neglect and sexual abuse. *Psychiatric Clinics of North America, 5*(2), 321–332.

Kempe, C. (1978). Sexual abuse, another hidden pediatric problem: The 1977 C. Anderson Aldrich Lecture. *Pediatrics, 62*, 382–389.

Kempe, C., Silverman, F., Steele, B., Droegemueller, W., & Silver, H. (1962). The battered-child syndrome. *Journal of the American Medical Association, 181*, 17–24.

Kramer, S. (1956). *From the tablets of Sumer*. Indian Hills, CO: Falcon's Wing Press.

Light, R. (1973). Abused and neglected children in America: A study of alternative policies. *Harvard Educational Review, 43*(4), 556–598.

Maher, D. (1985). Child abuse–the secret epidemic. *Early Child Development and Care, 22*, 53–64.

Martin, M., & Walters, J. (1982). Familial correlates of selected types of child abuse and neglect. *Journal of Marriage and the Family, 44*, 267–276.

Meier, J., & Sloan, M. (1984). The severely handicapped and child abuse. In J. Blacher (Ed.), *Severely handicapped young children and their families* (pp. 247–272). New York: Academic Press.

Merrill, E. (1962). Physical abuse of children: An agency study. In V. De Francis (Ed.), *Protecting the battered child* (pp. 1–5). Denver: American Humane Association.

National Center on Child Abuse and Neglect. (1981). *Study findings: National study of the incidence and severity of child abuse and neglect*. (OHDS 82-30325). Washington, DC.

National Center on Child Abuse and Neglect. (1986). *Child abuse and neglect: An informed approach to a shared concern*. (No. 20-01016). Washington, DC.

National Committee for the Prevention of Child Abuse. (1982). *Basic facts about sexual child abuse*. Chicago.

Ohio Department of Public Welfare (undated). *Open the door on child abuse and neglect*. Columbus, OH.

Ounsted, C., Oppenheimer, R., & Lindsay, J. (1974). Aspects of bonding failure: The psychopathology and psychotherapeutic treatment of families of battered children. *Developmental Medicine and Child Neurology, 16*, 447–456.

Park, R., & Collmer, C. (1975). Child abuse: An interdisciplinary analysis. In E. Hetherington (Ed.), *Review of child development research* (pp. 509–590). Chicago: University of Chicago Press.

Pettis, K., & Hughes, R. (1985). Sexual victimization of children: A current perspective. *Behavioral Disorders, 10*(2), 136–144.

Radbill, S. (1974). A history of child abuse and infanticide. In R. Helfer & C. Kempe (Eds.), *The battered child* (pp. 3–21). Chicago: University of Chicago Press.

Roscoe, B. (1985). Intellectual, emotional and social deficits of abused children: A review. *Childhood Education, 61*(5), 388–392.

Rosenburg, M., & Reppucci, N. (1983). Abusive mothers: Perceptions of their own children's behavior. *Journal of Consulting and Clinical Psychology, 51*, 674–682.

Russell, J. (1983). The incidence and prevalence of intrafamilial and extrafamilial sexual abuse of female children. *Child Abuse and Neglect, 7*, 133–146.

Ryan, W. (1962). *Infanticide: Its law, prevalence, prevention, and history*. London: J. Churchill.

Salzinger, S., Kaplan, S., & Artemyeff, C. (1983). Mothers' personal social networks and child maltreatment. *Journal of Abnormal Psychology, 92*, 68–76.

Sandgrund, H., Gaines, R., & Green, A. (1974). Child abuse and mental retardation: A problem of cause and effect. *American Journal of Mental Deficiency, 79*, 327–330.

Sarafino, E. (1979). An estimate of nationwide incidence of sexual offenses against children. *Child Welfare, 58*, 127–134.

Seattle Institute for Child Advocacy, Committee for Children. (1985). *Talking about touching: A personal safety curriculum*. Seattle.

Segal, J. (1978). *A child's journey*. New York: McGraw-Hill.

Sgroi, S. (1982). *Handbook of clinical intervention in child sexual abuse*. Lexington, MA: Lexington Books.

Sgroi, S., Blick, L., & Porter, F. (1982). In S. Sgroi (Ed.), *Handbook of clinical intervention in child sexual abuse* (pp. 9–37). Lexington, MA: Lexington Books.

Soeffing, M. (1975). Abused children are exceptional children. *Exceptional Children, 42*, 126–133.

Solomon, T. (1973). History and demography of child abuse. *Pediatrics, 51*, 773–776.

Solomons, G. (1979). Child abuse and developmental disabilities. *Developmental Medicine and Child Neurology, 21*, 101–108.

Starr, R., Jr. (1982). A research-based approach to the prediction of child abuse. In R. Starr, Jr. (Ed.), *Child abuse prediction: Policy implications* (pp. 105–134). Cambridge, MA: Ballinger.

Steele, B. (1976). Violence within the family. In R. Helfer & C. Kempe (Eds.), *Child abuse and neglect* (pp. 3–23). Cambridge, MA: Ballinger.

Steele, B., & Pollock, C. (1968). A psychiatric study of parents who abuse infants and small children. In R. Helfer & C. Kempe (Eds.), *The battered child* (pp. 89–133). Chicago: University of Chicago Press.

Straus, M. (1980). Stress and physical child abuse. *Child Abuse and Neglect, 4*, 75–88.

Summit, R., & Kryso, J. (1978). Sexual abuse of children: A clinical spectrum. *American Journal of Orthopsychiatry, 48*, 237–251.

Tyler, R., & Stone, L. (1985). Child pornography: Perpetuating the sexual victimization of children. *Child Abuse and Neglect, 9*, 507–519.

Vander Mey, B., & Neff, R. (1982). Adult-child incest: A review of research and treatment. *Adolescence, 17*, 717–735.

Wilson, M., Daly, M., & Weghorst, S. (1980). Household cooperation and the risk of child abuse and neglect. *Journal of Biosocial Science, 12*, 333–340.

Wolfe, D. (1985). Child-abusive parents: An empirical review and analysis. *Psychological Review, 97*, 462–482.

Young, L. (1964). *Wednesday's children: A study of child neglect and abuse*. New York: McGraw-Hill.

Zirpoli, T. (1986). Child abuse and children with handicaps. *Remedial and Special Education, 7*(2), 39–48.

Chapter 2

An Educational Perspective on Abuse

Renitta L. Goldman

Definitions

What is *child abuse*? It may be broadly defined as physical or mental abuse, emotional injury, sexual abuse, or exploitation, negative treatment or maltreatment of a child under the age of 18 by a person responsible for that child's welfare (Meier & Sloan, 1984). However, others would argue that there is no real definition of child abuse. Is malnutrition, failing to adequately feed and clothe, allowing a child to live in a depressed or deprived environment, or keeping a child outside of school to be defined as child abuse? According to Gelles (1982), child abuse is a political term, which is not useful in legal or scientific realms among different social and cultural groups. Practices of child rearing that are deemed acceptable vary greatly. This is a society that upholds sorority and fraternity hazing and promotes involved cosmetic surgery to promote beauty. This is a society that upholds corporal punishment. It is composed of adults willing to inflict physical punishment on its youth. According to Stark and McEvoy (1970), 93% of families in the United States use physical punishment with their children. Straus (1980) found that the percentage of families who spanked their children was as high as 82%. An interview of 232 school principals in 18 states revealed that 51% used physical punishment in dealing with exceptional children (Feshback & Feshback, 1976). It has been suggested that corporal punishment is not only ineffective but also counterproductive. Children do not seem to be protected under the law. The Eighth Amendment forbids use of cruel or unusual punishment, yet spanking persists. In China, where corporal punishment is nearly nonexistent, incidents of child abuse are rare (Sidel, 1972).

What is neglect? A widely accepted difference between physical abuse and neglect is that the former is associated with an act of commission, the latter with an act of omission (Kaplan & Pelcovitz, 1982). Relatively little research attention is paid to the condition of neglect. Toro (1982) has suggested that neglect may be more pervasive and possibly more important to the developmental problems of its victims. Neglect embraces such things as abandonment, lack of proper parental care or control, and failure to provide basic necessities. Medical neglect describes a situation in which parents fail to provide a child with the necessary medical care. In nonlife threatening situations, the court decisions have been split as to medical neglect.

Erickson, McEvoy, and Colucci (1984) have differentiated physical abuse and neglect from psychological or emotional abuse and neglect. While physical abuse includes physical harm or imminent threat thereof, psychological abuse encompasses intentional or negligently inflicted psychological injury. Some states interpret this form of maltreatment in broad terms that allows intervention to prevent *threatened* psychological harm. States that interpret psychological abuse in more narrow terms permit intervention only when a child is *actually suffering psychiatric symptoms* (Goldstein, Freud, & Solnit, 1979).

The two maltreatment conditions of abuse and neglect were compared with each other in a prospective follow-up of 219 physically abused children and 159 grossly neglected children. Most of the children were under protective custody and placed in out-of-home care. A third group of low SES children were assumed to be at risk for maltreatment but no reports had been filed was also studied. The investigator (Kent, 1976) found that both maltreated groups were at intake rated as manifesting a higher incidence of problem behaviors as compared with the third group. The group that had been physically abused was rated as more disobedient, more aggressive, having more tantrums, and having more peer problems than the group that had been neglected. By contrast, the neglected group showed more emotional withdrawal and greater intellectual and developmental delay than either the physically abused or comparison group. Teachers had rated the majority of maltreated children as having unsatisfactory peer relationships. Although methodological flaws have been noted concerning this study (Lamphear, 1985), it is particularly noteworthy in its attempt to differentiate the effects between abuse and neglect.

Prevalence

The Abuse Prevention and Treatment Act, Public Law 93-247 was first signed into law in 1974. It was renewed by Congress in 1984 and provides funds to help identify, report, investigate, and treat abuse cases. This law established the National Center on Child Abuse and Neglect located in the Children's Bureau, U.S. Department of Health and Human Resources. Much of our prevalence data comes from this resource.

The number of abuse cases shows remarkable variability — between 40,000 to 4.7 million a year. Estimates are that an even higher number are neglect cases. These cases included children who are shot, stabbed, burned, kicked, punched, or hit with an instrument by their parents, sexually abused, and emotionally neglected and abused. Although these figures include children between the ages of 3 to 17, significantly most abused children are *under* the age of 4. The National Center on Child Abuse and Neglect demonstrated an increase in the number of reports filed over an 8-year period in the U.S. In 1976, 416,033 reports were filed, whereas in 1983, 10,007,658 reports were filed (Zirpoli, 1986).

However, our prevalence data is unclear for many reasons. Estimates of child abuse have clearly increased through increased public recognition (Bourne, 1981). New laws exist that require reporting and expand who is mandated to report. Although all states and the District of Columbia have mandated reporting laws, six states do not have standard reporting forms on the characteristics of the child. Among the states that do have reporting forms, 18 do not identify preexisting handicaps of the child (Camblin, 1982). Many cases go unreported. Parents do not take the child for medical care, or if taken, many do not return to the same medical care facility. Some injuries are not detected. Some private physicians fail to report. Public health persons interpret abuse differently. School personnel come into daily contact with children and are mandated reporters. Yet, a low number of school officials report abuse and neglect (Goldman & Wheeler, 1986). The number of children who die by accidents, natural causes, or homicides is uncertain. Solomon (1973) reported that the average age of children killed by parents was under 3. Ironically, if all the cases were reported, the system could only handle one third of those cases (Zirpoli, 1986).

Although both boys and girls are equally likely to be abused, boys are more vulnerable at an earlier age. The highest incidence for boys occurred between the ages of 3 to 5; whereas, the highest incidence for girls occurred between ages 15 and 17. Preschoolers suffer more severely from physical abuse and are more likely to sustain permanent damage than older children. An only child is slightly more likely for abuse than a child with siblings although families with four or more children are more likely to physically neglect and sexually abuse children than smaller families (Light, 1973). Mothers are more likely to inflict physical abuse; fathers are more likely to perpetrate sexual abuse. Although men are more frequently associated with acts of violence, in physical abuse women as perpetrators are far beyond their usual representation in acts of violence. They are apt to inflict more serious injury (Johnson & Showers, 1985). Parents at home (unemployed or homemakers) are more likely to be abusive. Most abusive parents fall within the normal range of intelligence. Geographically, highest incidence of abuse is reported in the Midwest, the lowest in the South. Sexual abuse is more common in rural areas, and emotional neglect is more common in suburban areas. Abuse and neglect cross all ethnic and racial boundaries. Physical abuse is reported to be more prevalent among low income families; emotional neglect is found to be more prevalent with families with incomes greater than $15,000 a year (Kurtz & Kurtz, 1987). However, this difference between socioeconomic groups could be related to intrinsic problems in reporting. The poor and minorities have greater visibility among social service agencies. By contrast, the more affluent seek private professional services. Thus, they are less vulnerable to professional checks and labeling (Miller & Miller, 1979).

The Dynamics of Child Abuse

As to the etiology of abuse, the prevailing theory is that an interaction exists among a psychologically vulnerable parent, a child who is unique in some way, and environmental factors (Kaplan & Pelcovitz, 1982).

Helfer (1975) had identified three variables in the formula for child abuse:

1. Crisis(es) in the family.
2. Personality traits of the abuser.
3. Characteristics of the victim.

Earlier research efforts tended to focus on the personality traits of the abuser. Now greater focus has been on the characteristics of the victim. Meier and Sloan (1984) pointed out the mutual interaction among several factors that contribute to abuse. They identified ecological factors such as conflict between spouses, unemployment, and inadequate income, which help instigate abuse. They identified parental factors such as socioeconomic status, learned aggression, alcohol, and stress, as additional contributing factors leading to abuse. Child characteristics are another significant factor in the dynamics of abuse. Is the child a problem child? Does the child demonstrate colic, incontinence, mental or physical illness, or disability? Finally, there is precipitating situation or event such as the child crying or great frustration. Then the child abuse begins.

Characteristics of the Perpetrator

How can a parent abuse a child? Desirable mothering behavior is not a natural phenomena. Parents who themselves felt rejection in childhood are more likely to reject their offspring. Human animals like nonhumans at times act and react in a stressful situation with little conscious intent. Abuse, neglect, and infanticide of offspring occur regularly in some animal populations such as among the primate species of monkeys in Southeast Asia. Nonhuman species are programmed to review the resources and dispose of less viable offspring. It is the parents' nature to maximize "fitness" (i.e., to invest reproduction and nurturing efforts in their offspring). Investment is made to ensure that not only children but grandchildren thrive. However, this individual fitness scheme does not extend to nonbiological children. Therefore, the chances of abuse by a stepparent is two to six times more likely. Parents limit their investment in each child and, therefore, free themselves to invest in other offspring. Conflict results when offspring strive toward greater investment than the parent can provide. If a child is removed from the home by the court for child abuse, often a new pregnancy or dissolution of the marital bond occurs (Daly and Wilson, 1981).

Are abused and neglected children less appealing to parents than other children? Is this lack of appeal inherent in the child or the result of experience with a maltreating parent? Crittenden (1985) reported on the results of two studies undertaken with over 100 low SES mother-infant (1–19 months) pairs. The results offered evidence supporting a model in which the mother initiates the maltreatment, but both mother and infant behave in ways as to maintain the situation. No difference in congenital characteristics was found between maltreated and adequately reared infants. However, the maltreated youngsters displayed deviance in characteristics that had been affected by environmental conditions. Some abused infants were more difficult and angry when stressed. Other abused infants were more passive and somewhat helpless when stressed. When interventions were made with the mothers to stop the maltreatment, the infants' behaviors improved.

Besides inflicting physical abuse, abusing and nonabusing mothers seem to differ in other ways when dealing with their children. Allen and Wasserman (1985) studied infants ranging in age from 8 to 25 months who had been physically abused by their mothers. Mothers and infants were videorecorded as they were told to "play with your baby as you would at home." Analysis of the communication indicated that abusing mothers are likely to ignore their infants and are less likely to use verbal means to teach their children about the world. The abusing mothers' limited verbal stimulation and availability do not encourage language development. These mothers may provide physical needs, but their interactions appear as covert neglect. Simultaneously the abused infant may be less responsive and communicative, behaviors which may cause the mother to feel less effective and to withdraw even further.

Factors within the perpetrator who commits sexual abuse have been identified. These include prior abuse, isolation, aggressive impulses, stress, and cultural forces such as pornography (Schor, 1987). Conte (1984) proposed that few data support the belief that all incestuous abusers abuse only their own children.

Finkelhor (1979) described 4 preconditions of abuse:

1. The individual is motivated toward abuse.
2. The individual overcomes internal (societal) inhibitions.
3. The individual overcomes external (situational) inhibitions.
4. The individual overcomes the child's resistance.

The moral dilemma involved in why parents abuse their children and the moral reasoning that people undergo have been analyzed. Frequently a lack of attachment in the abuser's own history exists. In a simplified explanation of Kohlberg's paradigm, individuals undergo stages in moral reasoning. An initial stage is premoral, which is characterized by the attitude, "might is right." A higher stage is the conventional or social conformity stage. The desired stage is the principled stage in which a universal principle of morality is adhered to. Abusers fail to reach higher stages of moral reasoning (Kohlberg, 1984).

The median age of the abuser is 25. Frequently cited characteristics among abusive families are that the perpetrator has observed abuse and violence, has *perceived* stressful life experiences, is emotionally insecure, has marital and/or financial problems, and experiences social isolation and high mobility. The family member may have undergone minor criminal offenses and unemployment (Spinetta & Rigler, 1972). Often the family has no support system and no extended family or social reinforcement for appropriate parenting behavior (Garbarino, 1982). The abusing parent may have a negative self-image and unrealistic expectations of the child (Kaplan & Pelcovitz, 1982; Sangrund, Gaines, & Green, 1974).

Many abusive and neglectful parents have had negative childhood experiences so that they have developed inappropriate childrearing behaviors and practices. Their histories reveal that they have lived with parents who have undergone episodes of alcohol abuse and mental illness. They were exposed to emotional maltreatment and excessive physical discipline (Kurtz & Kurtz, 1987). These parents' expectations of their children are often unrealistic. A child may be unresponsive to a mother's inept or ill-timed feeding attempts. The mother then perceives the child as negative, cold, and unworthy of care. Steele (1980) has described some parents' inability to show "empathetic caring" for their child. This term refers to the ability to be sensitive to a child's needs and to meet those needs. Abusive parents during stress periods place their needs before those of their children. Although the general public perceives abusive parents as "crazy," only 5% are psychotic. Children in their care are at extreme risk. For example, psychotic parents will show paranoia, indicating that the child is "out to get them" (Spinetta & Rigler, 1972).

Abusive parents are often socially isolated, a situation which they seem to prefer. They frequently shun social interaction and resist help from human service or educational agencies. They lack supportive, reciprocal relationships with family, neighbors, church, or other helping agencies. Without support services, parental abuse of children is far more likely.

To understand child abuse is to recognize the critical roles of stress and social isolation. The preponderance of lower socioeconomic groups in reported child abuse statistics may well represent the greater likelihood that violence will be used by those who do not have the same environmental support that the more affluent enjoy.

Conditions of a damaged fetus have been associated with drug and alcohol abuse among pregnant women. These women are likely to neglect their own welfare and ultimately, the welfare of their fetus. Many families with drug or alcohol addiction had abused their children. The addiction had interfered with the ability to be responsible, caring parents.

Single-parent families are at higher risk for child abuse than are two-parent families for several reasons. They tend to be poor and come in contact with human service agencies who are likely to report child maltreatment. The single parent has the sole responsibility for child rearing and may have fewer resources to depend on for support. Being a single parent and adolescent can even be more stressful. The adolescent parent is struggling with his/her own sense of being and lacks the knowledge to be an effective parent (Kurtz & Kurtz, 1976).

Johnson and Showers (1985) identified some common characteristics of abused victims. These were that the victim was likely male, under four years of age, and had been exposed to battering from 1 to 3 years (Solomon, 1973). The victim was likely to be of low birth weight (Lynch & Roberts, 1982) and had behavioral problems and a difficult temperament (Bousha & Twentyman, 1984). Additional characteristics noted were messy and poor eating habits, crying (frequent/high pitched), sleep and toileting problems, and unresponsiveness to their parents' attention (Nesbit & Karagianis, 1982). Many of these characteristics were abnormalities, which were subtle, not obvious handicaps but disturbing to the parents nonetheless. Soeffling (1975) has observed that these child victims are different or perceived as difficult to raise. All of these children required special and/or additional parental care and attention. Interestingly, only one child in a family is often the victim of abuse (Parke & Collmer, 1975).

A longitudinal investigation of the developmental sequelae of maltreatment in infancy was undertaken (Egeland & Sroufe, 1981). The researchers asked what were the developmental consequences of abuse and neglect over the first two years of the infants' lives. The mother, the child, and the home environment served as the sources for data collection. Kinds of maltreatment were grouped as physical abuse, hostile/verbal abuse, hostile/verbal abuse with physical abuse, emotional neglect, emotional neglect with physical abuse, physical neglect, and physical neglect with physical abuse. Mothers who provided adequate care were chosen as the control group. Results indicated that exposure to different forms of maltreatment resulted in different psychosocial outcomes. The physically abused group had significantly higher scores on ratings of observed aggressive behaviors, frustration, and noncompliance as compared with nonabused controls. Greater anger and frustration toward their mother were shown by both the verbal/hostile groups than the control group. Psychological unavailability also seemed to have negative effects. Whining and negative affect were greatest among the group who were emotionally neglected without physical abuse. Both groups experiencing emotional neglect displayed less positive affect and higher rating of child noncompliance than the control group.

The Role of Special Education

The population served by special educators seems to be at greater risk for all kinds of abuse. This population includes children with mental retardation and those who were premature infants and/or among other handicapped preschoolers. Children with undesirable psychosocial behavior may be enrolled in programs for the behaviorally disturbed. Children with physical handicaps receive special education services as do handicapped adolescents. The following discussion addresses the characteristics of special children that tend to make them more vulnerable to abuse.

Helfer (1975) suggested that the special education staff is in an excellent position to observe and identify cases of potential abuse. The staff could provide the families of special children with extra supportive assistance including help in developing realistic expectations for the child.

Characteristics of the Victim

As to the relationship between abuse and a handicapped child, extensive reviews of the literature in areas of medicine, psychology, education, law, and social work have revealed no established interaction. However, some studies indicate a correlation, and professional opinion suggests a relationship (Soeffing, 1975). Zirpoli (1986) noted that the majority of research shows some common characteristics among victims increase their vulnerability; however, others argue there are no definitive characteristics (Starr, 1982).

Historically, the birth of a handicapped child was interpreted as God's will, the interference of the devil, and punishment on the parents (Meier & Sloan, 1984). Having a handicapped child was equated with the dying of an "Idealized child" (Kubler-Ross, 1969), and parents underwent stages hopefully to resolve this loss. Stages of denial, anger, open grieving, acceptance, and resolution have been described in the literature (Baladerian, 1985b, Gargiulo, 1985, Meier & Sloan, 1984). If the handicapping condition is not perceived as the fault of the parent, greater social acceptance and more open acknowledgment is likely.

A debate persists as to whether the handicapping condition is accidental or inflicted. Daly and Wilson (1981) observed that the question often persists is the developmental disability a contributing factor to the abuse or a result of that abuse. In a comprehensive nationwide survey of 14,000 abused and neglected children reported to the National Clearing House on Child Abuse and Neglect in Denver, a disproportionate number of abused children were special children. More specifically, 4.8% of the 14,000 were reported emotionally disturbed, 2% were diagnosed as mentally retarded, 1.7% were deemed physically handicapped, 1.3% had congenital defects, and 1.8% had chronic illness such as diabetes (Soeffling, 1975).

Several investigators (Daly & Wilson, 1981; D'Onofrio, Robinson, Isett, Roszlcowsic, & Spreak, 1980) have commented on parent-child attachment issues. They found that parents often take children to larger institutions believing that the quality of care would be better than at home or in a small-care facility. These parents become less likely to interact with their youngsters and the number of visits steadily decline. Surrogate caretakers (e.g., foster or stepparents, babysitters, institutional childcare workers, single mothers' boyfriends) are more likely to abuse handicapped children than biologically related parents. Male caretakers, including natural fathers, are more likely to abuse these children than female caretakers. Sixty to 90% of these abusers were abused as children (Lightcap, Kurland, & Burgess, 1982).

Abused children are expected to be children with academic difficulties. Frisch and Rhodes (1982) studied students referred for an evaluation for learning problems during a 1-year period in Oahu, Hawaii. Of the 430 youngsters, 6.7% of them had been reported to the state protective agency for abuse. This number is a three and a half times higher rate than for all other children of similar age in Oahu. No difference in the types of abuse received or the kinds of learning problems was noted.

Baladerian (1985b) when describing the crisis the handicapped child creates for the family posed several thoughts the parent may undergo:

1. My life is more difficult.
2. You have underscored my inadequacy.
3. You frustrate me in caring for you.
4. You add pressure.
5. You add cost.
6. You take my spouse away from me.
7. You cannot protect yourself.
8. You won't be believed.

Children with cognitive or neurological deficits often demonstrate behavior that is particularly provocative and unmanageable (Elmer, 1967; Martin, 1972; Sangrund et al., 1974).

Handicapped children are particularly at risk for abuse. The children are less likely to defend against abuse nor articulate that abuse. They are less able to differentiate appropriate from inappropriate physical conditions. They are more dependent on the care of others and, therefore, more trusting of others. They are reluctant to report abuse for fear of losing the linkage to major caregivers. They are considered less credible.

Mental Retardation

A long history exists establishing a relationship between impairment of intellectual growth and language learning and child abuse and neglect. For example, in the nineteenth century a child was imprisoned in a feud over inheritance. He was rescued and tutored so that he could use language and recall the facts of his past (Money, 1982). In the early twentieth century following the invention of the intelligence test by Binet, various studies reported low IQs associated with social and intellectural impoverishment and neglect (Gordon 1923, Skodak & Skeels, 1945).

In the 1930s the American psychologist H. Skeels undertook a study of the effects of abuse, neglect, and deprivation and was able to document the benefit institutionalized infants received from being placed under the care of adult inmates. In a follow-up investigation 30 years later, Skeels (1966) studied the histories of the two groups who had been institutionalized as infants, the one who had received adult inmate interaction and the older group who had not. The first group had fared far better, having been taken into adoption, receiving normal schooling, and showing normal ability to earn a living and establish a family life. The second group had fared badly in becoming dependent on state welfare or custodial care. Their IQs were permanently defective versus the first group whose IQs fell in the average range.

Further evidence of the toll abuse and neglect play on intellectual development is revealed through a study by Dennis (1973), who investigated two groups of children who were inmates of an orphanage in Beirut, Lebanon. The first group was older, had been wards of the orphanage all their lives, and had been reared under extreme conditions of institutional neglect and deprivation. They had lost half of their mental growth. Instead of expected IQs of 100, theirs were around 50. In contrast, a younger group had been put up for adoption before age 2. Their average IQ was 100.

As stated earlier, statistics are unclear as to whether mental retardation is an antecedent to abuse. Brandwein (1973) has underscored that children frequently receive brain damage from abuse. Our numbers are dependent on the accuracy of preabuse medical and education records. Schilling and Schinke (1984) indicated that children of mentally retarded parents are at higher risk for abuse than those with normally functioning parents. They further observed that retarded persons exists in poverty — of income, experience, and opportunity. These unfortunate circumstances compound the likelihood of maltreatment of retarded individuals and children of retarded parents.

Retarded persons have a uniqueness that increases their risk for abuse. They have a prolonged, often lifelong dependency on caretakers. They are subjected to the cultural myths and misunderstandings about mental retardation. One such myth is that they have no feelings of sexuality or that they are overly charged sexually. In reality at times they suffer their parents' emotional reactions to their retardation, and they are frequently isolated from the mainstream of social life. They are subject to a unique form of sexual abuse, the denial of their sexual rights, which can range from punitive suppression of masturbation to enforced segregation by sex and forced sterilization (Szymanski, 1981).

In one group of abused children under study, 43% were deemed mentally retarded. Most of these children had been identified as retarded before the abuse occurred. The stresses placed on parents by having children with limited cognitive functioning were considered as important contributing factors to the violence that ensued (Friedman & Morse, 1974).

A study was undertaken (Goldberg, Marcovitch, MacGregor, & Lojkasek, 1986) to determine whether parents of Down syndrome children coped differently than parents of developmentally delayed youngsters. The hypothesis was that since the former parents had had a longer time to adjust to their children's difficulties than parents with developmentally delayed children, they would report fewer symptoms of distress, more support from others, higher self-esteem, and a greater sense of internal control than would parents whose children had problems of unknown etiology. Fifty-nine preschoolers' parents were asked to respond to interviews and questionnaires. The results were that all comparisons favored the Down syndrome group. Furthermore, fathers of Down syndrome children seemed to have fewer symptoms of distress, higher self-esteem, more internal locus of control, and less support than mothers. These findings would suggest a need to understand individual differences among families of handicapped youngsters. The effects of a child's handicap on fathers differ from those upon mothers.

Elmer (1967 and 1977) conducted a series of investigations on abused and nonabused, accident victims. These groups were studied during three time periods: (1) at the time of the trauma; (2) a follow-up after 1 year, and (3) a follow-up after 8 years. The 17 abused and 17 nonabused victims were matched in age, sex, race, and socioeconomic status. Evaluation measures include behavioral, physical, and intellectual indices. At the time of the trauma, while both groups suffered adverse health status, the abused children had more overall problems and showed more mood variations. No significant differences were noted in height, head circumferences, distractability, activity level, nor delay in mental, language, or motor areas. After 1 year, the abused population was directionally in worse shape on many developmental variables. The only statistically significant difference was that the nonabused accident children were more active. This finding seems to support the theory that abused children are generally more passive children than the general population. Both groups showed considerable deficits, perhaps reflecting the overriding influence of low socioeconomic status. After 8 years, fewer differences were noted between the two groups. Physically, both groups weighed more than the matched untraumatized comparison groups. Seventy percent of the traumatized groups had language problems. The abused group had more expressive language problems and some signs of verbal aggression and impulsivity as revealed by using a storytelling procedure. No statistically significant differences were noted in how the children rated self-concept, intellectual ability, visual-motor integration (Bender-Gestalt), academic achievement, or teacher ratings, although abused children scored poorly directionally on several of these measures. Those children who had been removed from their homes did not fare better. Elmer analyzed the inconsistency of the findings. While the abused group occasionally differed from either the accident or the comparison groups, the abused group never differed from both. Further, the number and strength of significant group differences diminished across the three times paths suggesting that stressful living conditions and pathology were shared by the two groups of traumatized youngsters. Elmer undertook additional data analyses to see which variables might predict outcomes. Five independent variables of family background characteristics, maternal perceptions of the child, child characteristics, and abused group membership were used to predict nine outcome variables: expressive language, intellectual ability, school achievement, achievement ability quotient, overall degrees of disturbance, separation problems, nervous mannerisms, overcontrol of aggression, and undercontrol of aggression. Analyses for the outcome variable indicated that abuse was not a useful predictor of child outcome; whereas a combination of other independent variables proved to be quite useful. Elmer concluded that SES and related social stress may be more important than the abuse in the determination of the course of child development.

Additional studies have indicated that abused youngsters have lower cognitive functioning. The cognitive status of abused, neglected, and nonabused (control) children ages 5 through 12 was studied. Results indicated that abused children were 10 times as likely to demonstrate significant verbal versus performance differences on IQ measures (Sangrund et al., 1974). Martin (1972) undertook a 3 year follow-up study of 42 abused children. Within this sample 18 had neurological handicaps, 14 scored below 80 on IQ measures, 14 indicated failure to thrive in terms of height and weight, and 16 were language delayed. In a 4½ year follow-up study of 58 abused youngsters, one third scored significantly lower on tests of intellectual performance (Martin, 1972).

Down syndrome infants have been found to be less ingratiating and demonstrated less frequent smiling behaviors than normally developing peers. Therefore, the youngsters were apt to develop weaker and defective bonding between them and their mothers.

Many studies have indicated that abused children have scored lower on standardized tests of intelligence. Sangrund et al. (1974) used a sample of 120 children, 60 of whom had been abused, 30 neglected, and 30 nonabused. Of the abused children, none had suffered head injuries. It was found that 25% of the abused population were retarded, 20% of the neglected population were retarded, and only 3% of the nonabused control group were retarded.

Buchanan and Oliver (1979) studied 140 children under the age of 16 who were admitted to two British hospitals. Thirty-one children had been victims of actual abuse before admission to the hospitals. A further 10% were at risk for abuse, having been threatened with injury or death by their parents. In terms of abuse and mental retardation, 3% had definitely suffered assaults as babies, which caused brain damage so intense as to render them severely retarded. An additional 11% could have been deemed mentally retarded as a result of abuse. In terms of neglect and mental retardation, 48% of the children were considered suffering from neglect — inadequate parental care. In 24% of the survey the neglect was considered a contributory factor in reducing intellectual potential.

Caffey (1974) identified the "whiplash" shaking of infants, which can cause later mental retardation and permanent brain damage. This casual, habitual manual shaking of infants often leaves no external signs of injury to the head, face, or neck. However, it does cause massive intracranial and intraocular bleeding. The damage may go undetected by parents and physicians. This syndrome may first be noticed at school age when minor motor defects are first detected. Permanent impairments of vision and hearing may first be noticed when the child is 5 or 6 years of age.

Physical abuse may well impact on the intellectual ability of its victims. Brandwein (1973) believes that physical abuse that causes neurological damage is a major contributor to the high incidence of retardation among abused youngsters. Abused children are often placed in special education classes.

Byrne and Cunningham (1985) examined the effects mentally handicapped children have on their families. Their study reached the conclusion that stress is not inevitable for families with mentally handicapped children. The effects are dependent on the number of stressors, family integration, and the family's interpretation of the situation. A major need for some families could be a liaison person who could explain, mediate, and interpret social, educational, and health services. Family adaption patterns for dealing with a mentally handicapped child fall across a continuum. Coping is influenced by such factors as social support systems and family environment.

Research has indicated a close relationship between child handicaps and child abuse. A handicapped child places a special strain on a family, and families with limited resources may not be able to cope with the burden. In a sample of 125 children under protective services, the children's handicapping conditions (such as mental retardation) apparently contributed to the abuse or neglect in 37% of the cases. By early identification of specific disabilities, earlier and more appropriate intervention might occur (Souther, 1984).

Undesirable Psychosocial Behaviors

Gil (1970) undertook a nationwide survey of 6000 abused children. Twenty-nine percent of these children had demonstrated abnormal social behaviors before being abused. A British researcher (Calam, 1983) conducted a follow-up study of 38 physically abused chilren, ages 5 to 12, matched on age and sex. Using teacher ratings on behavior and academic measures, the investigator found that the abused children were more reactive – hostile, had poor peer relationships, and were disruptive. These undesirable behaviors were more prevalent among males and with youngsters who lived with only one parent. In a study of psychosocial behavior of abused toddlers, George and Main (1979) found these youngsters showed more aggression toward peers and daycare staff. The Denver Department of Welfare stated that 20% of the 97 abused children reported were considered unmanageable by child welfare workers (Johnson & Showers, 1985).

Unfortunately, children who have grown up in an atmosphere of violence, because of imitation and identification become violent adults. An association between abuse and delinquency exists. King (1975) investigated the background of 9 adolescents who had committed murder and found that all 9 had histories of severe beatings as children.

Even gifted children with undesirable behaviors seem eligible for abuse. Freidman and Morse (1974) concluded that hyperactive or intellectually precocious youngsters displayed inquisitiveness and intellectual superiority – behaviors that caused vulnerability to abuse.

The syndrome of multiple personality has been identified with a high incidence of physical and/or sexual abuse in childhood. Those with multiple personality disorders occasionally abuse their own children. This syndrome is difficult to diagnose, particularly in childhood, and difficult to treat. (Coons, 1986).

Physical Handicaps

Children with orthopedic disorders, spina bifida, fibrocystic diseases, and cleft palates are children at risk for abuse (Daly & Wilson, 1981). Diamond and Jaudes (1983) undertook a study of 86 children with cerebral palsy. Twenty percent were abused and 14% were at risk for abuse. Nine others were abused after the onset of the cerebral palsy, which resulted from prior abuse.

Solomon (1979) surveyed the research literature to determine how cerebral palsy populations are affected by abuse. There is a possibility that parental abuse was a cause of the disability. MacKeith (1974) estimated that 400 cases of brain damage resulting from child abuse would occur each year in the United Kingdom. Each year 1,600 new cases of cerebral palsy occurred, and in one half of these cases, no apparent cause could be found. Over 200 children who met the criteria for a diagnosis of cerebral palsy were studied. Twelve percent had acquired their deficit. Injury to the head was the second most common cause of the acquired motor handicap. It is uncertain how much of the trauma recorded was definitely accidental since the data was collected on children born between 1959 and 1966, a period in which child abuse was not easily recognized (Nelson & Ellenburg, 1978).

Jaudes and Diamond (1985) wrote a descriptive paper that reviewed the problems of children whose development was affected by the compound influences of maltreatment and the presence of a handicapping condition. The authors based their conclusion from working with 37 children with cerebral palsy who had been abused. They also reviewed the literature in related areas. They concluded that the very medical, legal, and protective systems designed to care for the child often fail, leaving the handicapped child without the opportunity to reach developmental potential.

Premature Infants

For a period of their lives, low birth weight infants are indeed at risk and have received considerable attention in the literature. Although less than 8% of births are premature, they are overrepresented as a significant percentage of abused infants. Fontana (1971) found that 50% of the premature infant population he had studied had been abused.

Klein and Sterne (1971) reported about 25% of 51 premature infants they studied were abused. The high risk families revealed common sources of stress: isolation without adequate social support systems, financial problems, marital maladjustment, and inadequate child care arrangements.

Premature babies are prone to behaviors that are not desirable. They are prone to colic and general irritability, difficult to feed, and hypersensitive to parent handling (Bishop, 1971). They often are hospitalized for an extended period so that the prolonged separation between parents and child may have a profound effect on their lives. There is a delay in the learning about each other, and being able to recognize distress signs and to control irritable behavior.

Clinical research regarding attachment of normal versus handicapped children was reviewed. In general, the evidence suggests that attachments formation between young handicapped children and their mothers and caretakers may be delayed, dulled, or even absent. Severely impaired-handicapped infants, especially those who were premature and sickly often require prolonged hospitalization. These infants may develop characteristics that promote abuse (Blacher & Meyers, 1983).

Handicapped Preschoolers

At birth the human infant possesses far fewer behaviors than the human adult. During the forthcoming preschool years, the child acquires a wide range of behaviors that favorably compares with those possessed by an adult. The preschool years are a period in which children make rapid strides along several dimensions of development. They widely expand their language and communication skills, learn to play with others, develop a repertoire of preacademic skills such as learning numbers and letters, and develop sex roles (Waterman, MacFarlane, Conerly, Damon, Durfee, & Long, 1986). However, the acquisition of behaviors is contingent on the dialectic interaction between the growing child and the child's environment (Piaget, 1952). For most children, development takes place without serious problems. If a child starts out with a single deficit, complications can become progressively worse as the child matures. For example, if a child lacks some basic prerequisite skill such as a perceptual one, the child cannot acquire more complex skills which build on the basic skill. A hearing loss may make the imitation of speech sounds more difficult. The parents may consider this child unresponsive and, therefore, difficult to enjoy. The child may not be compliant with parental requests and thus more difficult to manage. Eventually, the child who has a hearing impairment will also suffer from speech and language delay, problems with behavior management, and a poor self-image. The child and the parents may suffer family dysfunction.

The developmentally delayed young child may not produce behavior that either maintains parent attention or elicits supportive parent behaviors. These children often display unattractive behavioral repertoires such as hyperactivity and limited social responsiveness. Support programs and personnel are not responsive to families with moderately disabled children who are not clearly deviant in early development. Children with mild or moderate (versus severe) disabilities appear to be at the greatest risk for family dysfunction (Martin, Beezley, Conway, & Kempe, 1974).

Language and speech delays among preschoolers appear to be the one area of child functioning that may have the greatest impact on the child-parent relationship. If the child has poor receptive language, he/she may not understand what the parent has said. Parents' efforts to interact or manage the child's behavior through verbal instructions may become a source of continued frustrations.

Handicapped preschoolers frequently are slower in acquiring social skills. They may exhibit maladaptive social behaviors that interfere with the opportunity to learn. Nearly 70% of parents with handicapped children report behavior management difficulties with them (Martin et al., 1974). Compounding the behavior problems are the unrealistic expectations parents may have for their handicapped youngsters. The parents often lack knowledge about alternative methods of handling disruptive children.

Problems among handicapped preschoolers may delay the parents willingness to initiate teaching interactions. Ironically, the at-risk or handicapped child needs more frequent learning opportunities and greater environmental support to acquire, integrate, and expand skills.

Sexual Abuse of Preschool Children

Waterman et al. (1986) addressed the prevalence of sexual abuse among preschoolers. The incidence is especially hard to pinpoint because of the child's lack of credibility and cognitive and communication skills. Further, crime statistics often do not differentiate victims by age. Although the peak age for child sexual abuse is generally 8 to 13 years, the duration of abuse, particularly in cases of incest, may affect the age so that it appears artificially high. Many long-term victims of child sexual abuse do not remember exactly when the abuse began partly because of the poor sense of time among preschool and young school age children.

Several authors have noted a small but significant number of sexually abused children of preschool age (Finkelhor 1979; Waterman et al., 1986). The Los Angeles County Mental Health Department reported that in 1983 about 22 percent of their sexual abuse cases involved children under five years of age (Waterman et al., 1986).

Sexual acts may vary from fondling to sodomy and intercourse. The type of act is likely to have a considerable differential impact on the child. Types of acts can be nontouching acts (e.g. exhibitionism), nonviolent touching acts, and violent touching acts (e.g., rape). Although generalizations are not possible, it is more likely that the preschooler will encounter a "molester" than a "rapist."

To ascertain whether abuse has taken place, it is important to understand the developmental level of the child and to make a judgment of the child's capacity to deal with the abusive incident. Previous and current theorists believe in Freud's theory of psychosexual development, which suggests children go through stages in the development of their sexuality (Waterman et al., 1986). For preschool children, control seems to be the major task. This control shows itself in the child's attempt to master certain aspects of the environment and develop a sense of self. During the ages 2 through 4, the anal stage, the child struggles to control his bladder and bowels. Freud postulated that between ages 4 through 6 the child undergoes the phallic stage. The child has become increasing aware of his/her genitals and why boys and girls differ. The child plays "doctor" with other children and engages in masturbation. At this stage children may demonstrate precocious sexual behavior. Little boys may tease or strut. Little girls may primp and dress up in mother's clothes. This behavior helps the identification of the child's own sexual imagery. According to Freud, the latency period sets in after the preschool years. Between ages 6 through 12, children possess and demonstrate less overt interest in sexuality. Obscene words and dirty jokes hold great appeal, but little acting-out occurs. Masturbation continues, but sexual play and demonstration become covert.

If Freud's psychosexual theory is correct, preschoolers demonstrate provocative behavior. If adults do not have good self-control and a firm sense of moral and social boundaries, a preschooler's flirting behavior may "incite" or provoke sexual advances. Perpetrators who admit sexual abuse frequently accuse children for "leading them on." Children are *never* at fault.

Early Intervention

Since handicapped preschoolers are particularly vulnerable to abuse, early intervention to aid these children and their families may help to alleviate abuse. Opportunity to help handicapped children and their families is increasing. Public Law 99-457 establishes a new federal program to assist coordinated, interdisciplinary, and interagency programs of early intervention services for handicapped infants, toddlers, and their families. An objective of the law is that it strengthens the incentive for states to serve all handicapped children ages three to five under the supervision of the public schools. The law further extends discretionary programs under parts of PL 94-142 including research, demonstration and outreach programs, and personnel preparation. Eligibility for early intervention services is extended to handicapped infants and toddlers, age 2 inclusive. These children need early intervention services because they have experienced developmental delays in one or more of the following areas: cognitive development, psychosocial development, and self-help skills. Services may include family training, counseling, and home visits as well as speech instruction, occupational therapy, physical therapy, and psychological services (Edwards, 1987).

Adolescence

Abuse toward adolescents is far more prevalent than previously realized. Recent literature suggests the dynamics involved is different than with younger children. Abuse against adolescents suggests major family dysfunction; whereas, abuse against younger children suggests environmental factors are to blame (Kaplan & Pelcovitz, 1982).

Twenty-five percent of abuse reports involve adolescents who are developmentally disabled according to Schor (1987). Developmental disability includes the mentally retarded, sensory impaired, the severe and chronically ill, and cerebral palsied. The disability must be manifested before age 22 and likely to continue indefinitely. The disability substantially limits function in three of the following areas: self-care, language, learning, mobility, self-direction, and capacity for independent living. Abrams (1986), when working with chemically dependent adolescents, found a high proportion of female patients had histories of sexual abuse.

The major task of early adolescence is to explore personal values, establish greater independence, and increase interaction with peers of the opposite sex. By midadolescence the youth has to begin to consider career options. Among the developmental disabled, high rates of social problems, adjustment disorders, and other emotional diagnoses appear. The mentally retarded have a relatively slower rate of learning, greater social isolation, and academic underachievement than their normal peers (Schor, 1987).

Society has difficulty in dealing with the developmentally disabled and consequently the disabled may have a lower sense of self-worth. Fortunately, in the past two decades, there has been more open discussion on the sexuality issues. Clearly, most disabled adolescents have wishes for affiliation and affection. Unfortunately, some handicapping conditions interfere directly on accomplishing sexual expression. For example, spinal cord lesions eliminate the possibility of erection or orgasm. However, alternate methods of giving and receiving emotional/sexual sensations are possible.

Historically, there have been myths about the sexuality of developmentally disabled. They have been viewed as totally asexual, innocent, or super charged. Parents are often less prepared in dealing with the sexuality of their handicapped children than with their normal offspring. Most children get their information from peers, and thus there is considerable misinformation. Certain behaviors associated with genitalia are more common among mentally retarded persons, such as obtrusive masturbation and menstrual hygiene management problems among severely retarded girls. Szymanski (1981) indicated that parents of institutionalized, severely retarded girls had great concern about their potential for abuse. In actuality, mildly retarded children were at far greater risk.

Schor (1987) reported on the sexual activities of 87 mentally retarded, noninstitutionalized girls. Half of the mildly retarded girls had had sexual intercourse; a smaller number of the incidents of sexual intercourse was reported among girls who were moderately or severely retarded. Rape or incest was reported among a third of the mildly retarded population studied and among a quarter of the moderately retarded females. When incest occurred, it was often repetitive.

Why are developmentally disabled adolescents particularly vulnerable to abuse? Childlike behaviors among these adolescents may be attractive to pedophiles, persons who prefer children as sexual partners. These adolescents are a devalued population. Fewer situational safeguards exist among them. They are victims of stereotypes that they are "sexually driven." They experience greater frustration because of lower school achievement. They are easily led and have a greater desire to please than their normal counterparts. They feel a greater need for affection because of prior rejection.

Strategies for intervention and prevention of abuse among developmentally disabled adolescents are several. Society must recognize the stress on families who must deal with children with difficult temperaments and numerous needs. Successful coping mechanisms must be given to these parents. The youngsters must be given basic training and information about human sexuality and relationships. They need direct information about exploitation, how to protect themselves, and to whom to turn for help. Many workers who deal with the developmentally disabled have little knowledge or training in human sexuality. Schor (1987) suggests the following:

- Allow these children activities that will allow for greater social competency through training and community outreach programs.
- Promote state protection groups and advocacy groups for the developmentally disabled.
- Establish self-help groups that will encourage learning social skills.

Long-term Conditions

As nonhandicapped children grow older, the chances of continued abuse decrease. In contrast, among the handicapped since the handicapping condition will not go away, they stand a greater chance that abuse will continue. Glaser and Bentovim (1979) observed that among normal populations, abuse decreases during the first 6 years of life. In a study of one hundred eleven abused children, 32 percent of the nonhandicapped children were abused after age two. In contrast 52 percent of the handicapped children were abused after age two. By age five only nine percent of nonhandicapped children were abused; whereas 29 percent of handicapped children continued to receive abuse.

Role of Schools

Educators have a vital role in the prevention of abuse as well as the identification of its victims. Schools are in the business of teaching children. Children need to learn of their vulnerability and their right to say "no." Children need to learn appropriate modes of behavior so that abuse will not be a part of their parenting experience. Schools have a professional responsibility to be involved in as significant a societal problem as abuse.

Roscoe (1984) suggested many important contributions educators can make toward helping the child who has been victimized. Some of the activities enhance the student's self-concept, allow self-expression, and serve as a model for appropriate child-adult relationships.

The Identification of Abuse

The classroom teacher plays a significant part in childrens' lives. The teacher is perhaps the single professional who is in the position to continuously observe children over an extended period of time. Gil (1970) upheld that the teacher can be the most important line in the preventive and protective chain. The teacher has daily contact with children and can note behaviors that might be indicative of stress and ultimately abuse. Children may display dramatic changes in behavior such as problems with social interaction, learning, passivity, depression, and destructiveness, frequent tardiness or absence from school, and fearfulness of adults. Teachers are encouraged to maintain anecdotal records on their children as well as progress reports. Teachers are encouraged to interact with parents and can discern parent-child relationships that may be stressful.

Children often keep quiet about being abused. Often the abuser frightens them and warns them not to talk. The child generally knows the abuser. In sexual abuse researchers estimate that 68% of child molesters are parents, 14% are other relatives, and 18% are other trusted adults or persons unknown to the victims (CBS, 1985). Many parents or other adults who deal with children do not know how to recognize signs of abuse.

Teachers need to understand the various types of child abuse and some reasons for their occurrence. It is also most important to be able to recognize the symptoms and signs of abuse among the children whom they teach. Physical abuse is the most easily recognized although sometimes the evidence is concealed by clothing. Since physical abuse is usually recurrent, the teacher has to wonder how many times the same bruised child can walk into doors or spill hot water.

Several forms of sexual abuse such as exhibitionism, incest, or inappropriate sexual behavior occur outside the home. Sexual abuse outside the home is more likely perpetrated by a person known to the child. The perpetrator may be a neighbor or babysitter. These offenders are usually pedophiles, adults who sexually prefer children. Although most sexual abusers are men, data is revealing a larger number of women than had previously been considered (Goldman & Wheeler, 1986; Herbert, 1985).

Emotional abuse is a very difficult form to identify. Evidence of extreme emotional deprivation is not easy to discern by the inexperienced observer. In infants, the symptom "failure to thrive" is noted. In older children, emotional abuse takes its toll in a variety of ways.

Neglect is often more evident to a classroom teacher. However, it is extremely difficult to remedy. These children are frequently absent or may be distrustful of adults in general. The causes of neglect need to be examined. Poverty, wherein a single parent is attempting to hold the family together without support, may be one cause. Parental ignorance of a psychiatric problem may play roles in the neglect of children.

Children who are abused often give signals. Chapter 1 lists characteristics of child abuse (Harrison, 1985; Herbert, 1985). However, not all of the children exhibiting these characteristics are victims of child abuse. Some of these signals can be a natural part of children's growth and development. However, if a child exhibits several of the listed characteristics on a regular basis, the teacher should be aware that something is amiss.

The long-term effects of child abuse have greater implications than imagined. Abused children often have low self-images and are retarded in academic and social development. It is to be wondered if they are able to fulfill their potential in being productive adults. Child abuse is often intergenerational. Abused children may grow up to be abusive parents and/or spouses.

School Policy

It is imperative that each school district formulate written policies to guide its school personnel in the details of what they can and should do regarding child abuse and neglect. Specific procedures and staff responsibilities must be addressed and communicated to teachers, school counselors, and administrators. Otherwise prevention and treatment are ineffective (Erickson, McEvoy, & Colucci, 1984). In dealing with the maltreatment of children, two important areas of concern exist: (1) how to achieve a workable policy and (2) what elements should that policy include.

Many schools have not developed policies on child maltreatment. According to the Education Commission of the States (1978), only 44% of the largest school districts in the United States had adopted written policies on child abuse. Levin (1983) reported only 5% of the nation's schools have working policies and procedures for reporting abuse and neglect. Schools are very poor reporting agents (Garbarino, 1982), a fact which seems as testimony to lack of developed policies. In a questionnaire sent to school administrators, 49% indicated that their district had some type of standard operating procedure. In contrast, only 24% of the staff (teachers and school nurses) were aware of such a procedure. Beezer (1985) reported that research indicates that educators are quite reluctant to report child abuse and neglect. They are unsure as to what constitutes abuse and neglect, are unsure how to make a report, lack confidence that the report will be acted on, and fear legal repercussions. Neglect in the year 1982 indicated only 10% of reports came from the schools (Zirpoli, 1986).

Erickson et al. (1984) suggested a format for a child abuse and neglect policy for a school district. Components of this policy include: (1) a rationale for the policy, (2) legal obligations, (3) professional obligations, (4) building teams, (5) primary prevention policy, and (6) continued evaluation of the policy. The manner in which the policy is developed should reflect a multidisciplinary approach to the multidimensional problem of child maltreatment. The collective expertise of relevant community professionals and volunteers should be used for the schools to develop an effective team. Child abuse is not an individual problem but a community one. Protection of a child can be a community-wide social movement in which troubled families can be a benefactor.

Reporting Abuse

Most states expressly name teachers and other school personnel as among those required to report suspected abuse or neglect incidents. The reporting requirement, often called "mandated reporter," indicates that the individual has a prescribed degree of knowledge about a particular child. How sophisticated must the educator be about signs and symptoms of abuse and neglect? The law does not require educators to have the level of knowledge possessed by physicians, nurses, and child protective service workers. The law does require that they report *immediately*. School administrators may consult local law agencies to determine whether teachers are required to report suspected abuse directly or to supervisory personnel such as principals. However, the law is implicit that a report must be made. Persons who report abuse situations in good faith, without malice and with the intent to protect the child, are immune to civil or criminal liability (Zirpoli, 1986).

Towers (1987) suggested that an educator needs three kinds of knowledge *before* encountering a case of child maltreatment. These are (1) knowledge of the reporting laws of the state in which they teach, (2) knowledge of the school reporting policy, and (3) knowledge of the protective agency designated to accept reports. He further recommended a checklist a teacher might utilize when preparing to report abuse. The checklist includes a series of questions such as:

- Have I written down the information?
- Have I analyzed the data as to the cause and listed the symptoms?
- Have I had an opportunity to see the interactions between parent and child?
- Have I spoken with other professionals within the school and do they have reason to suspect abuse/neglect and if so, why?

If a child protective worker, juvenile officer, or police detective comes to the school to interview a child who is an alleged victim of abuse or neglect, a private setting should be provided. Investigators usually prefer to conduct interviews on a one-to-one basis, which would allow children to feel more comfortable to discuss difficult issues, and more information is likely to be gathered. However, there may be times when a younger child may feel more comfortable in the presence of a school person with whom the child is very familiar.

Debate persists as to what steps are involved in the notification of parents. In cases of child abuse and neglect, parents should not be notified before or after the interview by school personnel. Notification of the parent(s) should not be the responsibility of school officials but rather that of the investigator and will be done as soon as feasible following the interview. If parents contact school personnel before the investigator notifies the parents, school officials should acknowledge the purpose of the investigator and refer the parents to the investigator. Cooperation among the schools, social agencies, and law enforcement officials should make a more thorough investigation possible, lessen the child's anxiety, and result in helping the child – the goal of all concerned.

Talking to a Child

The teacher may be the child's source of disclosure in cases of abuse and neglect. Although formal interviewing to gather data for possible prosecution of the perpetrator is not the role or responsibility of the teacher, being able to talk to the child about the revealed abuse in a way which will be helpful to the child is important. Several suggestions on effective communication have been made. The child should never be made to feel that he/she is at fault. Although guilt is a natural sequel of abuse and neglect, it is *never* a child's fault. The child needs additional reassurance that the teacher cares and respects this child regardless of what the disclosure has revealed. A child needs to be told that the information will not be shared with classmates, other children, or teachers. However, the teacher should be honest in describing what legal steps need to be followed and who needs to be notified once the disclosure has been made. Only those persons directly involved in the process of child protection should be informed. The child's right of privacy is paramount.

If the teacher suspects a child is being abused, it is important to remember that the child may be feeling hurt or afraid. It is recommended (Goldman & Wheeler, 1986; Harrison, 1985) that a quiet nonthreatening place, free of interruptions, be selected where the child can feel as comfortable as possible. The teacher should sit with the child, not behind a desk. During the discussion, the teacher might consider making physical contact; a hand on the shoulder or a hug can be reassuring to a young girl. Repeated questioning of the student should be avoided. The role of school personnel is to report, not investigate. School staff should not call or visit the child's parents or relatives when questions of abuse or neglect arise unless specifically directed by a protective agency staff. Regardless of how upsetting the situation may be, the teacher should approach the child with a sense of warmth and understanding. A sense of judgment should be absent from communication. One should avoid conveying the impression that the child's parents are inadequate or unloving. Teachers should not display pity. The teacher is not expected to resolve the conflicts a maltreated child may experience. However, giving the child the opportunity to vent frustrations can be therapeutic. Consistency can provide guidance and convey clear-cut expectations to children. One of the problems maltreated children face is inconsistent child-rearing practices by their parents. This inconsistency can be a source of mistrust for all forms of adult authority.

Hughes (1988) observed that interviewing children can be quite different from interviewing adults. These differences may include the centrality of the relationship, questioning strategies, the initiation stage, and developmental considerations. In terms of the centrality of the relationship, adults often have a wide range of motives for cooperation with the interviewer. Children do not often refer themselves for assistance, and they may see the entire experience as coercive. As to questioning strategies, with adults the examiner may use open-ended questions to "tell your own story" with a minimal of direction from the interview. With children the questions may be too abstract and require more structure and organizational format. Typically, children need more time to adjust to the interview situation than adults. In addition to differences in interviewing behavior, children's developmental levels differ among themselves. The use of language, understanding of social relationships, ability to think logically, and understand the causes of their own and others' feelings, have implications for the interviewer.

A teacher who is concerned about abuse and neglect may want to talk directly with a child. This direct approach may not be advisable since some children are afraid of being hurt further by the abuser or may feel loyalty to the parent. The child may feel the abuse was deserved. Some children may be threatened by a teacher's inquiry and withdraw from that teacher. A better approach may be to assure children that a teacher can be approached when they are ready to talk. Movies, filmstrips, and puppet shows are useful to show in the classroom since they may elicit reports from children by helping them realize that a problem exists, and it is all right to talk about it. The use of art or play techniques are also methods that may encourage a report, especially from young children. To ask children to draw pictures of themselves and their families can be quite revealing. Towers (1987) recommended that the teacher consult a school psychologist for the analysis of such drawings.

Prevention of Abuse

Primary Prevention Programs

Rosenberg and Reppucci (1985) examined three categories of child abuse primary prevention programs: (1) programs that enhance competencies of families, (2) programs that prevent the onset of abuse, and (3) programs that target high-risk groups undergoing the transition to parenthood.

The use of television and live theater to communicate information on parenting are proving to be exciting approaches to child abuse prevention. The creative arts are used as a media to inform parents who do not usually come into contact with traditional service systems. One prevention program used videotaped skits or live performances in a variety of settings such as shopping centers, alternative high school classes for teenage parents, military bases, and battered women's shelters. The program was evaluated by pre- and post-questionnaires. Overall, the general audiences showed the most pre-post attitude change. Professionals next showed the most attitude change. Then high-risk viewers followed professionals in showing the most attitude change. The skits focused on such themes as anger control, support systems, and child rearing issues. The high-risk viewers changed most positively around the child rearing issues (Grady, 1983a).

Different cultural groups have been targeted as potentially abusive parents. Gray (1983b) studied Hispanic families in an attempt to improve the children's school performance as well as to prevent child abuse. Parents were exposed to a curriculum that included parent education classes, a home visiting program with regular filming of parent-child interactions, and involvement in a practicum in the project's daycare center. Curriculum evaluation was assessed by questionnaires of both an experimental and control group. Program participants (relative to controls) were found to be significantly more knowledgeable about a variety of child rearing areas, more willing to use support systems during stress, and were more optimistic about the future.

To prevent the onset of abusive behavior, programs typically involve information, crisis and referral services, media campaigns, and efforts at the neighborhood and community levels to empower social networks to provide support and feedback to families (Cohn, 1982). The underlying assumptions of such programs are that understanding about the problem and where and how to get help alleviate potential abuse.

A multifaceted public awareness project was undertaken in Washington State. Four rural counties were selected that had significant service delivery programs. A high percentage of residents in these counties were living in poverty, in social and physical isolation, with little public awareness about child abuse, and no available hotline services. One county resisted. However, the other three counties reflected the successful realization of the project goals of providing professional and community education, developing referral and information systems, and networking within the community. A secondary outcome of increasing public awareness resulted in a massive reporting of suspected abuse (Gray, 1983b).

Since the 1960s telephone hotlines have been available as a crisis intervention service for a variety of mental health concerns. Recently, these hotlines have emerged as a viable strategy to prevent child abuse. Although, the goal is to reach parents before abuse occurs, in reality, the calls are used mainly for other purposes. In Connecticut, the welfare association reported that out of approximately 9,000 calls received, 59% were information and referral, 40% were reports of abuse or neglect, and only 1% was primary prevention stress calls. It is rare that follow-up information is collected because of the volume of calls and the anonymity of many callers. An inherent problem with evaluating the effectiveness of a hotline call is that a parent might receive help from a resource other than an abuse hotline. For example, a call to a medical resource might reduce the stress of living with a sick child (Boratynski, 1983).

Crisis services are designed to give immediate help to parents under stress. They function as a major referral source to long-term services as needed. These services may be part of a multifaceted service program or a free standing entity.

The "rooming in" concept following a child's birth has been utilized as a means of increasing contact between mother and child following delivery. This concept is based on the assumption that prolonged separation of mother and newborn in the postnatal period may have detrimental effects on relationships (Klaus & Kennel, 1976). However, the effectiveness of early bonding as a useful child abuse prevention strategy needs further research (Rosenberg & Reppucci, 1985).

Another type of family support program includes health visitors and parent aides. Gray (1983b) studied 100 mothers deemed high risk for abuse. Half of these women were subjected to a comprehensive pediatric follow-up by a health visitor; the other half were assigned to routine procedures. Five children from the high-risk routine procedure group were abused and needed hospitalization for serious injuries. No hospitalization occurred in children of the high-risk intervention group.

A crisis center is another resource for parents who need relief or are in crisis. Parents Anonymous groups provide support and an outlet for expression of feelings. Mother's Day Out or similar programs may provide care for young children during the day and give parents the opportunity to engage in activities by themselves.

Prevention Programs for the Very Young

Providers of care for children and parents are better educated about the symptoms of abuse than 10 years ago. However, the focus on saying "no" must be augmented with other information and skill training. Because young children are small and have a respect for authority figures, it is unlikely that they will be able to say "no," although they know it is the correct response. Children will be abused. Therefore, they need to receive messages that they must tell someone when abuse has taken place and that they are not at fault. They need to know that they will be believed, that they are safe, and that they are still loved. Presentations to young children should be given over a period of several sessions. Language should be used that will help them understand (Waterman et al., 1986).

Because young children are so vulnerable to abuse and sexual molestation, better societal controls over child care facilities need to be exercised. More daycare facilities in this country need licensing. Employees in these facilities need to be better screened and held accountable. Education needs to be extended beyond parents to preschool and daycare administrators, teachers, and other staff about how to recognize signs of abuse and neglect.

A crisis in many daycare facilities exists because of unfounded allegations of sexual abuse. This fear may drive some qualified workers out of the business or inappropriately limit their interactions with children. For example, workers may be unwilling to change diapers or hug children. Ideally, prevention programs should stress encouraging affection as well as warding off abuse.

Experts in the field of abuse and neglect have suggested that once the report has been made, the abuse may well increase (Goldman & Wheeler, 1986; Waterman et al., 1986). Our systems' response to abuse reports should ensure sensitive and effective handling of the cases.

Little is known about the sexual abusing perpetrators against small children. For future prevention, it is important to know how these perpetrators differ from those who abuse older children. Can these perpetrators be effectively treated? Perpetrators frequently themselves have been abused. Treatment programs for youthful abusers are important to attempt to halt this cyclic nature of the problem of abuse.

Research needs to be undertaken as to the effectiveness of prevention programs on young children. What further programs need to be initiated and when are the most beneficial times in a child's development should these programs be presented?

Extended treatment programs are needed for child victims. These programs would serve to ward off potential abusive behavior on the victims' part as well as help resolve conflicts that may arise that are related to the victims' current age. Treatment programs and counseling centers for abusers need to be developed. These resources could hopefully prevent abusive behavior.

Surveying Current Needs and Resources

In planning a comprehensive child abuse prevention program, an inventory of existing community resources and needs is an essential first step. What ongoing programs or services provide information and/or intervention for child abuse? Would the personnel in these facilities be willing to lend their knowledge to help in the inservice training activities for school personnel? Is there an active child abuse task force in the immediate community? Often a task force is composed of professionals, mental health specialists, child protective workers, law enforcement workers, and lay citizens. Major goals of this group are to coordinate activities of community groups and disseminate information. The abuse task force may serve as a vehicle to promote inservice training for teachers. School boards need to approve the time and money allocations that a school program for prevention of child abuse will require.

Schools potentially have a vital role in the identification and prevention of child abuse and neglect. The experiences of several school projects suggest this important role and impact. For example, in Syracuse, New York, the school district undertook a prevention program. Since its inception 5 years earlier, the program has been the greatest single referral source in the city (Murdock, 1970).

Education has its greatest potential to help deal with the problem of child abuse and neglect in the areas of identification, precrisis intervention, and primary prevention. Activities that schools could pursue follow:

- Offer courses in the primary, intermediate, and secondary curricula on relational skills such as assertiveness and listening, on child development, discipline, aggression, and other topics potentially useful to future parents. How to problem solve, cope with stress, and responsibilities associated with parenthood could also be included.

- Offer courses for both secondary students and adults on appropriate parenting skills, coping with stress, child behavior and development, and feelings and attitudes associated with parenthood.

- Identify suspected cases of abuse and neglect.

- Provide special attention to the educational, developmental, and emotional needs of abused and neglected children.

- Offer preservice and inservice training for all school personnel.

Program for Teachers

A well-trained, knowledgeable staff is critical to prevention of child abuse. Educators can be sensitized to the issues surrounding abuse through preservice and inservice training. Educators need to know how to identify abuse, what reporting steps need to be followed, and how abused children can be treated successfully.

Teacher-training programs seldom offer units on the abuse of children in its prescribed curriculum. Topics such as abuse are considered nonacademic and not integral to a teacher's training. Colleges and universities have just begun to offer courses that address child abuse. Curriculum specialists have difficulty adding coursework to an already crowded bachelor's degree program and meeting state and national accreditation standards. Bartlett (1978) reported that only two thirds of degree granting programs in education include information on child abuse in their curricula. Furthermore, the quality of that training has been questioned.

Gladbach and Wheeler (1986) have suggested an inservice teacher training program that is based on four functions of the schools' role in addressing abuse and neglect: (1) identification, (2) prevention, (3) reporting, and (4) treatment. In the identification part of the curriculum, the educator is given information concerning the physical and mental characteristics of abused and neglected children. Also educators are encouraged to examine their own feelings and attitudes toward abuse and neglect. Prevention focuses on the recognition of early warning signs of high risk children and teaching the child about appropriate adult behaviors and the children's responses. The reporting section points to the legal responsibilities of the teacher and the policy and procedures. Treatment deals with remediation of academic difficulties and emotional support.

Curriculum Ideas

An effective program must address the needs of the students in that school or district. Activities can be modified depending on the specific age and development level of the group. Parents also need information about abuse.

Training parents. Lutzker, Megson, Webb, and Dachman (1985) reported that schools have a vital role in training parents. This training can be achieved through viewing videotapes that show models of appropriate parent behavior, role-playing activities, and feedback mechanisms. Parents need training in how to cope with anger and frustration through relaxation methods and problem-solving skills (Denicola & Sandler, 1980).

Special educators can communicate to parents children's training needs. These parents need positive feedback about their children. Teachers should balance information about students' handicaps with their strengths. They need to help parents see beyond the children's handicaps. Positive reinforcement parents receive from educators may help facilitate positive attachment and parent-child interaction.

Effective child management skills were taught to abusive parents. The curriculum included reading materials, role playing, problem-solving activities, and feedback. Parents were rewarded (contingency contracting) for the use of appropriate child management techniques. Appropriate techniques continued to be demonstrated at least 12 months later (Wolfe & Sandler, 1981).

Teaching children. Schools should provide all children with quality education at regular intervals for different age groups. Certain basic principles need to be taught such as children's rights, how to protect oneself, and that it is not the child's fault. A variety of child abuse prevention materials are available (Goldman & Wheeler, 1986; Pettis & Hughes, 1985).

Abused and neglected children can be helped by the teacher. These children often have a very poor self-image. They need to succeed and know they have rights, too. Children with loving parents are typically trustful of adults. On the other hand, maltreated children, exposed to inconsistent parenting, are not convinced that grown-ups mean well. The teacher needs to be especially conscious of how children react to commands. Teachers may need to make referrals for assessment for special learning. Children need to improve their self-image and to do something right. The teacher can assign tasks that meet these needs. For example, the child may be given a task that offers a feeling of authority in the classroom or on the playground. The task may be as simple as erasing the chalkboard. The child might be assigned a caretaking task such as feeding the gerbils. This enables the child to learn ways to properly care for another living being as well as feeling important. Older students also need to be given tasks of importance. The teacher may wish to comment on the student's little successes as they are accomplished.

Wells and Canfield (1976) cited numerous exercises for the classroom that can help a child feel important, thus enhancing one's self-image and feelings of worth. Topics such as "What's the Best About Me?" or for the older student "What Have I Accomplished About Which I Am Most Proud" can be used for discussion. Teachers need to find activities that encourage children to think in terms of their own potential rather than of their limitations, to look for positive attributes and strengths.

Towers (1987) suggested several ways to encourage reporting. Audio-tapes such as "A Dragon in My Closet" (for younger children) or "Deborah Wore Designer Jeans" (for older children) may generate discussions about abuse as well as about whom to turn when children feel they have problems. Training programs geared to personal safety and the prevention of sexual abuse are available. These programs address privacy and assertiveness issues as well as abuse.

The hope for the future is to prevent abuse. When selecting material, there are several issues to be addressed. Ideally, the material can be integrated into the classroom curriculum, into a variety of subjects. For example, in English classes, students could write about feelings. In science classes, discussion can focus on how remarkable the body is as a machine. The material should be appropriate to the age of the students. Children in the early grades, for example, can be taught about good and bad touch. As children grow older, they are ready to understand more about how people treat children. A prevention program should elicit input from the children themselves. It should be able to be taught by someone familiar and trusted by the children, namely the teacher (Towers, 1987).

Parents and teachers will find many resources available. Organizations that are dedicated to preventing child abuse are also helpful in providing materials. Goldman and Wheeler (1986) provide a comprehensive listing of resources.

Conclusion

Schools have a unique opportunity to aid in the dilemma of child abuse and neglect. By teaching students of their rights and appropriate strategies for coping with stress, hopefully they will not be victims or perpetrators of abuse. They will gain the necessary knowledge and insight to interact with others in an appropriate manner. They will have gained strength rather than have suffered the immeasurable toll that abuse takes from its victims.

References

Abrams, M. (1986). *Adolescent sexual abuse: Clinical discussion of community treatment responses*, New York City: Medical Publishers.

Allen, R., & Wasserman, A. (1985). Origins of language delay in abused infants. *Child Abuse and Neglect, 9*, 335–340.

Baladerian, N. (1985a). Prevention of sexual exploitation of developmental disabled adults. Paper presented at the 1985 Convention of the California Association of Post Secondary Educators of the Disabled. Sacramento, CA.

Baladerian, N. (1985b). Family reactions to the child with learning disabilities: Abandonment and loss and abuse and neglect. Paper presented at the meeting or the Association of Children with Learning Disabilities Conference, Irvine, CA.

Baladerian, N., Dankowski, K., & Jackson, T. (1986). *Survivor: For people with developmental disabilities who have been sexually assaulted*. Los Angeles: Los Angeles Commission on Assaults Against Women.

Bartlett, R. (1978). An investigation of child abuse/neglect instruction offered in early childhood and elementary education pre-service programs. *Dissertation Abstracts, 38*(10-A): 6064–6065. (University Microfilms No. 7804506).

Beezer, B. (1985). Reporting child abuse and neglect: Your responsibility and your protection. *Phi Delta Kappan, 67*, 434–436.

Bishop, I. (1971). Children at risk. *Medical Journal of Australia, 1*, 623–628.

Blacher, J., & Meyers, C. (1983). A review of attachment formation and disorder of handicapped children. *American Journal of Mental Deficiency, 87*(4), 359–371.

Boratynski, M. (1983). *Final report: The child abuse primary prevention project*. New Haven, CT: Yale University, The Consultation Center.

Bourne, R. (1981). Child abuse and neglect: An overview. In R. Bourne & E. Newburger (Eds.), *Critical perspectives on child abuse* (pp. 1–14) Lexington, MA: Lexington Books.

Bousha, D., & Twentyman, C. (1984). Mother-child interactional style in abuse, neglect, and control groups: Naturalistic observations in the home. *Journal of Abnormal Psychology, 93*, 106–114.

Brandwein, H. (1973). The battered child: A definite and significant factor in mental retardation. *Mental Retardation, 11*, 50–51.

Buchanan, A., & Oliver, J. (1979). Abuse and neglect as a cause of mental retardation. *Child Abuse and Neglect 3*, 467–475.

Byrne, E., & Cunningham, C. (1985). The effects of mentally handicapped children on families: A conceptual review. *Journal of Child Psychology and Psychiatry, 26*(6), 847–864.

Caffey, J. (1974). The whiplash shaken infant syndrome: Manual shaking by the extremities with whiplash-induced intracranial and intraocular bleedings linked with residual permanent brain damage and mental retardation. *Pediatrics, 54*, 396–403.

Calam, R. (1983). *The long-term effects of child abuse on school adjustment.* Paper presented at the 91st annual meeting of the American Psychology Association, Anaheim, CA.

Camblin, L. (1982). A survey of state efforts in gathering information on child abuse and neglect in handicapped populations. *Child Abuse and Neglect, 6,* 465–472.

CBS Presents Kids' Don't Tell (1985). New York: CBS Educational and Community Services.

Cohn, A. (1982). Stopping abuse before it occurs: Different solutions for different populations groups. *Child Abuse and Neglect, 6,* 473–483.

Conte, J. (1984). The justice system and sexual abuse of children. *Social Service Review, 58,* 556–568.

Coons, P. (1986). Child abuse and multiple personality disorder: Review of the literature and suggestions for treatment: *Child Abuse and Neglect, 10*(4), 455–462.

Crittenden, P. (1985). Maltreated infants: Vulnerability and resilience. *Journal of Child Psychology and Psychiatry 26*(1), 85–96.

Daly, M., & Wilson, M. (1981). Abuse and neglect of children in evolutionary perspective. In D. Tinkle & R. Alexanders (Eds.), *Natural selections and social behavior: Recent research and new theory* (pp. 405–416). Concord, MA: Chiron Press.

Denicola, J., & Sandler, J. (1980). Training abusive parents in child management and self-control skills. *Behavior Therapy, 11,* 263–270.

Dennis, W. (1973). *Children of the creche.* New York: Appleton-Century-Crofts.

Diamond, L., & Jaudes, P. (1983). Child abuse in the patient with cerebral palsy. *Developmental Medicine and Child Neurology. 25,* 169–174.

D'Onofrio, A., Robinson, R., Isett, M., Roszlcowsic, E., & Spreak, S. (1980). Factors related to contact between mentally retarded persons and their parents during residential treatment. *Mental Retardation, 18,* 293–294.

Education Commission of the States (1978). *Teacher education: An active participant in solving the problem of child abuse and neglect.* Denver: Education Commission of the States.

Edwards, G. (1987). P.L. 99–457: Law broadens services to handicapped children. Alabama State Department of Education, *Handicapped Children's Early Education Program, 1 & 10.*

Egeland, B., & Sroufe, L. (1981). A developmental sequelae of maltreatment in infancy. *New Directions for Child Development, 11,* 71–92.

Elmer, E. (1967). *Children in jeopardy: A study of abused minors and their families.* Pittsburgh: University of Pittsburgh Press.

Elmer, E. (1977). *Fragile families, troubled children: The aftermath of infant trauma.* Pittsburgh: University of Pittsburgh Press.

Erickson, E., McEvoy, A., & Colucci, N. (1984). *Child abuse and neglect: A guidebook for educators and community leaders* (2nd ed.). Holmes Beach, FL: Learning Publications.

Feshback, N., & Feshback, S. (1976). Punishment: Parents rites vs. children's rights. In G. Koocher (Ed.) *Children's rights and the mental health professionals* (pp. 149–170), New York: Wiley.

Finkelhor, D. (1979). *Sexually victimized children.* New York: Free Press.

Fontana, V. (1971). *The maltreated child.* Springfield, IL: Charles C. Thomas.

Friedman, S., & Morse, C. (1974) Child abuse: A five year follow-up of early case findings in the emergency department. *Pediatrics, 54,* 404–410.

Frisch, L., & Rhodes, F. (1982). Child abuse and neglect in children referred for learning evaluation. *Journal of Learning Disabilities, 15*(10), 583–586.

Garbarino, J. (1982), *Children and families in the social environment.* New York: Aldine.

Gargiulo, R. (1985). *Working with parents of exceptional children.* Boston: Houghton Mifflin.

Gelles, R. (1982). Child abuse and family violence: Implications for medical professionals. In E. Newberger (Ed.), *Child Abuse* (pp. 25–42). Boston: Little, Brown & Co.

George, C., & Main, M. (1979). Social interaction of young abused children: Approach, avoidance and aggression. *Child Development, 50,* 306–318.

Gil, D. (1970). *Violence against children: Physical child abuse in the United States.* Cambridge, MA: Harvard University Press.

Gladbach, R., & Wheeler, V. (1986). Child abuse and neglect: A curriculum proposal. *Teacher Education 21*(3), 9–14.

Glaser, D., & Bentovim, A. (1979). Abuse and risk to handicapped and chronically ill children. *Child Abuse and Neglect, 13,* 565–575.

Goldberg, S., Marcovitch, S., MacGregor D., & Lojkasek, M. (1986). Family responses to developmentally delayed preschoolers: Etiology and the fathers role. *American Journal of Mental Deficiency, 90*(6), 610–617.

Goldman, R., & Gargiulo, R. (1987). Special needs children: A population at risk for sexual abuse. *Reading Improvement, 24,* 84–89.

Goldman, R., & Wheeler, V. (1986). *Silent shame: The sexual abuse of children.* Danville, IL: Interstate.

Goldstein, J., Freud, A., & Solnit, A. (1979). *Before the best interests of the child.* New York: Free Press.

Gordon, H. (1923). *Mental and scholastic tests among retarded children. An Educational Pamphlet 44.* London: Board of Education.

Governor's Committee for Children and Youth, (1979). *Child abuse and neglect . . . An interdisciplinary approach to treatment and prevention.* Jefferson City, MO: Division of Family Services.

Gray, E. (1983a). *Final report: Collaborative research on community and minority group action to prevent child abuse and neglect. Public awareness and education using the creative arts* (Vol 3). Chicago: National Committee for Prevention of Child Abuse.

Gray, E. (1983b). *Final report: Collaborative research of community and minority group action to prevent child abuse and neglect. Information and referral programs* (Vol. 4). Chicago: National Committee for Prevention of Child Abuse.

Harrison, R. (1985). How you can help the abused child, *Learning, 14*(1), 74–78.

Helfer, R. (1975). *The diagnostic process and treatment programs.* Washington, DC: U.S. Department of Health, Education and Welfare, National Center on Child Abuse and Neglect.

Herbert, M. (1985). What principals should know about child abuse. *Principals, 65*, 9–14.

Hughes, J. (1988). Interviewing children. In J. Dillard and R. Reilly (Eds.), *Systematic interviewing: Communication skills for professional effectiveness* (pp. 90–101). Columbus, OH: Merrill Publishers.

Jaudes, P., & Diamond, L. (1985). The handicapped child and child abuse. *Child Abuse and Neglect, 9*(3), 341–347.

Johnson, B., & Showers, J. (1985). Injury variables in child abuse. *Child Abuse and Neglect, 9*, 207–215.

Kaplan, S., & Pelcovitz, D. (1982). Child abuse and neglect and sexual abuse. *Psychiatric Clinics of North America, 5*(2), 321–332.

Kent, J. (1976). A follow-up of abused children. *Journal of Pediatric Psychology, 1*, 25–31.

King, C. (1975). The ego and integration of violence in homicidal youth. *American Journal of Orthopsychiatry, 45*, 135–145.

Klaus, M., & Kennel, J. (1976). *Maternal-infant bonding.* St. Louis: C. V. Mosby.

Klein, M., & Sterne, L. (1971). Low birth weight and the battered child syndrome. *American Journal of Disabled Children, 122*, 15–18.

Kohlberg, L. (1984). *Essays on moral development.* San Francisco, CA: Harper & Row.

Kubler-Ross, E. (1969). *Death and dying.* New York: Macmillan.

Kurtz, G., & Kurtz, P. (1987). Child abuse and neglect. In M. Neisworth and S. Bagnato (Eds.), *The young exceptional child.* New York: Macmillan.

Lamphear, V. (1985). The impact of maltreatment on children's psychosocial adjustment: A review of the research. *Child Abuse and Neglect, 9*, 251–263.

Levin, P. (1983). Teachers' perceptions, attitudes and reporting of child abuse/neglect. *Child Welfare, 14*, 15–19.

Light, R. (1973). Abuse and neglected children in America: A study of alternative policies. *Harvard Educational Review, 43*, 556–598.

Lightcap, J., Kurland, J., & Burgess, R. (1982). Child abuse: A test of some predictions from evolutionary theory. *Etiology and Sociobiology, 3*(2), 61–67.

Lutzker, J., Megson, D., Webb, M., & Dachman, R. (1985). Validating and training adult-child interaction skills to professionals and to parents indicated for child abuse and neglect. *Child and Adolescent Psychotherapy 2*(2), 91–104.

Lynch, M., & Roberts, J. (1982). *Consequences of child abuse.* New York: Academic Press.

MacKeith, R. (1974). Speculations on non-accidental injury as a cause of chronic brain disorder. *Developmental Medicine and Child Neurology, 16*, 216–218.

Martin, H. (1972). The child and his development. In H. Kempe & R. Helfer (Eds.), *Helping the battered child and his family* (pp. 93–114). Philadelphia: J. B. Lippincott.

Martin, H., Beezley, P., Conway, E., & Kempe, C. (1974). The development of abused children. *Advances in Pediatrics, 21*, 25–73.

Meier, J., & Sloan, M. (1984). The severely handicapped & child abuse. In J. Blacher (Ed.) *Severely handicapped young children and their families*, (pp. 247–272). San Diego: Academic Press, Inc.

Miller, K., & Miller, E. (1979). Child abuse and neglect: A framework for identification. *The School Counselor, 36*, 284–287.

Money, J. (1982). Child abuse: Growth failure, IQ deficit, and learning disability. *Journal of Learning Disabilities, 15*(10), 579–582.

Murdock, C. (1970). The abused child and the school system. *American Journal of Public Health, 60*(1), 105–109.

Murphy, M. (1982). The family with a handicapped child: A review of the literature. *Journal of Developmental and Behavioral Pediatrics, 3*(2), 73–82.

Nelson, K. & Ellenberg, J. (1978). Epidemiology of cerebral palsy. *Advances in Neurology, 19*, 421–435.

Nesbit, W., & Karagianis, L. (1982). Child abuse: Exceptionality as a risk factor. *The Alberta Journal of Educational Research, 28*, 69–76.

Parke, R., & Collmer, C. (1975). Child abuse: An interdisciplinary analysis. In E. Hetherington (Ed.), *Review of child development research* (pp. 509–590). Chicago: University of Chicago Press.

Pettis, K., & Hughes, R. (1985). Sexual victimization of children: Implications for educators. *Behavioral Disorders, 10*, 175–182.

Piaget, J. (1952). *The origins of intelligence in children* (M. Cook, Trans.). New York: International University Press.

Roscoe, B. (1984). Sexual abuse: The educator's role in identification and interaction with abuse victims. *Education, 105*(1), 82–85.

Rose, T. (1983). A survey of corporal ppunishment of mildly handicapped students. *Exceptional Educational Quarterly, 1*(4), 9–19.

Rosenberg, M., & Reppucci, N. (1985). Primary prevention of child abuse. *Journal of Consulting and Clinical Psychology, 53*(5), 576–585.

Sandgrund, A., Gaines, R., & Green, A. (1974). Child abuse and mental retardation: A problem of cause and effect. *American Journal of Mental Deficiency, 79*, 327–330.

Schilling, R., & Schinke, S. (1984). Maltreatment and mental retardation. *Perspectives and Progress in Mental Retardation, 1*, 11–23.

Schor, D. (1987). Sex and sexual abuse in developmentally disabled adolescents. *Seminars in Adolescent Medicine, 3*(1), 1–8.

Sidel, R. (1972). *Women and child care in China.* New York: Hill and Wang.

Skeels, H. (1966). Adult status of children with contrasting early life experiences: A follow-up study monograph of the society for *Research in Child Develpment*, I-65 (Serial No. 105).

Skodak, M. & Skeels, H. (1945). A follow-up study of children in adoptive homes. *Journal of Genetic Psychology 66*, 21–58.

Soeffing, M. (1975). Abused children are exceptional children. *Exceptional Children, 42*, 126–133.

Solomon, G. (1979). Child abuse and developmental disabilities. *Developmental Medicine and Child Neurology, 21*, 101–108.

Solomon, T. (1973). History and demography of child abuse. *Pediatrics, 51*, 773–776.

Souther, M. (1984). Developmentally disabled abused and neglected children: A high risk and high need population. *In perspectives on child maltreatment in the mid 80s.* (pp. 33–34). Washington, DC: National Center on Child Abuse and Neglect.

Spinetta, J., & Rigler, D. (1972). The child-abusing parent: A psychological review. *Psychological Bulletin, 77*, 296–304.

Stark, R., & McEvoy, J. (1970). Middle class violence. *Psychology Today, 4*, 52–65.

Starr, R., Jr. (1979). Child abuse. *American Psychologist, 34*, 872–878.

Starr, R., Jr. (1982). *Child abuse prediction: Policy implications* (pp. 135–156). Cambridge, MA: Ballinger.

Straus, M. (1980). Stress and physical child abuse. *Child Abuse and Neglect, 4*, 75–88.

Steele, B. (1980). Psychodynamic factors in child abuse. In C. Kempe and R. Helfer (Eds.), *The battered child*, 3rd ed. (pp. 49–85). Chicago: University of Chicago Press.

Szymanski, L. (1981). Coping with sexuality and sexual vulnerability in developmentally disabled individuals. In A. Milunsky (Ed.), *Coping with crisis and handicap* (pp. 251–265). New York: Plenum Press.

Toro, P. (1982). Developmental effects of child abuse: A review. *Child Abuse and Neglect 6*, 423–431.

Towers, C. (1987). *How schools can help combat child abuse and neglect.* Washington, DC: National Education Association.

Waterman, J., MacFarlane, K., Conerly, S., Damon, L., Durfee, M. & Long, S. (1986). Challenges for the future. In K. MacFarlane & S. Waterman (Eds.), *Sexual abuse of young children* (pp. 315–332). New York: Guilford Press.

Wells, C., & Canfield, J. (1976). *One hundred ways to enhance self-concepts in the classroom: Handbook for teachers and parents.* Englewood Cliffs, NJ: Prentice Hall.

Wolfe, D., & Sandler, J. (1981). Training abusive parents in effective child management. *Behavior Modification, 5*(3), 330–335.

Zirpoli, T. (1986). Child abuse and children with handicaps. *Remedial and Special Education, 7*(2), 39–48.

Chapter 3

The Prosecution of Child Molesters

Robert P. McGregor

The sexual abuse of children is both a phenomenon as well as a horror story and is as old as civilization itself. It is also a crime in every state in the United States of America. The laws vary from state to state and their application from jurisdiction to jurisdiction, but nowhere in this country is child sexual abuse *not* a crime. Yet, sexual crimes against children are neither treated the same nor *thought* of the same as other crimes. Sometimes the crime is ignored, and the act is treated as some sort of psychological aberration on the part of the offender who is more to be pitied than scorned. Sometimes the wrath of society is so great that the murder of a child molester is not considered to be a crime and treated as a public service performed on behalf of the community and deserving of an honorarium to be paid to the avenging parent. Sadly, all too often the crime is treated as if it never happened, as if the admission that such a thing could happen somehow taints all of us. And if we say that it really did happen, we are admitting that it could happen to our own children. Finally, and perhaps as terrible as the realization that such an atrocity could happen to our own children, is the unspoken thought that we, or someone that we know and love, could commit such an act.

I write from the perspective of a prosecutor – a deputy district attorney who has prosecuted child molesters for several years. During that period of time, I have also tried murderers, rapists, burglars, robbers, and drug dealers. I have prosecuted five men who were sentenced to the electric chair because of the guilty verdicts returned by the men and women who sat in judgment of them. In none of these cases have I felt the same burden of responsibility, the same tearing at my gut, as when I try a child molester. Twice during that period of time I have suffered from the burnout that is a professional hazard to the prosecutors who try these cases. My viewpoint of what to do with these murderers of innocence has changed over the course of time. It has been tempered somewhat by my learning that there are degrees of evil and that we cannot put away all of these individuals forever. I have learned that distinctions must

---

Note. This chapter is presented from the personal perspective of a prosecuting attorney who regularly encounters cases of child abuse. The tone reflects not only considerable professional information but also emotional commitment when dealing with such sensitive issues.

be made among offenses and among offenders. I have also learned the truth of the maxim that a bird in the hand is worth two in the bush. In many cases a guilty plea to a sexual offense, even if the recommended sentence is for less time than such an offense deserves, is preferable to trying the case before a jury, which may not believe that the prosecution has proved its case. The criteria to be used in making the decision of what sentence to recommend to a judge in exchange for a plea of guilty will be discussed in some detail later in this chapter. For now, I merely will say that a bird in the hand — even a starving fledgling — beats having to look a little boy or girl in the eyes and tell this child that the jury did not believe him or her. That experience is devastating and is one of the major contributing factors to prosecutor burnout. That disease is an occupational hazard with which every prosecutor who tries these cases is very familiar. Most prosecutors are also afflicted with a characteristic that both helps us and hurts us in this line of work. We are cursed with the belief that the only thing standing between that molester and his victims is us. Too often that belief is true.

My philosophy as a prosecutor has changed during the 4 years that I have been prosecuting child molesters. I have already mentioned that I have learned that there are degrees of evil and that distinctions have to be made among offenses and among offenders. There is one facet of my philosophy that has not, and will not, change. Any sexual act committed against a child by an adult must be considered a crime. That is not to say that a prosecution should always result from the reporting of one of these acts. One of the maddening things about the law, as well as about life, is that it is filled with exceptions. And a prosecutor must learn to deal with those exceptions. Prosecutors, unlike private attorneys, have more than one client to represent in any given case. A criminal defense attorney, for example, has an ethical obligation to represent his client, and his client alone, when that person has been charged with having committed a crime. A prosecutor always has at least two — and sometimes more than two — "clients." In the strictly legal sense a prosecutor has just one client and that is the governmental entity against which a crime has been committed. But in a very real sense a prosecutor represents not only that cold sounding governmental entity, but also a flesh and blood human being who has been victimized by another person. In a more general, but no less real sense, a prosecutor represents an often fickle but ever-present client known as public opinion. On occasion the prosecutor must adopt the convictions, if not voice the actual words, of William H. Vanderbilt that "the public be damned." Therefore, not only must our judicial system *be* fair and just, insofar as can any institution of mortals, it also must *appear* to be fair and just. If the general public comes to believe that prosecutors are involved in a witch hunt, pursuing innocent and God-fearing individuals whose lives and reputations are going to be ruined by accusations that no reasonable person could believe to be true, then we have failed. If, however, we work hard, balance the sometimes competing interests and maintain a professional appearance and attitude, we can make a difference. Later in this chapter I will elaborate on how those interests can compete and conflict with each other and suggest some approaches to resolving those conflicts.

The Decision of Whether to Prosecute

Several legal and prudential considerations are involved in the decision-making process of whether to prosecute in any given instance of a report of child sexual abuse. I have three general rules that I follow when I am making such a decision. They are as follows:

1. Make sure that you are right; then go ahead.
2. Do not get into a fight that you cannot win.
3. If you *do* get into a fight, make sure that you win it.

Does the Act Constitute a Crime

The legal and prudential considerations that I distill down to those three basic rules are the subject of the next portion of this chapter. The most basic consideration for a prosecutor is whether a crime occurred. This consideration is not always as simple as it might appear. The prosecutor must determine what act or acts actually occurred. The younger the child, the more difficult this determination normally becomes. Once the prosecutor is satisfied that he knows what happened to the child, then he/she must look to the criminal statutes to pigeonhole the act under a particular violation. Rape and sodomy, obviously, are easier to focus, but even those crimes require close scrutiny before the act is labeled. For example, in Alabama, there is no statutory requirement for penetration for the crime of sodomy. All that is required is a "touching" of the appropriate body parts of one with the appropriate body parts of the other. The crime of rape still requires a penetration, a requirement that has been passed down to us from the common law of England. It makes no sense, and it needs to be changed; but it is the law until and unless the legislature decides to do away with this anachronism.

The age of the child and of the offender frequently are considerations in determining what grade of offense an act is, and sometimes whether it is even considered a crime. In Alabama any sexual act committed on a child under the age of 12 by any person over the age of 16 is a felony offense even if the child consents. If the child is 16 years of age or older and the act is consensual, no crime, with the exception of some rarely enforced misdemeanor statutes, has been committed. Whether to prosecute in a case like this goes back to those "prudential" considerations that I mentioned earlier. Children in my jurisdiction who are at least 12 years of age but under the age of 16 are still protected by the law but not to the same extent as those under the age of 12. Obviously, the age requirements may vary from state to state.

The sexual act itself needs to be discussed because it is subject to question. In my state it is a crime to touch a child on a "sexual or other intimate part of the body." The statute itself supplies some definition and some has been supplied by case law but much is excluded and left up to determination by prosecutor, jury, trial judge, and the appropriate appellate court if the jury convicts. An example would be instructive. It has been established by case law in Alabama that the inner thighs of a young child are an "intimate part" of the body. This definition resulted from a man's being convicted by a jury and appealing his conviction on the basis that the inner thighs of a child were not, in fact, what the legislature had in mind when it included that phrase "other intimate part" in the body of the statute. Yet, would it be a crime for a person to caress a young child on the arms or lower legs or even the back, particularly if the young child happened to be about 5 or 6 years of age and the person doing the caressing was a 50-year-old stranger in the park? Would the answer change if the adult happened to be the child's grandfather? What is the answer if this affectionate senior citizen is doing this in the living room in front of the child's parents? What if he is doing it at midnight in the child's bedroom?

Another dilemma is that a prosecutor has to determine whether the above described acts and situations were accompanied by the requisite *criminal intent* on the part of the actor — the person doing the touching. Rape and sodomy are strict liability crimes. Why should it be any different if you are touching a little girl with your hand on her vagina? Well, what if you're her daddy and you are giving her a bath? You *might* be committing a crime and you might just be trying to bathe your daughter. In this kind of situation, just as in my "stranger in the park" and "grandfather in the bedroom" scenarios, I must determine as a prosecutor whether the individual doing the touching intended to sexually gratify either himself or the child. I cannot read minds any better than the next fellow, so I have to use my experience and common sense to aid me in this determination. Children must be protected, but a prosecutor *cannot* charge someone with a crime of any kind — much less child molestation — without first having coolly considered all of the facts and possible defenses.

Everything that I have just written as to whether a given act constitutes a crime is predicated on one vital assumption — that the described act actually occurred. Put another way, it is predicated on whether the child is telling the truth. Let me say at the outset that I am not one of those prosecutors who believes that a child is incapable of lying about, or of fabricating in some fashion, an episode or episodes of sexual abuse. I will say that my education, my common sense, and my experience in working with children tell me that it is rare, indeed, for a very young child to make up a story where he or she describes in the most graphic detail an instance of rape or sodomy. I have interviewed scores of children, probably over 100, who allegedly have been sexually abused, and I see the same frightened faces, the same tears, the same whispers, the same embarrassment in virtually every interview. As a prosecutor I am always alert for the facile recitation of a sexual assault which, if the child is asked to repeat it, can do it almost verbatim as if reading from a script. That kind of recitation should not be dismissed without further investigation, but it should certainly raise the antennae of the prosecutor to really scrutinize the entire situation. I say that this kind of recitation should not be dismissed out of hand because it might be a legitimate defense mechanism of the child as a response to being made to repeat incessantly the lurid details of probably the worst thing that child has ever had to endure.

The Child's Credibility

What criteria should be used by a prosecutor in assessing the credibility of a child? Some of the more obvious ones should be whether the child can explain what it means to tell the truth, whether there is a motive for the child to lie, whether there is a motive for an adult, most often a parent, to tell the child to lie, or to program the child to lie, or whether the child has a reputation for lying. Again, the younger a child is, the less likely it is that the child is consciously lying. I realize that to describe a lie as "conscious" is redundant; nevertheless, I want to draw a distinction between that instance and the instance where a child is reciting an incident which is a criminal act, absolutely believes what he or she is saying, and either it never happened or what actually happened is far less than what the child is reciting. That situation is the nightmare of all prosecutors. It can happen, and it can happen without anyone consciously programming the child to lie. That is one reason to studiously avoid leading the child as much as is practically possible when questioning the child. Children are suggestible, and caution must be exercised in interviewing them about such delicate and inflammatory matters as sexual abuse.

A note of caution is that some teenagers can and will lie about many things including incest or having sex with the high school basketball coach. Most teenagers, the vast majority, who make allegations of sexual abuse are telling the truth. In fact, it is often more difficult to get a teenager to talk about being sexually abused than it is to get a 5-year-old to talk. The cautionary note for the prosecutor is merely to understand that teenagers are more capable of lying about these things than are very young children. Their motives, their track record for telling the truth, whether they have been experiencing any psychological difficulties, and any other factor which might influence them to fabricate such a report should be investigated. If there have been psychological difficulties, the most obvious explanation that the problems are a consequence of the abuse they have suffered cannot be discounted.

Benefits of Prosecution

A final consideration with regard to whether a case should be prosecuted is whether the benefits to be gained from prosecuting an offender outweigh the

detriments. The basic philosophy of a prosecutor should be that if a crime has occurred, the offender should be prosecuted. However, before jumping into the pond with both feet, it might best serve the victim and the community to first test the waters. With pure incest cases, my first consideration is what effect a prosecution — or lack of prosection — will have on the victim of the crime. Again, incest cases should be prosecuted and prosecuted vigorously, but in some instances, particularly where a very young child is involved, it might be best to avoid a prosecution, particularly where the chances of gaining a conviction are slim. This avoidance of prosecution should be the chosen course of action only when some alternative that ensures the future safety of the abused child and any other children in that family is available. These instances of alternatives to prosecution are rare, and prosecution should always be initiated when the offender poses any threat to the community at large.

Testifying in court can be a traumatic experience for a child, particularly when the offender is present in court. However, I have seen only a very few cases when it appeared that the possible trauma of testifying outweighed the benefits to be gained by prosecuting. If handled correctly, the child victim can benefit greatly from confronting the offender in court and openly accusing this person who has violated him or her. The operative phrases in the preceding sentence are "if handled correctly" and "can benefit greatly." While keeping within the basic guidelines, each case must be considered on its own merits. A prosecutor's job is to prosecute criminals while also keeping in mind that he/she has basic responsibilities toward both the victim of a crime and the people in the community. Even keeping all of those factors in mind, he/she must realize that it is a job that rarely will leave all parties satisfied.

In the case of sexual abuse committed against a child by a stranger, the stakes are raised and the decision of whether to prosecute will be predicated almost solely on the ability of the investigator and the prosecutor to make a case. The reason is obvious. A person who will molest a child not in his family poses a clear and present danger to the community. I am not saying that the incestuous abuser never poses a danger to the community. Given the proper circumstances, *any* abuser poses a threat to the community. Nor am I saying that a child molested by a relative has suffered any more or less than a child molested by a stranger. It all goes back, in terms of how much an individual child has been harmed by a molester, to examining each instance on a case by case basis. What I am saying about nonincestuous molestations is that the offender is a bolder individual than the incestuous abuser. Generally speaking, he presents more of a threat to the community than does the incestuous abuser. Therefore, the prosecutor's decision is a relatively easy one to make. If we have a case, then we proceed.

The two types of nonincestuous molesters are the stranger and the non-stranger. The strangers are easy to spot because everyone knows and fears them. They are the shifty-eyed, greasy-haired, foul-smelling, unemployed parasites, who wear raincoats stained with gravy from last year's Thanksgiving dinner

served by a mission. They have halitosis, a bag of candy, and always hang around parks, elementary schools, and movie theaters. If only these monsters really did all look that way my job would be much easier. For the record, I have prosecuted molesters who possessed almost all of those characteristics, but the vast majority of them look just about like anybody's next door neighbor. And, of course, just about every one of them is somebody's next door neighbor. The molester who is a stranger to a child usually knows exactly what he or she wants and how to go about getting it. These characters usually are non-threatening and smooth talking. Most child molesters are con men; that is how they get children to forget or ignore everything their parents and teachers have told them about avoiding strangers. One of the best ways to con a child is to use a pet as a lure and then as a distraction while the child is being molested. What child can resist a nice man in the park with a puppy or a kitty? Not too many. And that's what makes these type molesters difficult to prosecute success-fully. Often they engage only in touching, sometimes not even beneath the clothes. And they will do it in front of God and everybody, thus supplying themselves with an insidious but effective defense when piously mouthed by their defense counsel: "If this fine man were going to molest a child, do any of you good people on this jury honestly believe that he would do it in a public park with the child's mother talking to a friend only 10 feet from him and Susie? The poor child is a victim all right; not of my client, but of an over zealous prosecu-tor and of a neurotic mother." Maybe we cannot convict the offender the first time but at least we will get his or her attention and either slow this person down or get him or her on the next go around. And there *will* be a next time for some other poor child. A prosecutor should do all within his power to con-vince a reluctant set of parents that they should cooperate with the police and the prosecution in seeing to it that this offender is charged and brought to trial, unless he does the decent thing and pleads guilty.

The Investigator

Interviewing the Child Victim

I have discussed a number of criteria to consider in making the decision of whether to prosecute. I must now backtrack somewhat to demonstrate how a prosecutor arrives at the jumping-off point. In an incest case, generally speak-ing, the child will make a revelation of the abuse to a trusted friend, relative, or perhaps a teacher at school. That report normally will be forwarded to a social service agency or sometimes directly to the police. In the case of molesta-tion or sexual assault by a nonrelative, the report normally will be made by the child to her parents who will then call the police. It is most important that the child make only the initial report before a formal interview can be arranged.

The parents can render a hearsay report to all interested parties. There is no need — and it can be detrimental both to the child and to the prosecution — to have the child repeat the report to the examining physician, to the social service case worker, to the police officer who arrives at the house or hospital to generate a report, to the detective assigned to the case, and so forth down the line. It is unrealistic by a wide margin to believe that the story need be told only one time, but the incessant repetition of the episode can be eliminated with some planning. The importance of eliminating these multiple interviews cannot be overemphasized. Rarely does it occur that the first revelation by the child provides sufficient information on which to initiate a police investigation. The only thing that can occur from that point forward — until a trained interviewer can talk with the child — is to muddy the investigative waters and to continue to victimize the child by forcing him to relive what was most likely a horrible experience. From a prosecutorial standpoint multiple interviews or statements do nothing but provide a defense attorney material with which to impeach a child on the witness stand.

The interview of a child victim of sexual assault can make or break a subsequent criminal prosecution of the offender. Conducted properly, the interview should yield information, should not contaminate the child's recitation of what happened with what the interviewer thinks might have happened, and should not leave the child feeling as if he or she once again has been assaulted. An improperly conducted interview can harpoon a criminal prosecution before an indictment is ever returned against the offender. It can also leave a child devastated and with the resolve to never again trust an adult. Remember, this is a child who has already been brutalized by placing her trust in the wrong adult. If the interviewer comes on like he or she is interrogating a Nazi war criminal, what do you think the chances are of that child being able to testify in front of 12 strange jurors, a man or woman in a black robe sitting over her, and the person who did this to her sitting directly in front of her? And what do you think the chances are that this child will ever again trust any adult? The answer is slim and none.

Guidelines.   There is no one right way to interview a child anymore than there is one right way to prosecute a child molester. There are, however, guidelines to follow, both to ensure that the child is not given information about the allegations as well as to establish the kind of rapport with the child that will allow him or her to feel comfortable enough with the interviewer to make what will be very embarrassing and emotionally painful revelations. One has to assume that the interviewer is not going to talk with the child without first having read or been told by a person other than the child what the allegation is. The child will have made a revelation of abuse to one or more individuals before the interviewer ever meets with her for the first time. The child will have told a nonoffending parent, a teacher, a classmate or other friend, or any of a variety of other people before a formal interview is conducted.

Multiple Interviews.   There is no way to avoid this multiple telling of the abuse in most instances, except when that information is transmitted to someone in authority, and that is assuming that those in authority have a plan for dealing with child victims of sexual abuse. Unfortunately, such planning among the agencies who have the responsibility for dealing with sexually abused children too often lacks a component for retrieving information from a child without either subjecting that child to the trauma of multiple interviews or of contaminating that child's memory by conducting an overly suggestive interview.

A closer look at the typical way in which an allegation made by a child winds its way through the various agencies charged with investigating child abuse would be instructive at this point. Let us assume that the victim is an 8-year-old girl who has been molested by her stepfather and who has been told by him that if she tells her mommy, he will give her a whipping for being a bad girl and for making up a story. You have a child who believes that she is going to get in trouble for telling what happened to her to the person who is probably closer to her than anyone else in her life, her mother. The little girl typically then tells a friend, if she tells anyone at all. The friend tells her own mother who then may make a report to the local welfare agency charged with the responsibility of investigating reports of child abuse. Agency personnel ultimately will get to the child when they have worked their way through to that particular report, which is only one among hundreds. Often the child must work her way through the various individuals and bureaucracies charged with taking and investigating these reports. Included among that group are emergency room nurses, doctors, police officers, teachers, and prosecutors. It is an absolute wonder that any of these children are able or willing to tell anyone anything after being forced to run that gauntlet. Invariably, as a consequence of being subjected to multiple interviews at the hands of people who most often are not trained to interview a child, there are details left out from one interview to the next. The child is likely to become confused about dates, places, and types of abuse, particularly if this is a chronic situation. Any mistake or omission that the child makes during this process will be drummed into the jury's head by the defense attorney a year or two later when the case finally comes to trial.

The practice of engaging the child in multiple interviews by untrained people also leads to misstatements of fact, usually as the result of the interviewer asking leading questions, not asking the right questions in the right fashion, or of continuing to question the child when she is tired and wants nothing more than to be left alone. If I question a tired child with leading questions that require nothing more than a yes or no answer, I can probably get that child to agree to anything including the suggestion that the moon is made of green cheese and that we ate a piece of it for lunch. A skilled defense attorney can accomplish the same end by using this technique at a lengthy preliminary hearing at which the testimony of the child is taken down by a court reporter and which will be used to impeach the child later at trial. That is just one of the reasons why a good prosecutor will take these type cases directly to the grand jury and avoid a preliminary hearing if that is lawful in his/her jurisdiction. Also, by avoiding a preliminary hearing, the time span between the reporting of the abuse and the actual trial is somewhat reduced.

There is, of course, a remedy for the problems that result from multiple interviews conducted by untrained people. It is not perfect, but it is not difficult to implement. It depends on a willingness to cooperate among all of the professions and agencies who have an official interest in investigating and prosecuting a child molester. It also depends on the cooperation of the agencies and individuals who are involved in either the medical or psychological treatment of sexually abused children. The basic rule of thumb is that after the initial report is made to the adult person that must make an official report, the person to whom the report is made should not attempt to interview the child until a proper interview location is set up and until a trained interviewer can be available to question the child. Put more simply, if the police are notified of a possible abuse situation, they should take the hearsay version of what occurred and proceed from there. I am not suggesting the police should go out and make an arrest based on nothing but a hearsay report from a person who might not have the facts straight. But, in most instances of child abuse, the premium is on conducting a thorough investigation and not on making a quick arrest. There are obvious exceptions to that general rule. If a little boy or girl is forcibly raped or sodomized – particularly by a stranger – the police must act immediately. Even in these emergency situations, the investigator interviewing the child must know how to talk to children or the case may be damaged and the offender may never be caught. Patrol officers responding to a report of child abuse should never, except in emergency situations, attempt to interview a child. They should take the hearsay report from the adult on the scene and then get that report filed as quickly as possible to keep the investigation moving in a planned and swift fashion. Police agencies should anticipate both the routine report of child abuse – usually an incest situation – and the emergency situation where an immediate response is required. Patrol officers should be trained to recognize the difference in these two situations and to act accordingly. In a nonemergency situation, the patrol officer should never attempt to interview a child-victim. Patrol officers should be trained in the techniques of interviewing children when the officer must talk with the child in an emergency situation, such as getting a description of a rapist when the primary goal is to catch the offender as quickly as possible.

The desired kind of interview, and the kind that is most likely to yield good information, is conducted in a controlled environment. The environment is controlled to the extent that the child feels safe, comfortable, and at ease with those people present. A police station or a social services agency headquarters or a prosecutor's office normally will not be amenable to producing the kind of environment most conducive to yielding a good interview. If an interview must be conducted at one of these places or at a similar place, then the very least that can be done is to have a designated interview room which is quiet and out of the flow of traffic. It does not take a great deal of effort to designate a small room as the children's interview room and to stock it appropriately with a few toys that will serve both to entertain and to distract a frightened child.

Establishing Rapport.   Distraction and entertainment are two of the interviewer's most effective tools in relaxing a child to the point where he or she can trust the interviewer sufficiently to talk about the abuse. One obvious method of establishing this rapport is to compliment the child about how pretty she looks in her dress or to start talking with the young boy about football or some other age-appropriate topic. Showing the child the various toys or displays in the interview room can also be effective. After breaking the ice in that or similar fashion, getting the child to talk about friends or pets can get the conversation flowing. These preliminaries are aimed toward gaining the confidence of the child and *getting the child to talk to you.* It sometimes is easy to forget, particularly if the interviewer is inexperienced, that the object of the interview is to get the child to talk and not the other way around. Talking to the child is merely a technique to get the child to talk. It is not the object of the interview. It really does not matter *what* it is that the interviewer gets the child to talk about, at least at first. The big hurdle is to get the child feeling comfortable enough with the interviewer and surroundings that he/she ultimately will talk about the abuse even if there must be a second or even a third interview scheduled. If a child, particularly a very young child, will not talk with a social worker or police officer by the second interview, it is best to back off and let a therapist assume all of the responsibilities for interviewing the child. Therapy, when available, should be a very strong consideration for all child victims of sexual abuse.

Training.   Training is the key to a successful interview. A successful interview is defined as one in which the child relates to the interviewer what really happened or did not happen without subjecting the child to trauma. It is most helpful if the interviewer is experienced in working with children and is comfortable in talking with them. Interviewing techniques can be taught to just about anyone with the desire to learn them, but you cannot teach someone to feel comfortable around children or teach them to feel comfortable talking with children; that is a quality that a person either has or has not. A person can grow to feel comfortable with children after working with them for a period of time, but will not likely reach that level of understanding and ability to communicate that a "natural" already has. A top level interviewer has a significant level of empathy and has the ability to literally think and talk "child."

The Child's Perspective.   Regardless of the natural ability of the interviewer, anyone conducting the interview must remember that young children do not communicate in the same fashion that adults do. Even though the child may be speaking in English, the words themselves may connote different things than they would if spoken by an adult, or they may have a different meaning altogether than their dictionary meaning. Concepts such as time and even place are difficult for a child to grasp. Dates on a calendar mean almost nothing to a very young child. It is helpful to use events such as a child's birthday or a holiday such as Christmas to pinpoint when the abuse occurred. In cases of chronic abuse it is important to get the child to remember both the first episode of abuse and the last episode if at all possible. Very often the child will be able to remember only that she was "four or five years old" when the abuse began. The frequency of abuse should be established, and the last episode of abuse should be the focus of the interview. The last episode is so important because it likely will be the target crime of the prosecution and because it should be freshest in the mind of the child.

As is so often the case, if the child is unable to pinpoint with certainty the exact date of the last offense, it can be pinned down in many instances by asking the child when it was that he/she told a friend about it in relation to the episode itself. Certainly words like *episode* are not used in talking with the child. Age-appropriate words should always be used when interviewing a child. If the interviewer can backtrack through the various police reports and reports of other interested agencies—each of which should be dated as to when the information in that report was received—the child will only have to remember that it was a week or a month or whatever the time span was between the time that he or she was molested and the time that is was reported. Pinning down the incident on which the prosecution is being based is important because a defendant has the right to be fairly apprised of precisely with what it is he is being charged. That certainly includes a pretty close estimate of when it occurred. That requirement is not fair to a 5-year-old child with no sense of a time, but that is the law. The law was not designed to protect 5-year-old children in a criminal court. It was designed to protect adults charged with having committed crimes. By using this technique, a prosecutor normally can cope with that particular requirement.

Hearsay Testimony.   Another hurdle for the prosecutor to clear is the prohibition against hearsay testimony. In layperson's terms, hearsay is merely what one person says that another person told them. There are good reasons for excluding hearsay testimony from court proceedings, but there are also many good exceptions to the antihearsay requirement. In my jurisdiction there is no such thing as a "child hearsay exception," at least in the criminal courts. Therefore, in connecting all of the report links of the chain, one may ask only such very general questions as to whether a report of sexual abuse was made on a particular occasion. No details may be elicited by the prosecutor.

Anatomically Correct Dolls.   The bottom line of a prosecution of a child sex offender is that in most of these cases it falls on the shoulders of the child to sit before a jury of twelve strangers, in the presence of the abuser, and relate to them a horror story. One way to help the child tell, and show, the jury what happened is to use anatomically correct dolls. These dolls are exactly what their name states; they are little dolls with all of the appropriate body parts. The dolls are clothed and are of the proper sizes with regard to the differences between adults and children. They come in both genders and in various races. Aside from providing a graphic display for the jury as to what happened to the child, the dolls serve at least one other very important function. They distract the child from what is happening around him or her and from the alleged offender, sitting only a few feet away.

Before the trial, these dolls can be effective tools for an interviewer. One means of using these dolls during an interview with a female child who is reluctant to tell what happened is to introduce her to the little girl doll and to tell her something close to the following: "Susie, this is a friend of mine and her name is also Susie. But she has a problem and doesn't want to tell me about it. I want to help her, but I can't do that until she tells me her problem." The interviewer may then let the child get acquainted with Susie until she feels comfortable with the doll. It is nothing short of astonishing how a child will then focus on the doll and want to help her out. Ultimately, the offender doll can be introduced to the child. He or she can be given the same first name, last name, or title as the real offender. This approach with the offender doll presupposes the identity of the real offender. If a stranger is the offender or if the child knows the identity of the offender but won't reveal it, the approach is altered to fit that circumstance. The child should be allowed to explore the dolls and to see that they are just like real people. It is important that the dolls themselves have parts that are proportionate to the size of the rest of the doll and that the interviewer not place undue emphasis on the genitals of the dolls. It is just as easy to lead a child by using these dolls as it is by asking a child leading questions during the course of an interview. The person conducting the interview must exercise the utmost caution so as not to get the child to say things with the dolls that did not actually happen. An investigator interviewing a child must remember that he/she is a professional, and that the job is to arrive at the truth, not to influence a child to say things that might not have happened. It is not up to the interviewer to show the child what the investigator thinks happened based on the hearsay report of a parent or of a teacher at the child's school. It is the investigator's job to facilitate a child's use of the dolls so that the child may demonstrate what happened.

Drawings by the Child.   Another effective method of ascertaining the truth of what happened is to have the child draw pictures of herself/himself, of the offender, and of the body parts that were touched. Circles can be drawn around the place or places where the child was touched or around that part of the offender that touched the child. Pictures can also be drawn by the child of those parts on the offender that touched or penetrated the child. Consider the impact that such a drawing has on a jury. Although this kind of drawing can be introduced into evidence in court, it can be considered a form of hearsay if it has been drawn before the trial. A way around that problem is to have the child draw the offending body part right there in the courtroom. This kind of demonstration can win a case for the prosecution right on the spot. A note of caution for the ambitious prosecutor: you will be embarrassed if your star witness sits there and draws a happy face.

Interviewing Techniques.   All of these methods must be used cautiously by any responsible prosecutor. People should not be convicted on the basis of a child's testimony that is tainted by unnecessarily suggestive methods. The operative word in the previous sentence is "unnecessarily." I know of no way to interview any witness, much less a child, without being somewhat suggestive. An example would be my questioning an adult about a robbery report that I am holding in my hand during the interview of the witness. I must make certain assumptions as I begin the interview. I must assume that the witness has, in fact, observed something that at least resembles the taking of property by force from another person. Whether this person is lying about the entire incident that he claims to have some knowledge about, I will determine during the interview itself. I will also determine the witness's truthfulness by questioning other witnesses and by using what intuitive skills I have developed and honed as an investigator. I must start with the basic assumption that this person will tell me the truth unless I receive some indication to the contrary. Therefore, in an effort to get things moving and to avoid hearing this individual's life story, I will make some sort of opening remark such as the following: "Well, Mr. Jones, I understand that you may have seen something occur last Saturday night on Fourth Avenue South. Tell me about it." That very simple statement is suggestive, but it is not unnecessarily suggestive. It serves the purpose of setting the scene and directing the focus of the witness to the topic that I need to investigate.

The same general principle applies to questioning a child witness. The interviewer should already have read or been told about the substance of the original report of the child to a parent, teacher, or friend. If the interviewer has established sufficient rapport with the child to have a conversation about the abuse, he or she might say something like the following, "Linda, I think that I know what has happened to bring you to me today. I want to help you out with this problem. But, before I can help out, I have to talk with you about it. The only way that I know to help you is for you to help me. I need you to tell me what the problem is." If I am really lucky, and if the atmosphere is right, that ice breaker will be all that is necessary to get the conversation flowing. If the child is very young and very shy, then more than that very vague statement about my knowing about a problem will be required. The interviewer might need to mention something about the offender if he or she is known to the child. This mention could take the form of a question such as asking the child whether he or she likes this person. Regardless of the child's answer, the next question is obvious, "Why?" Sometimes a very direct question must be asked, although the "tell me" method is preferred for obvious reasons. Such a direct question could be in the form of asking the child whether this person ever touched him/her. If the answer is yes, then the next question must be "where?" The interviewer can always fall back to using the dolls, particularly in questioning the child about very sensitive topics such as oral sex. The interviewer can merely ask the child to "show me what happened." The interviewer should direct the interview, and never lead the child into agreeing with a suggestion simply because the child likes or is intimidated by him or her.

The Medical Examination

A medical examination (see chapter 4) of the child is an integral part of the investigation. It can either provide valuable evidence to corroborate what the child is saying about the abuse or it can make the investigator step back and take a good hard look at what the child is saying. Too many people who are chosen to sit as jurors in these kinds of cases think that they know, or can be persuaded by a smooth-talking defense attorney into thinking that they know, the medical consequences of child sexual abuse. These jurors do not know about people who very scrupulously avoid penetrating a little girl's vagina because they know what a torn hymen can mean to a physician. They do not know that most physicians are not qualified to render any kind of meaningful opinion about whether a child has been subjected to sexual abuse because most physicians do not have either the training or the equipment to detect the results of it. They do not know that an absence of this evidence is not conclusive as to whether the child was abused. It is left to the prosecutor to educate them as to these facts. Before the education can begin, the prosecutor must ensure that a medical examination is performed on the child. The examination should be performed as a matter of routine even if the abuse is of a kind that normally would not leave evidence such as — oral sodomy. Even if no evidence whatsoever of this nature is discovered during the course of the medical examination, the physician always should testify at trial if only to explain to the jury why there would not necessarily be any medical evidence given the nature of this particular kind of abuse. Prosecutors reading this chapter will recognize this technique as being analogous to putting the evidence technician on the stand to explain to the jury why there would not necessarily be any fingerprints left by the burglar.

The medical examination can also supply the investigator with evidence that a child is either lying about the abuse or is confused about what actually happened. For example, if a 7-year-old girl has told the interviewer that her uncle has put his penis into her two or three times a week for the past 2 years, and the medical examination shows that her hymen is intact, something is definitely amiss. Aside from the most obvious possibility that the child is lying, there are other possibilities. One is that the child is mistaken about the frequency of intercourse. Although given the fact that the medical report says that her hymen is intact, that is not likely. Another real possibility is that there has been some sort of miscommunication between the child and the interviewer. Perhaps the interviewer did not make clear what he or she meant when the child was asked whether her uncle had ever been inside of her. He had the idea of full penetration, and she thought that he meant just "inside," and not necessarily all the way in. Rarely does a young child have a real concept of penetration. The offender might just be rubbing his penis inside the lips of the vagina, and the child interprets that as being inside her. It is just this kind of situation that cries out for the abolition of the penetration requirement in rape cases.

Different kinds of examinations are performed by different kinds of doctors and for very different purposes. The rape kit exam is usually performed at the emergency room of the local hospital by an intern who has received some very basic training in the recognition of and examination for sexual abuse in children. If the prosecutor is very lucky, this particular intern has been trained in the art of preserving evidence and even understands the importance of maintaining a proper chain of custody. For the layperson that is nothing more than a list of people who have handled the evidence, people who the prosecutor fervently hopes will do nothing to disturb the purity of this evidence. If the prosecutor is lucky, all of those people will be available for trial in a year or two. These type examinations are performed only when the abuse has occurred a relatively short time before the examination. They are intended to see whether any trace of evidence such as semen or pubic hairs of the offender can be gathered from the victim. If the sexual abuse has involved force of any kind, or if the child is so young that penetration of any degree will result in bruising or tearing of the child, this kind of examination takes on great import. If an offender has committed oral sodomy on a child, swabs should be taken from the child's mouth and throat, particularly if there has been ejaculation. If the offender falls into that category of individuals known as "secretors," it is possible to type his blood from his bodily fluids. That kind of evidence can be invaluable during an investigation and later at trial.

Performing an examination more than a few days after a sexual assault can be a waste of time unless there has been chronic abuse of the child. In most instances of chronic sexual abuse, the evidence of the abuse is far more subtle than what might be noted during a casual examination, even one performed by a gynecologist. Doctors must be trained to look for certain signs of abuse, signs that might otherwise be dismissed by someone not trained in knowing what to look for and knowing what significance to attach to them if they are observed. Not only is special training required, most often special instrumentation is required to perform a proper examination. The presence of corroborating medical findings can mean the difference between a conviction and an acquittal in most jury trials. The absence of such corroborating evidence does not prohibit a guilty verdict being returned, but only if the absence is explained to the jury's satisfaction by the examining physician. Absence of such evidence can also prevent an innocent person from being charged with a crime. Some perfectly valid reason might explain why there would be no physical evidence in a legitimate sexual abuse complaint. There may also be perfectly valid reasons why physical evidence would be present in a false complaint. Prosecutors are paid to make themselves aware of all the factors that might affect their decision of whether to prosecute in a given situation. They also have a moral duty, which flows in two directions to make conscientious decisions.

Interviewing the Suspected Offender

Many investigators often overlook talking to the second most important person in any child abuse case. That person is the offender. Or I should say the purported offender, because he or she might be innocent. This interview might clear an innocent person. More often it can nail the coffin lid on a guilty party. One reason that investigators sometimes overlook this individual is that they have been trained in their police work to *not* interview a suspect until he or she has been arrested and is in custody. At least they have been trained to always advise a person of his or her rights if a suspect or if the focus of suspicion has fallen on the suspect. This overreaching by police to protect a suspect's rights was a product of the appellate courts of this nation stretching the *Miranda* decision of the U.S. Supreme Court into something far different from the rules of interrogation articulated by the Court in that decision. Basically, the *Miranda* (1966) decision stands for the proposition that a suspect of a crime must be advised by the police of certain Constitutional rights during any *custodial* questioning of the suspect conducted by the police. The operative word is "custodial." Guidelines as to what facts and circumstances constitute a custodial interrogation have been developed from other cases following *Miranda*. If a police officer is in doubt as to whether his or her questioning of an individual is being done in a situation that could later be interpreted by a court as custodial, then the officer should advise the suspect of his or her rights. Many lower courts interpreted *Miranda* as holding that a suspect should be advised of his or her rights under basically any circumstances, even when the person obviously was not in custody. And so it was that police took to advising all people of their rights, sometimes even when a person was not suspected of having committed any crime. And it was just a short step from that posture to not questioning a suspect until he or she was arrested, if then. This practice not only prevented good investigators from getting incriminating statements, and in some cases outright confessions from suspects, but it also resulted in the arrest of some innocent people who could have cleared themselves if they had been given the opportunity.

The proper way to handle one of these interrogations is to treat the report of abuse as an unsubstantiated report. There are always exceptions to this general rule of thumb. In the case of a violent rape by a stranger where a good description of the offender has been supplied by the child or any other witness to the crime, a police officer should make an arrest if he or she has probable cause, should advise the suspect of his or her rights, and should follow all of the other prescribed police procedures that apply when a suspect has been arrested. In the more typical molestation case, be it by a family member or otherwise, a more calculated approach is the preferred method. Some investigators prefer to notify the suspect by telephone and to advise him or her that they (the police) have a matter of importance that they would like to discuss and then make an appointment with the suspect at the investigator's headquarters to have this discussion. There are several advantages to this approach. It gives the investigator more time to work as opposed to driving all over town looking for people who need to be interviewed. It allows the investigator to conduct the interview on his or her own turf rather than on the suspect's. It allows time for anxiety to build up and perhaps cause the suspect to make a mistake that ultimately will result in his conviction. The chief disadvantage to this approach is that it gives the suspect time to think about what is going on and to call a lawyer who will advise him or her to keep his mouth shut.

An alternative approach is to pay a surprise visit to the suspect at his or her own home. This must be done in a very professional manner with the investigator identifying himself or herself with his credentials and telling the suspect that there is a serious matter that has been brought to the attention of the police and that needs to be brought to the attention of the suspect. In this kind of situation it sometimes helps if the investigator has another officer with him or her to act as a witness as to what is said and done. The suspect invariably will invite the officer into the home where a discreet conversation can be held. It is very difficult for a person questioned in this fashion to claim in court, at least successfully, that a statement made during this conversation was made during a "custodial" interrogation. It is particularly difficult when the officers leave the house after the questioning, and the suspect is not arrested until indicted by the grand jury.

Probably the best thing to be gained from interviewing the suspect, however, is eliminating his or her chance to invent an alibi right before trial time. If the suspect makes a statement to the investigator admitting that he or she saw the child on the day in question, even if the suspect denies molesting the child, the possibility of using an alibi is eliminated. One other very important piece of information to be gained from interviewing the suspect is admission to having had some personal contact with the child on the day in question. With this, the suspect has proven for the prosecution through this statement to the investigator the date of the offense. The child will then have to testify only in general and descriptive terms the occasion that the abuse occurred. Alibi defenses normally are used in nonfamily cases of abuse. In the family cases, alibi is usually not the defense of choice. The "vindictive mother" defense or the "power mad prosecutor" defense are seen far more often in cases of incest.

If the suspect does supply the investigator with names of people who can supposedly provide an alibi, this person or these people must be interviewed as soon as possible so that the suspect does not have the opportunity "to get the story straight" with them. If, however, the alibi is corroborated by one or more credible individuals, the case could be over before an innocent individual is arrested. A good investigator should never discount the possibility that the suspect may be telling the truth. On the other hand, a good investigator should never accept at face value an alibi even if the witness seems to be very credible. The offender may even have been clever enough to set up his or her alibi before the offense occurred. It all goes back to examining each case on its own merits.

Interviewing Other Witnesses

To ensure a thorough investigation and a successful prosecution, every possible witness, not just the alibi witnesses, must be interviewed. Every person to whom the child has made a statement must be interviewed, and what the child told them must be recorded in the investigator's notes. Any person who may have seen the child just after the offense occurred is a potential witness for the prosecution for several reasons. A child who has been molested by a stranger will probably be more inclined to make a statement to the first available person, particularly if this person is a parent. That statement, if it is made very soon after the incident, likely is admissible at trial as being an exception to the general prohibition against hearsay testimony. A prosecutor should always be looking for ways in which to bolster the testimony of a child witness. Juries, even though they may affirm to the prosecutor during the examination of all prospective jurors that they would just as readily believe a child as an adult, will rarely be inclined to convict if all the prosecution presents to them is the child victim. This very human tendency of jurors is made all the more likely to manifest itself if a credible looking and credible sounding defendant takes the stand and coolly denies the allegations. It is a bonus to the prosecution to be able to put as many adult witnesses as is feasible on the stand even if their testimony is limited to reciting what they did during the investigation. Their very presence lends force and credibility to the prosecution if only in a subconscious way of telling the jurors that all of these adults believed this child. That little extra often can mean the difference between conviction and acquittal.

The Prosecution

Once the prosecutor has made the decision to prosecute, a decision must be made as to whether to arrest the offender immediately or present evidence to the next available grand jury. If the prosecutor is not required by law to present evidence to a judge before proceeding to the grand jury, then that prosecutor should avoid arresting the offender and forcing the child to testify at a preliminary hearing. Obviously, if the offender presents a clear danger to the general public, then this person should be arrested as soon as possible. In most cases of incest or of molestation by a family friend, this kind of action will not be required. Even in the case of molestation by a coach, teacher, or other person who has access to many children, immediate arrest may not be the wisest course of action. That kind of person normally is respected in the community, and the typical reaction by the general public will be one of disbelief. A premature arrest can cause the prosecutor to go into court with slim evidence, and a not guilty verdict is the likely outcome of the prosecution.

Children in Danger

The prosecuting authority loses credibility with the public, and the molester is right back in a position to continue to molest children when the furor dies down. Failure to arrest the offender as quickly as possible may result in the abuse of one or more other children. There is no easy answer to this dilemma. The best possible solution is to have trained investigators, prosecutors, and other professionals who are a part of a community's plan for dealing with just this kind of problem. If the plan is in place, and if the agencies and individuals charged with addressing this kind of problem are properly prepared, then there will be a minimum of hand wringing and wasted motion. Safety of children from a molester is always the first concern of any responsible prosecuting authority, but this goal does not have to conflict with a proper investigation designed to result in the conviction of a guilty party. The basic rule of thumb is that if the individual child and the community at large are not in danger from the offender, it is always preferable to present evidence directly to the grand jury if that strategy allows the prosecutor to bypass a preliminary hearing.

If the police and prosecutor deem that it is in the best interest of the community to make an immediate arrest, that arrest and subsequent interrogation should be designed to produce an atmosphere favorable to yielding an incriminating statement or outright confession by the offender. There are many schools of thought on the interrogation of suspected criminals, but in any case where a suspect is actually in the custody of the police, Miranda rights must be recited and explained to him or her. Failure to take this very important step will render any subsequent statement made by the offender inadmissible at trial. Most people charged with having committed a crime want to make some sort of statement. Hardened criminals and other people who carefully plan their crimes very often will refuse to make a statement, but most other people want to "tell their story." Obviously not every person who invokes his or her right to remain silent is guilty of having committed the crime, and not every person who talks to the police is innocent. However, the presumption of innocence is a legal doctrine that protects both the guilty as well as the innocent. Further, most people who are arrested are factually guilty; it is up to the prosecutor to convince a jury that they are both factually and legally guilty. If a person is arrested by the police, that interrogator is going into his session with the defendant with the presumption that this person is the one who committed the crime. A good investigator is one who can be persuaded by the defendant of the possibility of his innocence, but that persuasion must be able to overcome the evidence that the investigator already has gathered. The investigator who interrogates the defendant must be tough minded, skeptical, and adaptable to various approaches taken by the defendant. In a child sexual abuse case the investigator must be patient enough to stay up all night with a defendant if that person keeps talking and does not request a lawyer. Regardless of how good a witness a child victim is, and regardless of how good the medical evidence is, a confession is more valuable in this kind of case than in any other crime. This fact is demonstrated time and again when juries fail to convict a molester simply because they do not want to believe that such a terrible crime could be committed by such a "nice man."

Preliminary Hearing

After a defendant has been arrested by virtue of an individual signing a warrant as opposed to being arrested by a writ issued by a grand jury, he or she normally will be entitled to a preliminary hearing. The prosecution is obliged to present sufficient evidence at this hearing to convince a judge that there is reasonable cause to believe that a crime has been committed and that the defendant is the one who committed it. The advantages to the defendant in having a preliminary hearing are not insubstantial. The prosecution must "show its cards" to a certain extent, and this allows the defendant to gauge the strength of the prosecution's case. If the defense can see any weak links and can see just how weak they are, that fact alone may make the defendant bold enough to try his or her luck with a jury. Any reasonable chance that the prosecutor might have had to negotiate a reasonable settlement may be gone as soon as the child takes the witness stand. Even if the child is a particularly strong witness, a good defense attorney can have a court reporter take down every word of the child's testimony to use months later to impeach the child in front of a jury. Unless witnesses memorize what they have said on a prior occasion, they will never testify exactly the same at a later time. This truth applies to both children and adults. A defense attorney does not have to bend over backward at a preliminary hearing to be nice to a child, because there is no jury. The defense attorney will attempt to ask questions that are confusing to the child or ask the same question a number of different ways so that the child will give contradictory answers later. All of this will be done with an eye toward impeaching the child at a later time during the trial. Again, some jurisdictions will require, by law, that the defendant is entitled to a preliminary hearing regardless of whether the prosecutor wishes to take the case directly to the grand jury. This kind of requirement delays the jury trial, subjects the child to yet another forced telling of the sexual abuse, and really does nothing positive toward arriving at the truth of the matter.

Grand Jury

The alternative to arresting the defendant with a warrant and having a preliminary hearing is to thoroughly investigate the allegations and then to present evidence to the grand jury if such action is warranted. The defendant is not entitled to be at the grand jury, and the child is not subjected to the cross examination of a defense attorney. Normally this procedure is not too traumatic for the child, and the procedure can be over for the child after just a few minutes of questioning by a prosecutor in front of the citizens who comprise the grand jury. Members of the grand jury are free to ask questions to the child but normally are not abusive in their questioning. The grand jury may request additional evidence from the prosecutor and is free either to indict or not indict the defendant. Defense attorneys who believe that a prosecutor can somehow control a grand jury and coerce that body into indicting an obviously innocent person do not give enough credence to the collective backbone of their fellow citizens. Most prosecutors want to do the right thing and want to give themselves the best opportunity to do it. Aside from the moral implications, it simply does not make good sense for a prosecutor to seek an indictment in a case where there is no reasonable chance of gaining a conviction.

Plea Negotiations

Most criminal prosecutions in the courts of this country never go to trial. The cost of hiring enough judges and prosecutors and paying all the jurors necessary to carry out such a Herculean feat would be impossible for any community or state to bear. Most defendants plead guilty. They plead guilty for two reasons: (1) they *are* guilty and (2) they know that in most cases the prosecution must provide some incentive for them to plead guilty. They would rather plead guilty and take the prosecutor's recommendation of 5 years than take a chance of being convicted by a jury and being sentenced by the judge to the 10 years that they really deserve. This second reason is, of course, a very brief example of the widely condemned and little understood process known as plea bargaining. In a perfect world we would have enough money to pay all of the judges, prosecutors, and jurors to give defendants their day in court. In a perfect world every jury would have the wisdom and insight necessary to allow them to convict the guilty and free the innocent every time. We do not live in a perfect world. So we plea bargain.

In negotiating a plea with a defense attorney in a child sexual abuse case the prosecutor must take into account a number of factors before making an offer. Some of the more important factors are the prior record of the defendant (particularly any prior record of sexual offenses), the seriousness of the presently charged offense, the danger that this person may present to the community, the impact that a protracted court proceeding will have on the child victim, and the strength of the prosecution's case. The last factor is one that prosecutors do not like to acknowledge as being part of the calculus of determining what an offer should be, but it is there and definitely affects most prosecutors. However, there are some offenses for which no offers except the maximum sentence are appropriate. These cases and the others for which particularly high offers are made are the ones that are decided by juries. Obviously, there are also some cases that are tried because of the defendant's insistence of innocence. Although sometimes the defendant actually is innocent, there are cases in which the defendant insists upon a trial even though guilty but cannot or will not admit guilt. These cases are also decided by juries. But the vast majority of cases can be settled by making the defendant a reasonable offer, one that will satisfy both the state and the defendant. For the layperson reading this chapter, an offer merely is a *recommendation* made to the court by the prosecuting authority as to the sentence that a defendant should receive if a plea of guilty to the charged offense is entered. The judge is free to accept or to reject the recommendation of the state. If the offer is rejected by the court, the case will be tried by a jury.

It should be made clear what is meant by making an offer that will satisfy a person pleading guilty to the offense of sexually molesting a child. No one will be satisfied going to prison for having pled guilty. But the defendant knows that going to trial with a jury of 12 unknowns is always a gamble and that the prosecutor will, in effect, give discount points for a plea of guilty. That is why they call it a bargain. Sexual abuse of a child under 12 in my jurisdiction is punishable by no less than a year and a day in the penitentiary or by more than 10 years. Rape or sodomy of a child under 12 is punishable by a minimum of 10 years and a maximum of life, which generally means about 10 years behind bars before a lifer is eligible for parole consideration. The sentencing range for each of these three offenses is broad. This broad range allows a prosecutor or a judge to take into account all of the factors previously described as having some bearing on what sentence that an offender should receive. A person should not be punished by a judge for insisting the right to a jury trial; neither should the defendant be rewarded for it. That is why it is incumbent on prosecutors to make fair offers. And a fair offer is one that is *less*, to some extent, than what a defendant deserves. There has to be some incentive for a guilty person to plead guilty and not to insist on an expensive and time-consuming trial, a trial that could result in a guilty person being set free by a jury that was not convinced beyond a reasonable doubt of the defendant's guilt.

For example, a prosecutor evaluates a case of sexual abuse as being deserving of 5 years in the penitentiary, based on all of the factors previously discussed in this chapter. The prosecutor should make the defendant an offer of 2 or 3 years as an inducement for a guilty plea. The defendant declines, insists on a trial, and is found guilty. The prosecutor should then insist on a sentence of 5 years instead of the 2 or 3 years that he offered. The judge should give that sentence. The defendant has not been punished for insisting on the right to a trial; the defendant would be punished only if the judge gave this person more than 5 years. It is obvious that some sort of consensus must exist among

prosecutors, defense attorneys, and judges for the system to work – and sometimes it actually does work.

Settling any criminal case is a delicate matter that on occasion brings criticism to the prosecutor and the prosecutor's office. Settling a child abuse case
is always a delicate matter, and any prosecutor who handles these cases will
sooner or later be subjected to criticism. Harry Truman once made a statement
that these prosecutors need to keep in mind, "If you can't stand the heat, get
out of the kitchen."

The Trial

Trial Preparation

The trial of a child sex offender requires sound preparation. A prosecutor must
be able to present the case to a jury in a fashion that will both give it a *reason*
to convict and make it *want* to convict. In most any other kind of case, the
prosecution has but one hurdle to clear. That is the hurdle of reasonable doubt.
In a child sex abuse case, the prosecutor must clear a hurdle before ever reaching
a reasonable doubt. This hurdle is the disbelief that anyone, much less this
particular defendant, could do such a thing. This hurdle is a very formidable
obstacle in cases of incest and in cases where a scoutmaster, teacher, or minister
is charged with the offense. The American public has no trouble whatsoever
envisioning child sex abuse in the abstract, but it seems to have a great deal
of difficulty when it comes down to specific individuals whom it must judge.
There is a disquieting tendency of not wanting to believe that it could really
happen, at least not in this particular instance where it must sit in judgment
as jurors. Any prosecutor who goes into one of these trials lacking a firm realization of that tendency will be in for a rude awakening come verdict time.

Trial preparation is important in every case that a prosecutor tries. Realistically, a prosecutor does not have the time to give every case the attention it
deserves. However, any competent prosecutor should be able to pick up the
average burglary file or dope file, for example, and go into court and get a
guilty verdict after having read through the file one time. Other cases, child
sex abuse cases chief among them, require much more than that minimal preparation. At the very least, the prosecutor should have established rapport with
the child so that the child will not "freeze up" in court. The prosecutor should
have taken the child into court a day or two before the trial and let the child
get familiar with the physical surroundings. Sometimes, a victim's advocate can
do this task for the prosecutor, but the advocate should be trained to act merely
as a guide and not discuss the case with the child.

Every witness must be interviewed before the trial, and this interviewing
process should include defense witnesses if they are known. Alibi witnesses
normally will not be issued a subpoena by the defense for the very purpose

of avoiding an interview with the prosecution. If a defense witness refuses to be interviewed, that refusal can be used against this witness at trial. The prosecutor may ask whether a police investigator asked to interview the witness before the trial and whether the witness refused to be interviewed. When the witness answers in the affirmative to both of these questions, the prosecutor normally should not ask the logical follow-up question as to why the witness refused to be interviewed. The witness may have been prepared by a good defense attorney, and the answer may not be to the prosecutor's liking. A good prosecutor will let the jury wonder why and then supply it with the answer during the closing argument.

But the most important witness of all, the child, should not be over interviewed. The defense can argue that the child has been coached or "programmed" by the prosecution and that what the child says is merely words put into the child's mouth by a prosecutor. The child should appear as natural as possible in front of the jury and should be able to answer truthfully that the only thing the prosecutor has told him or her is to tell the truth.

Selecting the Jury

Jury selection in one of these cases is more crucial than it is in most criminal trials. If a prosecutor is not careful, the case could be lost before the opening statement. The questioning of the entire *venire* by the prosecutor during the *voire dire* examination of all of these prospective jurors is used for two purposes: (1) to begin "selling" the case to the jury and (2) to identify those jurors who will be favorable to the case and those who will be unfavorable to it. The selling of the case is a process that begins as soon as a prosecutor enters the courtroom regardless of whether the prospective jurors are in court. A prosecutor must put on a "game face" just as a football player must. That does not mean that the prosecutor has to go around with a dour visage starting 2 days before a jury is selected; it merely means that the prosecutor must be serious about the task at hand and not be lulled into complacency by a sharp defense attorney who wants the jury to think that the prosecutor has a job to do and that is the only reason that everybody is in court. When those prospective jurors enter the courtroom, they must see a prosecutor who projects professionalism and who obviously believes that the defendant is guilty. Throughout the trial that prosecutor must maintain an air that says three things to the jury: (1) this defendant is guilty, (2) this child is telling the truth, and (3) it is your sworn duty to convict the defendant.

The actual choosing or striking of the jury is always a subjective matter, and every prosecutor has his or her own rules, preferences, and quirks in this phase of the prosecution. Personal experience, common sense, and the shared experiences of other prosecutors have provided a few guidelines in these types of cases. Although the prosecutor usually prefers jurors to be older, in child sex abuse cases, the younger the juror the better. Whether it is merely because a younger juror can identify with a child victim or whether it is because younger jurors may be better educated in this area than older adults, they seem to be more oriented toward the prosecution. People who are better educated are more likely to be aware of the pervasiveness of child sexual abuse in our society and thus are good prosecution jurors. My personal preference is to have female rather than male jurors in these cases, but many experienced prosecutors would disagree with that bias, and, in fact, are biased in the opposite direction. However, in an incest case, female jurors definitely are preferred over their male counterparts. Each group of people is different from the next, and sometimes a prosecutor should make an exception to the general rules. Specific questions asked during the *voire dire* examination are helpful in identifying general attitudes among the potential jurors about child sexual abuse, about whether any of the potential jurors believe that children fantasize about sexual abuse, and whether a juror would *not* convict on the word of a child even though this juror might believe the defendant guilty beyond a reasonable doubt. Again, the prosecutor is finding out about the potential jurors while asking these questions as well as beginning to convince the jury of the defendant's guilt even though no testimony has been presented to them. A good prosecutor will remind a jury during his closing argument that each of them took a sacred oath to return a verdict based on the evidence, and that each of them said that he or she could convict on the word of a child alone.

Opening Statements

After a jury has been selected, the respective parties make their opening statements to the jury. The prosecutor gets to make a statement first and should never miss the opportunity to strike a hard blow right off the bat. The opening statement is supposed to be an opportunity for each side to outline for the jury just what he or she believes the evidence will be in the particular case before the jury. It is not intended to be an argument, merely a sketch, or outline of the evidence that the prosecution expects to be presented to the jury. However, not only must the jury be given a preview of what is coming, it must be done in a manner that catches their attention and at least has them leaning in the right direction before it hears the first word of testimony. One thing that a prosecutor should not do in the opening statement is to get too specific as to what the child's testimony will be. That technique can blow up in a prosecutor's face if the child does not say exactly what the prosecutor has told the jury the child will say. Keeping the crime itself general is a good rule of thumb for a prosecutor to follow in a case where a child is the main witness. By keeping it general and avoiding the specifics of the crime, the prosecutor will pique the curiosity of the jurors while still giving them an outline of what to expect in the way of testimony. By outlining the expected testimony in this general fashion, the child witness will remain the focus of the jury's attention as opposed to having the prosecutor's opening statement being the apex of the trial.

The tone that the prosecutor adopts during the opening statement is also crucial to the success of the prosecution. The prosecutor should project seriousness and conviction without becoming overly dramatic. The delivery should be characterized by controlled emotion on the part of the prosecutor. The jury should be able to pick up on both the control and the emotion. But a prosecutor should never spend all of the emotional energy that should be in reserved at the beginning of the trial. The prosecutor should save the best shots for the second closing argument when the emotion should be apparent to all who are present in court. An overly dramatic opening statement can make a jury feel uncomfortable and can be exploited by any reasonably competent defense attorney. The prosecutor must never forget, when delivering the opening statement, when doing a direct examination of the child, or when presenting either of the two closing arguments to the jury, two very important facts about these kinds of cases: (1) emotion and conviction are *almost* essential elements in winning one of these cases and (2) losing control of your emotions at any point during the trial of a child sex abuser can turn a winning case into a not guilty verdict. Facts win cases. A jury must be reminded both during the opening statement and the closing argument that they are being asked to convict the defendant based on the facts, not on personal beliefs. A prosecutor, however, must be totally convinced that the defendant is guilty.

One needs to emphasize the strong suit during opening the statement. If the strong suit is the child, a picture should be painted of that child that will last throughout the trial. That picture should be brought back in the closing argument. If there is great medical evidence, and that rarely will be the case, let that jury know what is coming and what the significance of that testimony will be. If the child is going to be a weak witness, *tell* the jury that they are going to see a scared, young child whose testimony will be difficult to follow. Tell the jury to listen carefully to the testimony and to put themselves in that child's place as they listen to and evaluate the testimony. By this time, the defense attorney will have objected, but the prosecutor will have nurtured an idea that was planted during the *voire dire* examination of the entire pool of prospective jurors, namely that a child is different from an adult. That fact sounds simple enough to grasp, but it is nothing short of amazing how a group of adults can lose sight of this fact while sitting on a jury. Turn a weakness into a strength without being apologetic about it, and the jury will be leaning in the direction of the prosecution before the defense attorney has had an opportunity to try to undo the damage.

Trial Tactics

The evidentiary part of the trial is the only part of it that the jury is to take into consideration in its deliberations as to the guilt or the innocence of the defendant. As has been previously stated, every part of the trial is important because the jury will be affected by everything that it has heard. But a prosecutor would rarely win a case, regardless of a brilliant opening statement or closing argument, if the evidence is not presented in a logical and understandable fashion.

The order of witness presentation is important and affects the way that a jury views a case. Normally the child victim will be called as the first witness. There are advantages and disadvantages to leading off with the child. A strong favorable impression can be made with the jury immediately if the child is credible and sympathetic. But there is also a case to be made for having the child testify last for the prosecution for the simple reason that it is desirable to leave the jury with the picture of that child testifying and with the child's words still fresh as the jury begins its deliberations. Practical considerations, however, most often militate against this strategy. It is difficult, if not impossible, to predict how long the testimony of the other witnesses will take during the prosecution's case. Judges do not like to be kept waiting while a lawyer has a witness brought to the courtroom. The last thing that a prosecutor wants to have happen in one of these cases is to put on the witness stand a tired and cranky little boy or girl who has had to sit around all day in a waiting room. It is much easier to predict when the first witness will be called to testify. Thus, the choice of putting the child on as the first witness is the safest way to begin calling witnesses. Also, without the testimony of the child preceding other testimony, such as the medical testimony, the other testimony probably is legally irrelevant. Many judges will allow a prosecutor to call witnesses out of order with the prosecutor's assurance that all testimony will be tied together, but that is by no means a certainty. If those two problems could be eliminated, it would be far more desirable to call the child as the final witness. The jury could be prepared by way of expert testimony for many of the stumbling blocks in these type cases, such as the child's failing to reveal the abuse for a long period of time. The tendency of the jury to forget the testimony of the child would be reduced by a significant extent.

The order of the other witnesses should be done chronologically with one exception. The expert witness should be called last. An expert witness should be a good witness. The basic rule of thumb in calling witnesses is to start strong and to finish strong. Calling an expert witness in a child sexual abuse case is imperative if one is available who can explain the dynamics of child sexual abuse to a group of citizens who are ignorant of this phenomenon. My personal bias is to call an expert who has never seen the child victim in the particular case being prosecuted. This expert should be someone with both the appropriate academic credentials and the requisite practical experience in working with sexually abused children. Ideally this person should not be a paid witness and should give no hint whatsoever to the jury of being some sort of professional do-gooder who has an axe to grind. This person should *be* a professional, should *project* professionalism, and should be able to *educate* in a fairly short period of time a jury of people who have no idea at all about the dynamics of child sexual abuse. Education of the jury is at least half the battle in a successful prosecution of a molester. If an expert is not available to testify in the case, the jury must be educated by the prosecutor in closing argument by the prosecutor's skillful use of common sense examples with which the jury can identify.

The Child Witness

As has been stressed earlier in this chapter, the child victim has got to be the star of the show. A prosecutor does not exist who, after having tried a number of these cases, has not talked to a juror after the jury returned a verdict of not guilty and been told by that juror something along the lines of the following, "Well, all of us believed the little girl; we just didn't think that you proved your case beyond a reasonable doubt." The child's testimony must be so vivid, so real, so riveting, that the jury will at least remember the testimony when it begins its deliberations. Leading questions are allowed by courts in most jurisdictions when a child is the witness. The normal rule is that leading questions may not be asked by the lawyer who calls a witness to the stand. Leading questions are generally allowed only on cross examination, and that is done by the opposing lawyer. The exception generally is that the lawyer who calls a child as a witness may ask leading questions in his direct examination. The better practice for a prosecutor is to refrain from asking leading questions to a child so as to avoid the accusation by the defense attorney that the child did not testify at all. The defense attorney could claim that the child parroted the answers that the prosecutor fed him or her during direct examination. This approach in closing argument by the defense attorney generally is very successful. If a child is unable to answer nonleading questions asked by the prosecutor, the case likely should never have been made. There are exceptions. If another child who can testify in a straight forward manner has witnessed the abuse, then the victim's testimony will not have to stand on its own. Or if there is particularly good medical evidence, a reticent child may be led by the prosecutor without that leading being fatal to the case. Normally speaking, however, the child should be able to tell the jury what happened without having to be prompted by the prosecutor.

The location of the child during her testimony is also a consideration for the prosecutor. It is good to have the child sit in the witness chair just like any other witness. This placement of the child emphasizes the isolation of the child and can underscore how brave this child is to come into the courtroom and face the person who was the abuser. The prosecutor should stand at the far end of the jury box in this situation and direct the child to speak loud enough so that everyone in the jury box can hear. This technique also helps focus the jury's attention on the child and not on the prosecutor. If the child is too afraid or too shy to sit alone in the witness chair, most judges will allow the prosecutor to set up a couple of chairs directly in front of the jury box. This placement has several advantages. The prosecutor can sit in the chair opposite the child and can shield the child from the defendant if facing the defendant is a real problem for the child. This placement also puts the child directly in front of the jury box. The jurors invariably will lean forward in an effort to see and to hear the child. The prosecutor even can set up a small table between the two chairs to allow the child to draw pictures in front of the jury, pictures of what the defendant did. This technique will have them literally falling out of the jury box to watch the child. The same arrangement can be used when the prosecutor has the child demonstrate with the anatomically correct dolls precisely what was done to him/her. Use of the dolls in the courtroom also removes much of the force of the defense attorney's argument that the child was somehow coached into using these dolls in a particular fashion. Removing the unknown from jurors' minds with regard to the use of these techniques, drawings, and anatomically correct dolls takes away a powerful defense weapon for the closing argument.

Keeping the child in the witness chair emphasizes the child's isolation and that fact can be used by the prosecutor in his closing argument by pointing out to the jury how incredibly difficult it must have been for this child to sit in that chair alone and tell a group of strangers about the most frightening and humiliating moments of his or her life. The prosecutor can then make the point that most adults would find it difficult, if not impossible, to do the same thing. Some prosecutors have even been known to deliver part or all of their closing argument from the witness chair to emphasize that particular point. Bringing the child down in front of the jury box, besides resulting in the jury focusing on that child and what the child is doing and saying during the entire testimony, almost always will force the defense attorney to follow suit and sit in the chair opposite the child. This action is good for two reasons. First, it forces the defense attorney to be nice to the child, and the child will have an easier time answering questions. Second, regardless of how nice the defense attorney may be to the child, the jury still will be impressed with the child's being able to handle adverse questions while looking the defense attorney square in the face from a distance of only two or three feet. The particular placement of the child in any given trial depends on the child, the prosecutor, the kind of case it is, and any number of other factors that are learned through experience.

Witnesses

The number of witnesses called by the prosecution during a child sex abuse case is very important. Jurors have a tendency, regardless of how prepped they were in the *voire dire* examination and in the prosecutors opening statement, to say to themselves, "Is that all there is?" The only essential witnesses are the child and the doctor, unless you have an expert on child abuse. However, in a case of this nature, the more good witnesses that can be put on the stand, the better chance the prosecutor will stand with the jury. The natural *caveat* to that rule is to not forget that there is another rule called the law of diminishing returns. A prosecutor must always keep in tune with the jury's moods and feelings. The prosecution should put on a police officer, a social worker, and as many lay witnesses as is feasible. Obviously, never put any witness on the stand that would be harmful to the case. The idea is to sell credibility with sheer force of numbers. The more times that a jury hears a different witness say that the child made a report of sexual assault to him or her, the easier it is for a jury to accept the fact that the assault really occurred. The assault becomes believable, particularly if each witness who testifies to such a report is able to describe the demeanor and appearance of the child when the report was made. Having a nurse describe a crying child making a report of sexual assault shortly after the assault occurred is worth the testimony of 5 ministers acting as character witnesses for the defendant.

If the defendant decides to testify, which will most assuredly happen unless the defendant is a convicted murderer, child molester, or rapist, the prosecution's cross examination can put the defendant away if the examination is conducted with some skill and a great deal of restraint and common sense. At the same time, if the jury has already focused on some irrelevant issue, such as the prosecutor having failed to call a particular witness who really has nothing to do with the case, the prosecutor could absolutely undress and dissect the defendant with brilliant cross examination, and it would make no difference whatsoever that sexual abuse has taken place.

Attacking a defendant who testifies is rarely a productive strategy for a prosecutor to adopt. Many times the defendant will appear as a very sympathetic figure in front of the jury, notwithstanding his or her true character. A prosecutor must exercise restraint during this cross examination and must be civil to the witness, although a little thinly veiled contempt might be in order. If the defendant has made a statement to the investigator, even if there are no admissions in the statement, that statement can be used to the prosecution's advantage in many instances. Particularly useful are those statements in which a defendant has tried to explain the situation. Having the defendant repeat that explanation in front of a jury can be most entertaining. Caution must be exercised in these situations; a clever defendant can impress a jury even with the most ludicrous of explanations. There are many ways to cross examine a defendant charged with sexually abusing a child, but a general rule to follow is to pin the defendant down and then to wait until that second closing argument before unloading on the contradictions of that testimony.

Closing Argument

After both sides have presented their respective cases to the jury, each has the opportunity to sum up its case in the form of a closing argument to the jury. The prosecution, because it bears the burden of proof, actually has two chances to convince the jury of the guilt of the defendant. The first closing argument of the prosecutor should be used to very carefully review the evidence and its significance for the jury. A good rule to remember in trying one of these cases is one espoused by the old country preacher in delivering sermons, "Tell them what you are going to tell them. Then tell them. Then tell them what you told them." Opening statement, presenting the actual testimony, and summing up in closing argument are the analogues to the country preacher's rule in delivering a sermon. Repetition of a concept, an idea, or a fact is a very effective means of getting a group of people to believe what you are trying to get across to them. Any good defense attorney knows the truth of the principle of repetition and how it applies to convincing juries of your point of view. Any good defense attorney will make use of that principle in trying the case. A prosecutor should never allow the adversary to win using this principle.

The second closing argument of the prosecution is supposed to be a rebuttal to the argument made by the defense attorney. Although it should be used for that purpose, it should not be limited to that purpose. Key facts should be repeated for the jury even though they heard those same facts recited in the first argument. This is the opportunity for the prosecutor to let the jury know with his heart and soul of the truthfulness of that child and of the guilt of that defendant. A lawyer may not express personal opinion to a jury; if there is any doubt in a jury's mind after closing arguments as to what a prosecutor's personal feelings are, however, he/she should strongly consider taking up another line of work. The prosecutor must vividly remind the jury of the little child that testified before them. Some prosecutors prefer to have the child in court during closing argument, whereas some want the child outside of the courtroom. That choice should be made based on how comfortable a prosecutor feels about having the child present during arguments. Regardless of whether the child is actually in the court, the jurors should feel that the child is sitting right there with them. The prosecutor should paint a picture of that child that is so vivid that every member of that jury should actually see that child in court during the argument even if the child is nowhere around the courthouse. Juries are so uncomfortable with the fact of child sexual abuse that they literally will forget the child even if they believed every word that child said. The prosecutor should take the opportunity during the second closing argument to remind the jury as a group that each juror took an oath before any evidence was presented to "well and truly try the facts" (or whatever other words are used in any given jurisdiction) and that each should abide by this oath in judging the defendant. They should also be reminded that not one juror indicated in the *voire dire* examination that he or she would fail to convict on the word of a child alone if convinced of the defendant's guilt beyond a reasonable doubt.

Whatever words are used, the prosecutor really is seeking to do one thing in the second closing argument and that is to make the jury believe that there is no choice other than to find the defendant guilty. If the jury does find the defendant guilty after being instructed by the judge as to what the law is, jurors should walk out of that courtroom convinced that they found the defendant guilty because of the facts and not because of the brilliant argument made by the prosecutor. The prosecutor should never forget that facts are what win cases.

Neither should the prosecutor forget that all the facts in the world will not produce a guilty verdict if those facts are not presented in a logical and coherent fashion and if the prosecutor does not make the jury want to convict the defendant. Making a jury want to convict a defendant in a child sexual abuse case is really what successful prosecution is all about. If the prosecutor has done a good job and has fortune smiling down, the jury will want to convict for one of two reasons: (1) out of a sense of outrage and (2) out of a sense of duty.

Conclusion

Conviction by jury is what these cases are all about. When a jury foreman pronounces that verdict of "guilty," all of the preparation, worry, and pretrial anguish in the world will have been worth the sound of that word to the prosecutor at that moment. The elation is difficult to describe. By the same token, the heartbreak, disgust, and emptiness produced by the sound of the foreman pronouncing the words "not guilty" will take a prosecutor just as low. As low as the prosecutor feels at the moment of first learning of a not guilty verdict, it cannot begin to compare with the absolute despair felt by the mother or father of the child as well as the child. Mercifully, many very young children do not know the impact and consequences of an adverse verdict. Those old enough to understand feel a sense of betrayal that rivals what they felt when they were being abused. It is imperative that a prosecutor or victim's advocate prepare the parent or parents and the child for such a moment. Obviously, different approaches must be used with parent and child. An adult must be told very candidly that the chance of a not guilty verdict is great in one of these cases. A child must be told that the jury will believe him or her, but that the verdict that the jury renders depends on many things. And even then the child will still be heartbroken and feel the deepest sense of betrayal imaginable. Contact by the victim's advocate must be maintained after a verdict is rendered, particularly a not guilty verdict. The child likely will need counseling regardless of the verdict, but especially so after a verdict of not guilty. A prosecutor will get over a loss, no matter how bitter. An abused child must wear that additional scar for the rest of the child's life.

Glossary

Appellate court — A court of review that determines — from the written record of trial — whether the trial court correctly interpreted the law.

Case law — Law that is not passed by a legislative body; it is established by appellate courts that have the power of reviewing the written record of a criminal conviction to determine whether the trial court correctly applied the statutes, evidentiary principles that are part of our judicial system, and other case law in reviewing the written record of the conviction of a given defendant. Case law is the *interpretive* law of the land. Part of the reason for the judiciary's relying on case law is to ensure that there is a remedy to correct unconstitutional acts that have been passed by a legislative body.

Criminal intent — The purpose for which the act is committed must be for a bad purpose that amounts to a criminal purpose. In a child sexual abuse case, there may be a touching that is accidental or that is done for a noncriminal purpose, such as touching a child's genitals while bathing the child. Criminal intent must be proved by the prosecution and normally is proved in one of these kinds of cases by showing that the circumstances surrounding the touching were not such as could be explained by either an accidental touching or an intentional touching for a noncriminal purpose.

Grand jury — A body of citizens convened by operation of law to hear sworn testimony by witnesses called by the prosecuting authority to determine whether a criminal indictment should be issued against a person.

Hearsay — Hearsay is any out-of-court statement offered as evidence in court to prove the truth of the matter that is asserted within the statement itself. More simply, it is what one person says that another person said about what happened with regard to a particular thing or incident. There are numerous exceptions to the hearsay prohibition including, at least in some states, a child hearsay exception. Most of the statutes creating this particular hearsay exception contain certain indications of reliability that must be met before the out-of-court testimony is deemed to be admissible in court. Some of these indications of reliability commonly include requirements that the statement be made to a police investigator or to a certified psychologist. The statement must also be made under conditions that must tend to ensure its reliability.

Impeach — Generally speaking to impeach a person in court is the act of attacking a person's credibility as a witness by using one of several means including a demonstration that the witness has made statements before the court hearing that are inconsistent with the witness's in-court testimony on this particular occasion.

Incest — This crime consists of having sexual intercourse with a member of one's own family. The closeness of the familial relationship is determined by state law. Normally speaking, a prosecutor gains no advantage in charging incest as opposed to rape unless precluded by law from charging rape. This preclusion would occur in a nonforcible situation where the child was older than the maximum age allowable for charging statutory rape.

Indictment — A legal document issued by a grand jury charging an individual with having committed a specific criminal offense.

Leading question — A question that contains the answer within the question. "Isn't it true that you...?" Such questions normally may be asked in court by the party who did not call a witness to testify and are part of the cross examination of that witness. The court has it within its discretion to allow the party who calls a child as a witness to ask leading questions in its direct examination of the witness.

Misdemeanor — A crime that traditionally is punishable by a maximum sentence of one year in a penal facility, usually a city or county jail. Any crime punishable by more than one year in a penal facility traditionally is considered to be a felony, which is more serious than a misdemeanor, and the time imposed for punishment would be served in a state or federal prison.

Penetration — A requirement in the crime of rape that, for the act to be considered rape, and not merely an attempt, there must be some penetration of the penis into the vagina. The penetration may be slight, but it must have occurred for a rape to have occurred. In some states there is no penetration requirement for the crime of sodomy; a mere touching is sufficient.

Preliminary hearing — A legal hearing before a judge in which the prosecuting authority must present sufficient evidence to the court to legally justify the court binding the defendant over for either consideration by the grand jury or for trial. The measure of proof that must be met by the prosecuting authority is less than that required before a jury can convict a defendant at trial.

Rape — A criminal offense that consists of a male having sexual intercourse with a female by use of force, either direct or implied. A second definition of rape is intercourse by a male with a female child under a certain age. Children are considered under the law to be incapable of granting consent. The degree of force required and the age requirement are established by each state and may vary to a certain extent.

Sodomy — A criminal offense that consists of having one person touch his mouth to the genitals of another, or touch his genitals to the mouth or anus of another. Sodomy may be committed either by use of force, either direct or implied, or by virtue of the child being below a certain age and the age of the offender being above a certain age.

Statutory requirement — A requirement of the law that is mandated by a written statute (law) passed by the appropriate legislative body.

Strict liability crime — Any crime for which there is no requirement to prove a specific criminal purpose or intent. Rape and sodomy are strict liability crimes; if the prosecution has proved that the alleged act did occur, it has no burden to prove the specific intent of the offender when he was engaging in the act.

Venire — The pool of people from which the jury is selected.

Voire dire — The questioning process that is conducted by the court and by both the prosecution and the defense to help select an impartial jury from among the member of the *venire*.

References

Miranda v. Arizona, 384 U. S. 436 (1966).

Chapter 4

Medical Evaluation of the Sexually Abused Child

Kristi M. Mulchahey

The medical evaluation of the child or adolescent who may have been sexually abused presents the health care provider with special challenges. This is an extremely common problem, yet few professionals have received the special training needed to sensitively and appropriately deal with this difficult issue. Physicians from a wide variety of medical disciplines, including pediatrics, gynecology, and family medicine, along with nurse practitioners, nurse clinicians, and physicians associates, may be called on to provide this care. These health care professionals must be properly trained.

There is a great deal of reluctance among the general population to acknowledge the existence of sexual abuse in children and adolescents. Approximately 100,000 cases of sexual abuse are reported each year in the United States, with a conservative estimate that the reported numbers represent only the "tip of the iceberg" (Depaufilis, 1986). The actual incidence has been estimated by Woodling and Kossoris (1981) to be over 300,000 new cases each year, well over 3 times the reported incidence. Several studies have suggested that the prevalence of previous childhood sexual abuse in adults may be between 6% and 30% for women and 5% to 20% for men (Peters, Wyatt, & Finkelhor, 1986). Such studies have generated the often quoted prevalence figure of 1 in 4 girls and 1 in 10 boys as victims of sexual abuse at some time during childhood or adolescence. Nevertheless, it may be difficult for physicians to acknowledge signs of sexual abuse in their own patients, especially with families where a longstanding physician–patient relationship may exist. Also, many physicians have not been adequately trained to discuss sexuality with children and adolescents and may feel especially uncomfortable in doing so.

Physicians may have the same misconceptions regarding sexual abuse as the general population, such as ideas about social class or sex of the victim or the traditional view of the perpetrator as the "dirty old man." These misconceptions may impair the physician's ability to diagnose and effectively treat sexual abuse. In addition, children may be victimized by a number of different

---

Note. This highly technical and complex treatment of sexual abuse is written from the perspective of a practicing physician. Nonhealth care professionals may find it advantageous to consult a medical dictionary in addition to the glossary of terms provided at the end of the book.

forms of sexual abuse. Sexual victimization of children may include sexual assault, child rape, incest, child molestation, as well as commercial exploitation of children, such as child pornography and child prostitution. Health care professionals working in a setting with physically or mentally handicapped patients must be especially alert to signs of sexual abuse in their patients. Thomas Elkins, M.D. (1988) recently reported a 50% incidence of sexual abuse in his series of 300 girls and adolescents presenting for care at the University of Michigan Model Clinic for Reproductive Health Concerns of Mentally Handicapped Persons.

The education of health care professional students is another issue of great importance. Although current students are receiving more didactic and clinical training than ever before, this is still an area where continued efforts are vitally important. In the *American Journal of the Diseases of Childhood*, Orr (1978) reported significant inadequacies in the medical record documentation by resident physicians evaluating sexually abused children in the emergency room setting. Should all children be evaluated by specialized teams within the hospital setting, and, if so, what role should students play? If medical learners are not exposed to some of these issues during their training where close supervision can optimize their learning experience, many of the problems previously mentioned will never be corrected.

Clearly, the medical evaluation of the sexually abused child presents the health care professional with challenges in a number of different ways. These challenges are present regardless of whether the examiner is a student, an experienced health care professional who is confronted with sexual abuse on an infrequent basis, or a trained specialist working with sexually abused children every day. However, the search for solutions to these difficult problems will clearly benefit the person at greatest risk, the sexually abused child or adolescent. In this chapter, the medical approach to the sexually abused child will be discussed; current medical literature will be reviewed, as well as a discussion of active areas of investigation.

Presentation

The health care worker may be the first professional with whom the sexually abused child has contact; therefore, it is the responsibility of those who care for children and adolescents to be aware of the signs and symptoms of sexual abuse, both obvious and subtle. It may be easy to suspect sexual abuse in the child with gonorrhea, but difficult to entertain that possibility in the pregnant 13-year-old prostitute or the 16-year-old male involved with substance abuse or running away behavior.

Behavioral Changes in Sexually Abused Children

The physician is often confronted with behavioral changes, rather than physical symptoms, as the presenting complaint in the sexually abused child or adolescent. A wide variety of symptoms have been described and were summarized at the National Summit Conference on Diagnosing Child Sexual Abuse (1985).

As shown in Table 4.1, the behavioral changes may range from nightmares or depiction of precocious knowledge of sexual acts in doll play of the preschool child, to school difficulties, eating disorders, or substance abuse in adolescents.

The American Medical Association included behavior indicators in their Council Report entitled "Diagnostic and treatment guidelines concerning child abuse and neglect" (1985). The authors also included indirect disclosures of abuse which may be feelings of guilt or shame, as well as changes in the child's perception of body image; the presence of a sexually abused child in the home was also stressed as a marker for the possibility of sexual abuse in the other siblings.

Although the evaluation of such complaints may be considered by some to be the responsibility of a psychologist or social worker, these complaints may be the first indication of sexual abuse in the child. Certainly the presence of such symptoms in a child would warrant exploration of the possibility of sexual abuse, either past or present.

Physical Findings in the Sexually Abused Child

The sexually abused child may also present with physical complaints in the absence of any specific history of abuse. For example, the child may present with vaginal discharge, bleeding, or symptoms of vulvitis, such as itching, burning, or irritation. Such symptoms could be related to a sexually transmitted disease, but may also be seen in the absence of any specific infection. A history of recurrent urinary tract infections presenting as dysuria with negative urine cultures may actually represent pain from urination over injured vulvar tissues. Children also may present with recurrent vulvar complaints, despite normal findings on physical examination. For the very young child who may lack the verbal skills to communicate the story of abuse, or the older child who is afraid or ashamed to tell the story of abuse, such complaints may be the child's only means of making the victimization known.

Recurrent complaints of abdominal pain, much like complaints of recurrent headaches in the older child, may occur in the absence of any abdominal pathology. Such complaints most likely represent a somatization of psychological distress. A very dramatic and unfortunate example of this is provided by an adolescent patient who had been a victim of incest, starting at the age of 5 with the remarriage of her mother and the introduction of the stepfather into the home. She subsequently developed recurrent bouts of abdominal pain and underwent exploratory surgery twice during her elementary school years, always

Table 4.1 Behavioral Changes Seen in Sexually Abused Children

---

Young children, 4 years and under
Sleep disturbances
  Insomnia
  Nightmares, especially with specific content
Premature eroticism
  Excessive masturbation
  Seductive behavior
  Depiction of sexual acts in play
Fearfulness of normal nudity (diapering or bathing)
Somatic complaints
  Unexplained abdominal pain
  Vulvar discomfort
Regressive behavioral changes
  Increases in separation anxiety
  Bed-wetting, after nighttime dryness

Children, 5–10 years
Sleep disorders
Premature eroticism
  Drawing of genitals
  Seductive behavior/pseudomaturity
  Sexual aggression toward other children
School phobia
  Changes in school performance
Somatic complaints
Destructive behavior
  Substance abuse
  Running away
  Prostitution

Adolescents, 11–18 years
Sleep disorders
Destructive behavior
  Substance abuse
  Running away
  Prostitution
Eating disorders
Pregnancy
School phobia
Somatic complaints

---

with negative findings. She was about to undergo the third major surgical procedure in her young life when the long history of incest was finally discovered.

The physical findings associated with sexual abuse in the child or the adolescent may be fairly subtle and easily overlooked during the course of a routine exam by a health care professional. Especially with victims of incest, where the use of force is unusual, physical findings may be minimal or absent. Some authors have suggested that up to 50% of children who have been sexually abused will have no confirmatory physical findings. A health care provider who is familiar with the evaluation of sexually abused children may be able to increase the yield of such examinations by searching for subtle, yet significant, findings which could be easily overlooked by a less experienced examiner. In addition, the use of diagnostic tools, such as a hand-held magnifying glass, an otoscope, or a colposcope, can be an aid.

The colposcope, first developed for the evaluation of abnormal cervical cytology, aids the examination by providing an excellent source of light and magnification. This noninvasive instrument provides a variable degree of magnification without actually touching the patient (Figure 4.1). With the colposcope, the physician can obtain a very thorough examination of the external genitalia of even a very young child without causing distress to the child. Although many feel this instrument is not necessary to adequately evaluate these patients, the colposcope is a great visual aid and provides a simple means of photographing the physical findings for documentation, research, and teaching purposes.

With the assistance of such visual aids, in particular the colposcope, a number of investigators have significantly increased the percentage of abnormal findings detected in children suspected of being sexually abused. The use of colposcopy in the evaluation of sexual assault victims was first described by Teizeira (1980) in a series of over 500 patients, including both pre- and post-menarchial girls and women. This technique was further refined for use in childhood victims by Woodling and Heger (1986). Using this technique, they described abnormal colposcopic findings in over 75% of children who reported painful genital abuse. Subsequent to this, larger series have been published using colposcopy in the evaluation of the prepubertal sexual abuse victim. Emans, Woods, Flagg, and Freeman (1987) recently detailed anatomical variants and abnormalities discovered by examination with colposcopy in prepubertal girls.

McCauley, Gorman, and Guzinski (1986) have also adapted the use of toluidine blue dye to the pediatric sexually abused patient. This technique has been well described for use in the adolescent and adult population of sexual assault victims. The application of the toluidine blue dye to the area of the posterior fourchette enabled the examiner to detect lacerations in this area that were otherwise not visible to the unaided eye. The use of the dye increased the detection of lacerations from 10.2% to 32.6% in a group of prepubertal girls presenting with a chief complaint of sexual assault. As well, the application of the dye was well tolerated and did not interfere with interpretation of other forensic studies.

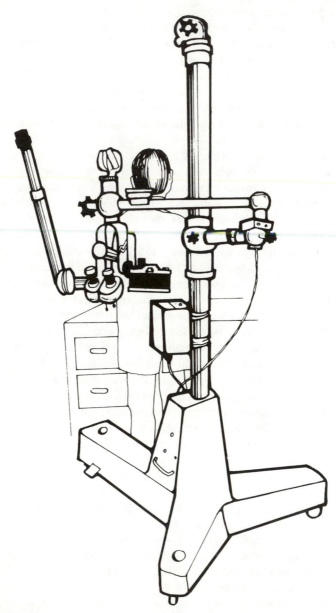

Figure 4.1 Colposcope. *Note*. From "Abnormal Pap Smear." Birmingham, AL: University of Alabama. Reprinted by permission.

Interpretation of the physical findings noted in sexually abused children depends a great deal on knowledge of normal anatomy in childhood. In addition to describing abnormal physical findings in sexually abused children, the colposcope has been very helpful in further detailing normal anatomy in children along with the common variants found.

Careful attention to the genital exam of normal children during routine well child care can enable the examiner to acquire a greater appreciation for the normal hymen and its variants. There may be a great deal of individual variation in the appearance of the hymenal ring in normal children. Pokorny (1988) has published a detailed study of hymenal anatomy in both normal and sexually abused children. Her observations have classified normal hymenal anatomy into three basic variants. The most common form was described as "posterior rim" (Figure 4.2). The hymenal tissue in these children was described as a crescent shaped rim of hymen present posteriorly, with little tissue visualized anteriorally. The "circumferential" hymen (Figure 4.3) consists of a smooth circular configuration of hymenal tissue, with a centrally placed opening. Another common, although less frequent, finding was the fimbriated hymen (Figure 4.4). This variant presents as abundant hymenal tissue that is thrown into folds, which are often said to resemble the "petals of a flower." Dr. Pokorny's careful

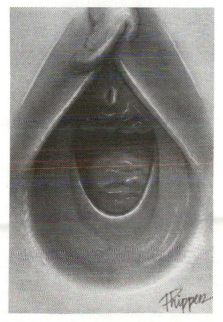

Figure 4.2 Posterior rim hymen. *Note.* From "Configuration of the Prepubertal Hymen" by S. Pokorny, 1987, *American Journal of Obstetrics and Gynecology, 157,* 950–955. Copyright 1987 by C. V. Mosby. Reprinted by permission.

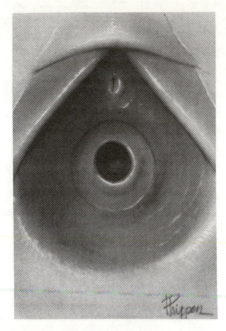

Figure 4.3 Circumferential hymen. *Note.* From "Configuration of the Prepubertal Hymen" by S. Pokorny, 1987, *American Journal of Obstetrics and Gynecology, 157,* 950–955. Copyright 1987 by C. V. Mosby. Reprinted by permission.

descriptions of normal children have been very helpful in interpretating abnormal findings in sexually abused children.

A number of abnormal physical findings have been reported in the prepubertal female sexual abuse victim. Bruising and abrasions of the external genitalia may be seen in the child with a recent episode of abuse. Information regarding the dating of the age of bruises is available in the forensic literature and may be helpful in determining the timing the assault in children. Bruises that are reddish-blue or purple are generally felt to be less than 24–48 hours old, whereas yellow, yellow-brown, and fading bruises are greater than 5 days old (Durfee, Heger, & Woodling, 1986).

Other findings documented in sexually abused children have included erythema of the vulva, vaginal discharge, lacerations of the posterior fourchette, and labial adhesions. Although these findings may not be specific for sexual abuse, they are found more commonly in sexually abused girls when compared with normal children. Although labial adhesions are commonly seen in young girls, especially with poor hygiene and chronic irritation in the face of a hypoestrogenic state, McCann, Voris, and Simon (1988) have described labial adhesions in a family of sexually abused girls. In a larger study, Berkowitz,

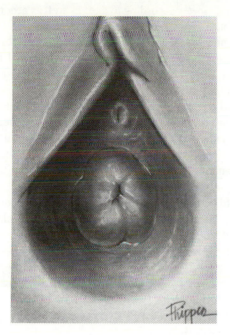

Figure 4.4 Fimbriated hymen. *Note.* From "Configuration of the Prepubertal Hymen" by S. Pokorny, 1987, *American Journal of Obstetrics and Gynecology, 157,* pp. 950–955. Copyright 1987 by C. V. Mosby. Reprinted by permission.

Elvik, & Logan (1987) retrospectively reviewed the charts of 500 girls present-ing to the pediatric clinic of Harbor/University of California Los Angeles Medical Center for evaluation of possible sexual abuse. They found 10 cases of labial fusion, unassociated with any history of vaginitis, straddle injury, or dermatitis; all of these children also have other physical findings consistent with sexual abuse. Muram (1988a) also reported a similar incidence of labial adhe-sions in sexually abused girls evaluated in Shelby County, Tennessee. The investigators encouraged examiners to consider the possibility of sexual abuse in the differential diagnosis of labial adhesions in prepubertal girls.

More specific physical findings suggestive of sexual abuse may include dilatation of the hymenal ring, as well as injury to the hymenal ring itself. Measurements of the transverse diameter of the aperture of the hymen ring have been used in the assessment of sexually abused girls. The normal hymenal ring diameter in the prepubertal child has been reported to be 0.4 cm or less. Cantwell (1981) reported that a hymenal diameter of greater than 0.4 cm correlated with the presence of sexual abuse in 75% of the children evaluated. However, there may again be a range of normal, including larger diameters in the older school age child. Adams, Ahmad, & Phillips (1988) reported an increase in hymenal diameter according to age, as well as according to the reported extent of sexual abuse. The diameter of the hymenal ring may vary with the positioning of the child for the examination, as well as the ability of the examiner to encourage the child to relax. Nevertheless, the hymenal ring in the unestrogenized, prepubertal female should measure less than 1.0 cm (rarely, more than 5–7 mm) and certainly should not admit an examining finger.

Although visual inspection is generally sufficient to determine the diameter and tone of the hymen, direct palpation may at times be helpful. Levitt (1986) has described the palpation of the hymenal ring as helpful in determining the possibility of vaginal penetration. She describes the child in whom the hymen provides no resistance to attempts at penetration with the examining finger or is felt to painlessly stretch to allow the examining finger to enter the vagina. Although this would certainly not be attempted if it caused any pain to the child, this technique may be helpful in certain situations, especially if the question of actual vaginal penetration is pertinent.

Especially with the aid of colposcopy, consistent changes within the anatomy of the hymenal ring itself have been described in children with a history of sexual abuse. These changes generally result from old, healed laceration(s) in the hymenal ring and may appear as transections of the hymen, attenuated or "worn away" hymenal rings, as well as synechiae attaching the hymen to the vaginal mucosa (Figure 4.5).

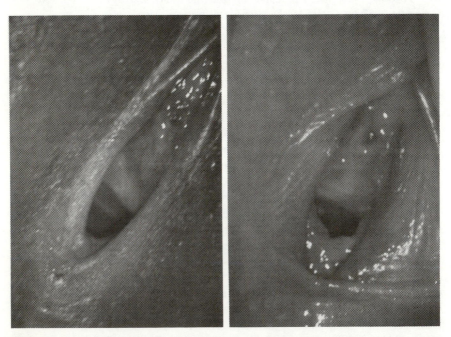

Figure 4.5 (A, *left*) Attenuated hymen in 5-year-old sexually abused girl. (B, *right*) Hymenal disruption in 8-year-old girl with *Chlamydia vaginitis*.

To facilitate interpretation of the physical findings in the prepubertal child, Muram (1988b) suggested a classification system that distinguishes between nonspecific and specific findings (Table 4.2). Nonspecific findings are seen not only in sexually abused girls, but also in girls with a history of infection or irritation. Specific findings strongly suggest the possibility of sexual abuse and are rarely seen in other situations. Such standardization will facilitate research as well as communication between physicians and in legal proceedings.

Much less is known about physical findings among young boys who are victims of sexual abuse. Authors are beginning to address the issue of anal findings in both male and female children. Sodomy in child sexual abuse may be more common than presently recognized. The young child's limited knowledge of anatomy, as well as insufficient verbal skills to describe the episode of abuse makes the assessment of either vaginal or anal penetration difficult to determine with certainty. The presence of perianal scarring and anal dilatation have been reported with increasing frequency in sexual abuse victims of both sexes. Other reported findings have included hyperpigmentation in the perianal area, anorectal skin tears, perianal skin tags, as well as gaping of the rectal sphincter or evidence of disruption of the anal sphincter. This may result in a sphincter with a key-hole appearance. Funneling with loss of the subcutaneous fat in the perianal area may also be seen (Sanfilippo, 1987).

Reinhart specifically addressed the issue of sexually abused prepubertal boys in 1987. In this group of boys, abnormal physical findings were noted in the genital as well as the perianal area. However, genital abnormalities were noted in only 5% of boys, compared to anal abnormalities in 29% of the boys. Abnormal genital physical findings included bite marks, bruises, urethral discharge, and skin changes such as rashes or redness. Perianal findings were especially common in the very young male child (i.e., 2 years old or younger) and included anal laxity, fissures, erythema, bruises, scarring, and skin tags, along with other findings.

Table 4.2 Classification of Physical Findings in Prepubertal Sexually Abused Girls

Category I	**Category III**
Normal exam	Specific findings
Category II	Hymenal lacerations
Nonspecific findings	Hymenal diameter $\geq$ 1 cm
Erythema of vulva	Sexually transmitted disease
Vaginal discharge	Bite marks on genital area
Labial adhesions	
	Category IV
	Definitive findings
	Presence of sperm

Although the question of vaginal or anal penetration may be a difficult one to determine, this question will become nevertheless an important legal issue if criminal proceedings result from the child's disclosure. The definition of penetration may vary from state to state, and each health care professional will need to be familiar with local statutes. A very interesting study recently reported by Muram (1988c) compared childhood victims' disclosures and physical findings with the confessions of their assailants. Even when the perpetrator confessed to penetration, specific findings were found in only 61% of the girls. Thirty-nine percent of the girls had nonspecific findings or normal examinations. This certainly stresses that the absence of physical findings should not negate the child's disclosure of sexual abuse. The presence or absence of physical findings in the child who reports an episode of sexual abuse should not be used to determine the validity of the child's statements.

The Medical Interview of the Sexually Abused Child

In the evaluation of the child suspected of being sexually abused, several special aspects in the history of the child will need to be evaluated, in addition to the usual aspects of medical history familiar to all health care professionals. The history of the episode(s) of abuse may be obtained by a health care professional from a medical, nursing, social service, or psychiatric background. It is also important to remember that requiring a child to repeat stories of sexual abuse, after the initial disclosure, may be very painful. In many areas, attempts are being made to coordinate legal, law enforcement, social service, and medical professionals so that the children involved are not required to repeat their stories to many different individuals.

Certainly the health care professional is trained to perform the medical evaluation of the sexually abused child and not to initiate psychotherapy. However, children may be unpredictable where and to whom they choose to disclose their story of abuse. The medical evaluation should be conducted in a manner appropriate for the developmental stage of the child. The individual who will be involved in any aspect of caring for the sexually abused child needs to learn to talk to children about sexual matters in an appropriate way that will facilitate future interactions that child will have with therapists in the counseling process. A well-meaning health care professional may cause a great deal of harm to the child and future therapy by seemingly "innocent" statements during the course of the history and the examination. For example, a question such as "You didn't let him do ____, did you?" gives a clear statement to even a young child that certain activities may be inappropriate to discuss or might be the fault of the child rather than the perpetrator.

Obtaining a history of sexual abuse requires an individual who is comfortable talking to young children about sexual matters. Learning from the caretaker the names that the child uses for genital parts and bodily functions may help the examiner to communicate more effectively with the child. Questions to the child should be posed in a way to avoid leading the child; specifically, avoiding "yes/no" questions will help to obtain an accurate history from the very young child. It is also important that the examiner have some knowledge of child development and the developmental level of the child being evaluated. For example, the very young child may have difficulty with the concept of time; attempting to date an event in relation to the seasons or the weather may be more successful than dealing with specific months or dates. Even more important, the interviewer may inadvertently communicate to the child his/her own sense of shock or disbelief at the events disclosed by the child. This is often an area of difficulty for the physician or nurse who is not involved in the evaluation of childhood sexual abuse on a frequent basis. Often, the strong feelings that the examiner may have regarding the events described may be apparent to the child and interpreted as feelings of disapproval, leaving the child with the feeling, "I must be very bad." In this setting, it is crucial to avoid communicating such feelings to the child, even unintentionally.

In addition to skills of communication that may be learned, there are also other simple tools that may be helpful to the examiner. Anatomically correct dolls are available, although they may be prohibitively expensive for the office or clinic that sees these children infrequently. In fact, some have even suggested that anatomically correct dolls may be frightening or too graphic for some children. In their place, nearly every child enters the office with a well-worn "lovie" that may be used during the course of obtaining the history and performing the exam. For example, the young child who cannot describe the episode of abuse (or does not have the language to explain the events) may be able to demonstrate with the doll or stuffed animal that accompanied him/her to the office.

For the older child who is reluctant to describe the events of abuse, simple drawings may be helpful. The child may be able to draw a description of the event. In addition, the child who cannot describe what a "boo-boo" is may be able to draw a "boo-boo" on a stick figure drawn by the examiner. The availability of toys such as a doll house or play telephone may also be helpful. The school-age child, who may be very embarrassed by the abusive episodes, may be willing to whisper an especially difficult portion of the account into the ear of the examiner, rather than recite the events out loud. Jones and McQuiston (1986) have a very thorough and practical review of interviewing techniques and tools published by the C. Henry Kempe National Center for the Prevention and Treatment of Child Abuse and Neglect.

As always, obtaining a careful past medical and surgical history is important. Special attention is due to certain aspects necessary to provide the child with good medical care and to prepare the health care provider for questions which may be asked in court at a later date. In addition to asking about the usual medical illnesses, the caretaker or older child should be asked about a history of vaginal bleeding, vaginal discharge, or vulvar complaints. In the child with a history of recurrent urinary tract infections, the health care professional should attempt to determine how these urinary tract infections were documented. It is not unusual to see the child with a presumed diagnosis of cystitis based on complaints of dysuria, when the dysuria was actually caused by pain from the urine on an injured vulvar area. A history of bowel habits is important in both male and female children. If a dilated anal canal is discovered during the course of the physical exam, it will be pertinent to know if the child has a history of severe constipation. Information regarding previous surgical procedures is pertinent; especially in the child who has undergone vaginoscopy, abnormal findings in the area of the hymenal ring may be related to prior surgical procedures for investigation of vaginal bleeding or removal of foreign bodies.

Information regarding medication taken by the child or any allergies the child may have should also be obtained. Current use of antibiotics could influence results of cultures obtained in screening for sexually transmitted diseases. Family history and social history should also be obtained. A brief social history may reveal pertinent information that may not be volunteered by the child or the historian in other areas of the history. Again, the health care professional is generally not trained to evaluate the social setting of the child, but there may be situations where this will be necessary. For example, a physician seeing the child in the emergency room late at night may need to become involved in assessing whether the home situation is safe for the child to return to or if the child should be admitted to the hospital until a more thorough evaluation can be done in the morning.

Physical Examination of the Sexually Abused Child

The physical examination of the pediatric sexual abuse victim requires a patient and often creative examiner. The physical examination is an extremely important part of the complete evaluation of the child when sexual abuse is known or suspected. The examination may well become an essential component of subsequent legal proceedings. In addition, detection of injury or a sexually transmitted disease is important for the overall health of the child. Jason (1982) reported that many childhood victims of sexual abuse receive no medical evaluation, despite its importance. The examination should be performed in a gentle, thorough manner with the child setting the pace for the examination, if possible. There is no justification for restraining or sedating the child! It is imperative that the medical personnel avoid compounding the trauma the child has already experienced from the sexual abuse. A hurried, rough examination may be actually more frightening or painful for the child than the sexual abuse. One young child, when asked about an episode of sexual abuse, could only reply, "Five people held me down on a cold table and hurt me." Later, it was realized that the child was referring to the medical examination. In her mind, this was a more frightening experience than the sexual abuse itself. Clearly, such situations are not in the best interest of the children involved and are to be avoided.

A general physical examination, serving three roles, is performed. First, the examiner will detect any physical abnormalities associated with any acute or chronic illnesses and will assess the level of sexual development. Second, findings associated with physical abuse, such as bruises, bites, or burns, will be identified. Tilelli, Turek, and Jaffe (1980) reported on a series of 130 children presenting with a chief complaint of a sexually related offense. In these children, 4 of the younger children had signs of chronic physical abuse and 43 of the children had some evidence of trauma, including nongenital locations. Attias and Goodwin (1985) have also report a 15% to 25% incidence of physical signs of abuse or neglect in children who reported sexual abuse. Pharyngitis, which could be caused by *N. gonorrhea*, should also be identified. Third, and possibly most important, the general exam allows the child to become accustomed to the touch of the examiner and fosters the development of trust between the examiner and the child. The same dolls, puppets, or stuffed animals used during the history may be helpful in this setting.

A thorough examination of the external genitalia is next performed. This portion of the exam requires a different approach than used in the pelvic exam of the adolescent or adult female. Children will often not tolerate the dorsal lithotomy position, nor will this necessarily provide the best exposure. Because it is not necessary to visualize the cervix, the vaginal speculum is not used in children; in addition, the use of even a pediatric speculum would be very painful to the unanesthetized child.

A variety of positions have been described that allow a through examination of the external genitalia of the child. These techniques have been well summarized by Gidwani (1987). Although certain positions may be well suited to different age groups, it is helpful for the health care provider to be familiar with a number of positions. Pediatric patients may vary in their willingness to be examined in different positions. The examiner will obtain a greater degree of cooperation with the exam if the child is in a position that makes the child feel safe and secure; in fact, a child who strongly resists certain positioning during the exam may do so because it reminds him or her of the episode of abuse. It is crucial that the health care provider be sensitive to these possibilities. Although older children may feel that draping with sheets will preserve a sense of modesty, children will vary widely in this regard. In some younger children, the presence of a sheet, which hides the examiner from the view of the child, may generate a great deal of anxiety about the exam. The younger child may feel safer if he/she can see as much of the examination as possible.

The child's mother or advocate who accompanies the child to the visit may be a great asset during this portion of the examination. The young child (and often the older child, as well) will usually tolerate being placed in mother's lap. With the mother sitting on the end of the examination table, she can hold the child's knees apart in a flexed position, affording a very clear view of the genital area, especially if colposcopy is to be performed (Figure 4.6). The older child may assist by placing her hands on the inner portion of her thighs, actually helping with the examination. Although traditionally described for the very young child, this position is possible with even the older prepubertal child.

For the older child, the modified dorsal lithotomy or frog-leg position may be useful (Herman-Giddens and Frothingham, 1987) (Figure 4.7).

The traditional gynecologic stirrups are not necessary in the exam of the prepubertal child and attempting to use them in an uncooperative or frightened child may result in an inadequate examination. However, a modified version of the traditional dorsal lithotomy position has been described, again involving the help of the mother or significant other who acts as the support person for the child. In this modification, the adult places her feet in the stirrups, with the head of the examining table raised. This child is then placed on the abdomen of the adult, with legs resting on the thighs of the adult. The adult can help to support the child's legs and provide emotional support during the examination (Figure 4.8).

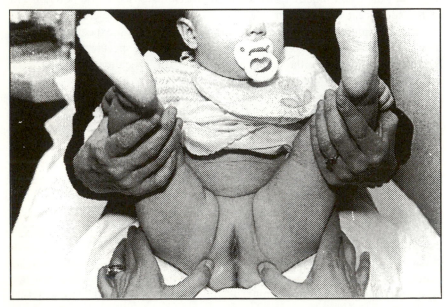

Figure 4.6 Examination of an infant, held in the mother's lap. *Note.* From "Approach to Evaluation of Premenarchal Child With a Gynecologic Problem" by G. Gidwani, 1987, *Clinical Obstetrics and Gynecology, 30,* pp. 643–652. Copyright 1987 by J. B. Lippincott. Reprinted by permission.

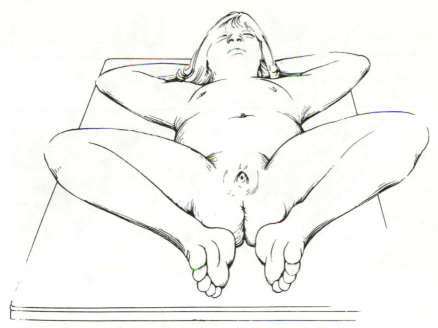

Figure 4.7 Examination of the child in frog-leg position. *Note.* From "Prepubertal Female Genitalia: Examination for Evidence of Sexual Abuse" by M. Herman-Giddens and T. Frothingham, 1987, *Pediatrics, 80,* pp. 203–208. Copyright 1987 by American Academy of Pediatrics. Reprinted by permission.

Jean Emans et al. (1980) has also described the examination of the prepubertal child in the knee-chest position (Figure 4.9). This position is especially helpful in visualizing the lower portion of the vaginal canal. As well, it may allow assessment of hymenal anatomy in children who cannot relax in the supine position or whose anatomy makes visualization difficult when supine. In the complete evaluation of the child, many authors have advocated examining children in both the supine and knee-chest position.

Again, it is important to be sensitive to the individual child being examined. For children who have been anally abused, this position may be reminiscent of the abusive episode, and, therefore, traumatic to the child. This may be especially true for the male child. Boys may be most comfortable being examined in the lateral decubitus position, grasping the knees to the chest (Durfee, Heger, & Woodling, 1986).

During the course of the examination, visual inspection of the external genitalia and the lower portion of the vaginal canal will be performed. By gently grasping the labia majora and pulling them apart, excellent visualization of the genitalia and the hymenal ring will be obtained. Careful inspection of

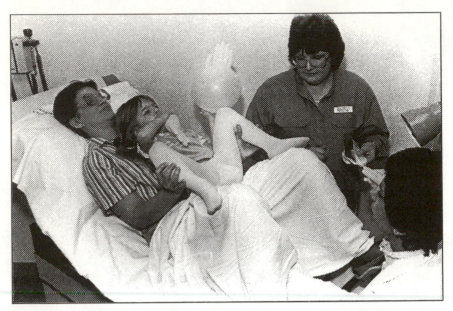

Figure 4.8 Examination of the preschool child. *Note.* From "Approach to Evaluation of Premenarchal Child With a Gynecologic Problem" by G. Gidwani, 1987, *Clinical Obstetrics and Gynecology, 30,* pp. 643–652. Copyright 1987 by J. B. Lippincott. Reprinted by permission.

the perianal area is important in children of both sexes. This portion of the examination is intended to detect abnormal physical findings that may suggest sexual abuse. Specimens may also be obtained during this portion of the examination to screen for the presence of sexually transmitted diseases, as well as to collect forensic evidence, if the assault has been a recent event.

These specimens must be obtained and handled in such a way as to yield accurate results, yet collected in a manner that will be atraumatic for the child. Although cultures may be performed from the lower portion of the vagina in the prepubertal child, even this will be uncomfortable to the child if a standard size, dry, cotton-tip applicator is used. Small, nasopharyngeal or urethral swabs can be moistened with a sterile solution and gently introduced through the hymenal ring of a small child without discomfort. Pokorny and Stromer (1987) also described an atraumatic technique for obtaining vaginal secretions, using a small double lumen catheter, which can inject a small amount of fluid and then aspirate secretions. Several other authors have described a technique using a small, soft plastic medicine dropper to accomplish the same purpose. The technique the health care provider chooses may be a matter of personal preference but should result in accurate specimens obtained simply and atraumatically.

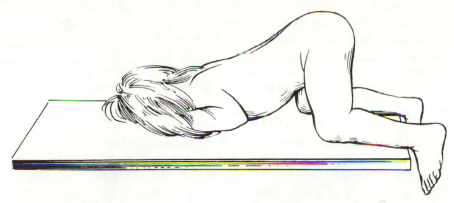

Figure 4.9 Examination of the child in knee-chest position. *Note.* From "Prepubertal Female Genitalia: Examination for Evidence of Sexual Abuse" by M. Herman-Giddens and T. Frothingham, 1987, *Pediatrics, 80,* pp. 203–208. Copyright 1987 by American Academy of Pediatrics. Reprinted by permission.

Just as a speculum exam is not a necessary portion of the pediatric gynecologic examination, the traditional vaginal bimanual exam is not necessary. Attempting to perform a bimanual exam would be very uncomfortable for the child; adequate information can be obtained from a rectal examination, including assessing the rectal tone and ruling out a pelvic mass.

Although it is important to emphasize that adequate information to evaluate the child suspected of being sexually abused can be obtained in the outpatient setting with a minimum of equipment and no discomfort to the child, circumstances may arise that require an examination under anesthesia. Although many might think that general anesthesia would be the simplest approach to examine the child who is frightened or uncooperative, an experienced examiner can generally accomplish an adequate examination without resorting to general anesthesia. In nearly every situation, the risks of general anesthesia would outweigh the benefits of the procedure.

The child who presents with acute trauma, with evidence of acute penetrating injury, should undergo an examination under anesthesia. The small, unestrogenized vagina of a prepubertal child is not distensible, compared to the estrogenized vagina of an adult, and may sustain severe lacerations. Even a small, fresh hymenal laceration, caused by an acute penetrating injury, could indicate a severe vaginal laceration. The posterior cul de sac is quite thin in the child and could be perforated with a penetrating injury. By this mechanism, severe intraperitoneal injuries (including damage to adjacent organs such as bowel, bladder, or major blood vessels) could accompany relatively minor appearing acute hymenal injuries (Huffman, Dewhurst, & Capraro, 1981b; Muram, 1986).

Several instruments are available for vaginoscopy, including a specially designed pediatric vaginoscope. However, it is not necessary to have specialized equipment to perform an adequate exam under anesthesia. A long nasal speculum, generally available in most operating rooms, along with an adequate light source, will provide good visualization into the vagina (Huffman et al., 1981a). A pediatric cystoscope, if available, can also provide excellent visualization.

Collection of Forensic Evidence

During the course of the examination, information is collected that is necessary for the health care of the child and documentation of any injuries that have occurred. Forensic evidence should also be collected during the examination, if the abuse is recent. Some authors have recommended that forensic evidence be collected if the interval of time between the assault and the examination is less than 72 hours, whereas others have recommended that the forensic exam be performed even if 5 to 7 days have elapsed. Each community has a forensic evaluation kit, generally referred to as a "rape kit," which is designed for the adult or the adolescent sexual assault victim. This kit, and its components, may be adapted for use in prepubertal children. Each local law enforcement agency may vary somewhat in the contents of the kit and the procedures for handling specimens. Therefore, each examiner should be very familiar with local procedures. The information collected in the forensic exam may become important evidence in legal proceedings. If not collected according to local standards, the evidence may be not accepted in court and may compromise the child's legal case. However, there are certain features common to nearly all rape kits, which are determined by standard forensic investigation.

The initial portion of the forensic examination involves collection of the clothing of the child, as well as any loose material that may be in the clothing. This is most easily accomplished by having the child undress over a large, clean sheet or piece of white paper, such as the paper used on the examining table. The articles of clothing, along with the paper or sheet, should be placed in a labeled container as possible evidence. The use of a Woods lamp, which emits ultraviolet light, may be helpful at this point. Areas on clothing or on the body of the child that fluoresce could represent seminal fluid; any such areas should be sampled with a moistened, cotton-tipped applicator. Scrapings from under the nails of the child, along with sampling scalp hair (or pubic hair from the older child or adolescent), will be necessary. Material from the assailant may be found under the fingernails of the child. As well, if any loose hairs are found in the clothing or on the body of the child, the hair collected from the child will serve as a standard for comparison. For example, a forensic lab can compare hair taken from the head of the child with hair found in the vulvar area to determine if the hairs are from the same or different sources.

Samples of clothing, dried stains on the surface of the child's skin, as well as smears from the mouth, vagina, and rectum of the child may be analyzed in a number for the presence of seminal fluid. The most commonly used is an analysis for acid phosphatase. Acid phosphatase is present in semen in concentrations 100 times higher than other body fluids. Acid phosphatase may be present in the vagina for up to several hours after ejaculation. On dried specimens, acid phosphatase may be stable for up to 3 years. With this method, even clothing which is many days or weeks old may be examined for the presence of semen (Schiff, 1975). Many males also excrete antigens from the ABO blood type into the seminal fluid. Standards of saliva from the alleged perpetrator, as well as standards from the victim, may be useful in determining the secretor status of the assailant (Woodling, 1977).

Recently, more specific markers for semen have been developed. For example, p30 is a protein found in seminal fluid originating only from the prostatic secretions. This will be present for up to 12 hours in vaginal secretions and for several years on dried specimens. In comparison studies, p30 has been located in specimens when acid phosphatase levels were too low to be diagnostic. This new marker has been extensively studied in the adult population (Polytz, 1984). Other new studies using DNA molecular biology techniques have been able to provide unique "fingerprints" of assailants from proteins found in seminal fluids. In situations where alleged perpetrators are known and seminal fluid has been found on the child, this new technology can identify the assailant, even in the absence of a clear history from the child (Dodd, 1985; Gill, Jeffreys, & Werrett, 1985).

Secretions from the mouth, lower portion of the vagina, and rectum should also be microscopically examined for the presence of spermatozoa. Motile sperm may be found for 12 hours in the vagina (Woodling et al., 1976) and nonmotile sperm for up to 3 to 5 days (Soules et al., 1978). The finding of sperm on microscopic exam is probably the most conclusive finding in the sexually abused child. This is a simple test to perform and should not be overlooked (Durfee et al., 1981). Studies in adult sexual assault victims have also shown a high degree of sexual dysfunction among assailants. Many victims with injuries consistent with penetration will fail to show any conclusive evidence of sperm in the vagina due to the relatively high frequency of retarded ejaculation and azoospermia among perpetrators (Groth et al., 1977).

Screening for sexually transmitted diseases in the abused child serves both a medical and forensic function. Just as the mouth, vagina, and rectum should be sampled for the presence of seminal fluid and sperm, all three sites should also be evaluated for the presence of sexually transmitted diseases. The preverbal child certainly cannot provide an adequate history of the abuse to determine the anatomical sites involved. However, the older child also may be unable to provide the examiner with accurate anatomical information, either from shame, fear, or lack of knowledge. It is, therefore, important that samples in all children be taken from the mouth, rectum, and vagina in the least traumatic method available.

Appropriate handling of all specimens collected is extremely important. A correctly collected positive culture or smear may be inadmissible in a court of law if the "chain of evidence" was not maintained according to local standards. Maintaining chain of evidence generally involves placing items of evidence in sealed and signed envelopes, which are then hand delivered to the appropriate authorities, for example, the police officers investigating the case. Appropriate diagnostic tools should be used in diagnosing sexually transmitted diseases in the pediatric age group. Sexually transmitted diseases are infrequent enough in this population that routine prophylactic treatment is generally not recommended, as in adults. The low prevalence of sexually transmitted disease in the population of sexually abused children makes the use of indirect, screening tests less reliable than in an adult population with a higher prevalence (Alexander, 1988). This is again a situation where the examiner is strongly encouraged to follow guidelines established by local authorities who designed the rape kit for the area. Furthermore, the examiner needs to be familiar with the limitations of the diagnostic tools at his/her availability.

Documentation in the medical record is becoming increasingly important in all areas of medicine, but good records are extremely important in the evaluation of the sexually abused child. The history provided by the child or accompanying adults should be carefully recorded, in the child's own words if possible. The examiner may think he or she will never forget what that child said, but there may often be many months between the examination and the subsequent legal proceedings. Careful descriptions of the physical findings on the general and genital exam are important. Drawings or photographs of the findings may be helpful at a later date. Written descriptions in the child's medical record should avoid the use of vague terminology such as "hymen intact" or "hymen not intact." Careful descriptions of the anatomy of the hymen, along with measurements of the hymenal ring and location of lacerations, will be much more useful. In teaching institutions, evaluation of the child and completion of the medical record should be performed by a licensed physician who will be capable of testifying in court at a later date. Finally, the examiner should be cautious in interpreting physical findings as supportive or not supportive of the child's history of sexual abuse. Remember that many children who have been sexually abused will have entirely normal exams; a well-meaning health care provider should not discount the child's disclosure in the absence of any supporting physical findings.

Sexually Transmitted Diseases

The sexually abused child may first come to the attention of the health care provider by presenting with a sexually transmitted disease. Table 4.3 indicates those diseases which may represent a sexually transmitted disease in children.

Table 4.3 Possible Sexually Transmitted Diseases in Children

Gonorrhea	Bacterial vaginosis
Chlamydia	Herpes simplex, Types I and II
Trichomoniasis	Molluscum contagiosum
Genital condyloma	Acquired immunodeficiency syndrome
Syphilis	

Although some of the infections listed in Table 4.3 may be perinatally acquired or possibly acquired through fomite transmission, the health care provider should remember that the Centers for Disease Control (1985) recommends that a sexually transmitted disease in a child be considered a sign of sexual abuse until proven otherwise.

The reported prevalence of sexually transmitted disease in abused children varies from study to study, dependent in part on the thoroughness of the screening and the age of the patients. White, Loda, Ingram, and Pearson (1983) reviewed the experience of the Child Medical Evaluation Program in detection of sexually transmitted diseases among children referred for evaluation of suspected abuse. They discovered one or more sexually transmitted diseases in 13% of the 409 children studied. These included gonorrhea, trichomoniasis, condyloma acuminata, and syphilis. Screening for chlamydia was not done during the years of their study. When specifically reviewing the cases of prepubertal male children, they found a sexually transmitted disease in 18% of the boys evaluated.

Other authors have found varying rates of sexually transmitted diseases among sexually abused children, ranging from 2% to 10% (De Jong, Emmett, & Herrada 1982; Marshall, Puls, & Davidson 1988; Rimsza & Niggemann, 1982; Tilelli, Turek, & Jaffe, 1980). The prevalence of sexually transmitted diseases in childhood victims of sexual abuse is generally felt to be lower than in adult victims of sexual assault. The activities involved in the sexual abuse of a child may be less likely to transmit a sexually transmitted disease. In addition, there are biologic factors which will effect the infection rate in a child exposed to a sexually transmitted disease.

Although the incidence may vary from study to study, the possibility of a sexually transmitted disease in the sexually abused child should be strongly considered and thoroughly investigated. Detection and treatment of the sexually transmitted disease is important for the general health of the child and is also important in documenting the episode of abuse. In many children, the presence of a sexually transmitted disease may be the only abnormal finding to substantiate the history of abuse. Since the prevalence of sexually transmitted diseases in children is so low, prophylactic treatment of the asymptomatic child is not recommended. In this situation, careful screening to determine those children in need of treatment becomes very important.

In evaluating the child for the possibility of a sexually transmitted disease, it is important to remember that children have anatomical and physiological differences, when compared to adults, which may affect the presentation of the disease. In prepubertal girls the epithelium of the vagina is unestrogenized, and, therefore, very thin. The alkaline pH of the vagina during childhood may also have an effect on susceptibility to infection. In the child, the exposed portio of the cervix does not contain exposed endocervical glands, as is common in the adolescent and young adult female. For this reason, the child exposed to gonorrhea or chlamydia will develop a vaginitis, rather than an endocervicitis. Female prepubertal girls are also not at risk for the development of upper genital tract disease, such as salpingitis. Therefore, cultures for sexually transmitted diseases in girls may be taken from the lower one third of the vagina, instead of from the cervix. These cultures can be done in the outpatient setting, without the use of a vaginal speculum.

Both male and female children may have rectal infection with a sexually transmitted diseases, making rectal cultures helpful in evaluation. Concurrent infection of the vagina and rectum may commonly occur in young girls. It is very unusual for a male child to have urethral involvement with gonorrhea or chlamydia, without a symptomatic discharge; for this reason, urethral cultures are unnecessary in the absence of specific symptoms. Children of either sex may also present with pharyngeal infection with gonorrhea or chlamydia, as well as asymptomatic colonization. Culturing all children from all three sites is the most reliable approach; as discussed earlier, it may be misleading to depend on the history of the child to guide which sites are cultured.

When considering each of the possible sexually transmitted diseases in childhood, all available diagnostic studies for each disease need to be considered. Indirect tests to diagnose sexually transmitted diseases have become increasingly available. Often, their cost may be lower than the more exacting culture methods. As well, these indirect tests may be more available to health care providers, especially those who practice outside of major cities. However, the use of these indirect tests may be inappropriate in children for several reasons. First, these tests were generally designed for use in an adult populations, where the primary site of testing was the cervix, not the vagina, pharynx, or rectum. There may be bacteria present at these other sites that will interfere with the correct interpretation of the indirect test. Second, these indirect tests were designed to be used in populations with a high prevalence of the particular infection being studied. In children, because of the low overall prevalence of sexually transmitted diseases, statistics regarding the specificity or sensitivity of the test in an adult population are not applicable to the pediatric population (Alexander, 1988).

Laboratories that handle specimens from children being evaluated for the possibility of sexual abuse should use appropriate confirmatory measures when positive tests are found. To provide results which will be admissible in a court of law, as well as avoiding the possibility of the misdiagnosis of a sexually transmitted disease in a child, the use of confirmatory tests is essential (Alexander, 1988).

Familiarity with the normal flora of the vagina in the prepubertal child is also necessary to accurately interpret culture results. Although the adult has *lactobacillus* as the predominant organism in the vagina, the unestrogenized vagina of the prepubertal child is usually colonized with *Staph epidermitis* and diphtheroids. These are organisms that colonize the skin in all age groups, as well as representing normal vaginal flora in the child. In younger children especially, the gram negative rods and other bowel flora are commonly found in the vagina. Hammerschlag and her colleagues (1978a, 1978b) conducted two detailed studies of normal vaginal flora in prepubertal girls. Her findings are summarized in Table 4.4. As will be discussed later, it is important to note that both Gardenerella vaginalis and mycoplasmas (*M. homines* and *U. urealyticum*) were found as normal flora in the prepubertal girl. A significant number of anaerobic bacteria were also cultured. In general, she found that the average girl was colonized with a mean of 8.7 species of bacteria.

Gonorrhea in Children

Gonorrhea has been one of the more commonly reported STDs in childhood, in part because of its prevalence in the adult population as well as the wide availability and low cost of cultures for *N. gonorrhea*. In adults, the risk of acquiring gonorrhea after an episode of sexual assault has been well studied. Hayman and Lanza (1971) studied 2,190 female victims of sexual assault. Of these women, 3.5% developed culture-positive gonorrhea when prophylactic treatment was not given. Such statistics about children are unknown. However, the sexually abusive acts involving children may be less likely to result in infection with gonorrhea, or other sexually transmitted diseases. White et al.

Table 4.4 Normal Vaginal Flora in Prepubertal Girls

Diphtheroids	78%
Staphylococcus epidermitis	73%
Streptococci	39%
Escherichia coli	34%
Klebsiella	34%
Gardeneralla vaginitis	13.5%

(1983) have reported an 11% prevalence of gonorrheal infections in their population of prepubertal children evaluated for sexual abuse. Rimsza and Niggemann (1981) found the positive rate of gonorrhea to be 7.4% in a large series of children cultured from multiple sites. In De Jong's evaluation (1982) of 532 sexually abused children under 14 years of age, gonorrhea was present in 4.7% of the children studied, with 44% of the infected children asymptomatic. Of interest, 32% of the positive cultures were obtained from anatomical sites not involved in the abuse as described by the child. This again points out the importance of culturing vagina, rectum, and oropharynx. The possibility of gonorrhea (as well as other sexually transmitted diseases), in the child who presents with vaginitis should also be considered. Paradise, Campos, Friedman, and Fishmuth (1982) reported on 52 prepubertal girls who presented with symptoms of vaginitis, but no specific history of sexual abuse. In this population, a 7.6% incidence of gonorrhea was incidentally discovered, with later investigations confirming the presence of sexual abuse.

The child with gonorrhea may present with symptoms of vaginitis or urethritis (vulvar pain, vaginal discharge, dysuria, or vaginal bleeding). Children may also present with symptoms of proctitis (diarrhea, tenesmus, or bloody stools) or pharyngitis. Vaginal cultures are most often positive in female children, while anal cultures are most often positive in male children. Vaginal gram stains looking for intracellular diplococci may be helpful in guiding therapy in the symptomatic child with vaginitis but should not be used for diagnostic purposes. Children of either sex may have positive cultures from the anus or oropharynx.

Cultures from any site may be positive in the absence of symptoms. The Prepubertal Gonorrhea Cooperative Study Group (Nelson, Mohs, Dajani, & Plotkin, 1976) studied 100 prepubertal children who presented with either vaginal or urethral discharge that cultured positive for gonorrhea. While none of these children had symptoms of rectal or pharyngeal involvement, rectal cultures were positive in over half of female children and 25% of male children. Pharyngeal cultures were positive in 15% of the children. Silber and Controni (1983) reported on 16 adolescent and pediatric patients with confirmed positive pharyngeal cultures for *N. gonorrhea*. Only 25% of these patients had clinical symptoms.

When a positive culture for gonorrhea in the prepubertal child is obtained, the possibility of sexual abuse should strongly be considered. As suggested, a positive culture in a child "raises the strong possibility of sexual abuse unless proven otherwise" (CDC, 1985). However, gonorrhea may be transmitted to a young child by a nonsexual means. Ingram, White, Durfee, and Pearson (1982) confirmed sexual transmission in all children over 4 years of age with gonorrheal infections in their study of children ages 1 to 12 years. In the age group less than 4 years, confirmation of sexual abuse was more difficult. However, sexual abuse was confirmed in at least 35% of these younger children. It is in this younger age group that the question of nonsexual transmission of gonorrhea is most important. Perinatal transmission of gonorrhea from an infected mother to her infant at the time of birth has been reported. But, persistence of such infection beyond the first 12 months of life is felt to be very unlikely. In Wald, Woodward, and Marston's study (1980) of prepubertal children with gonorrhea, positive cultures found in the 2-to-5-year age group were almost always a result of sexual abuse.

Transmission from child to child during play has also been reported (Potterat, Markewich, & King, 1986). Although this may explain nonsexual transmission of gonorrhea in some children studied, this is a much less common source of infection than sexual abuse. In addition, the contacts of the child who was innocently infected should be evaluated carefully for the possibility of sexual abuse. Nair et al. (1986) reported on the incidence of gonorrhea in household contacts on children younger than 12 years. Among 31 asymptomatic household contacts of the 10 cases evaluated, 29% also had positive cultures, with the most common site of positive culture the pharynx. In these situations, nonvenereal spread of the gonorrhea may be involved, as well as previously undiagnosed sexual abuse of more than one child in the home.

Sexual abuse in children is a common problem, and each reported positive culture deserves careful evaluation. However, false positive culture results have been reported. These false positive culture results could subject a child and the family to an unnecessary investigation and possible separation of the child from the family. Whittington, Rice, Biddle, and Knapp (1988) reported on a series of incorrectly identified pharyngeal cultures for *Neisseria gonorrhea* in infants and children. In their series, cultures plated on selective media still incorrectly identified *N. lactamica*, *N. catarrhalis*, and other species as *N. gonorrhea*. These other strains of *Neisseria* are commonly found as normal flora in children (Gold, Goldschneider, & Lepow, 1978; Wald, 1983). As these investigators have demonstrated, it is important that an additional confirmatory test(s) be used when *N. gonorrhea* is suspected.

Gram stains, as well as rapid tests with monoclonal antibody reagents or direct fluorescent antibody tests, have been used in adults for rapid diagnosis of infection. Again, the usefulness of these tests in children is doubtful and could easily lead to a false positive result. Diagnosis of *N. gonorrhoea* in children should be made only by a positive culture result, confirmed by several different procedures. As suggested by Whittington et al. (1988), isolates may be frozen at −70°C for confirmatory tests by a reference lab in areas where these tests are not easily available.

Information regarding the treatment of *N. gonorrhea* infection in infants and children is well covered in standard pediatric textbooks. Antibiotics (amoxicillin and probenecid) given orally are equally efficacious as intramuscular injections, as shown by the Prepubertal Gonorrhea Cooperative Study. Oral antibiotics are certainly much less traumatic for the child than an injection! The prophylactic treatment for gonorrhea after reported sexual abuse is not recommended by most authors. Kramer and Jason (1982) estimated that 96% of such children would be treated unnecessarily. The rate of positive cultures in children is low, and children are not at risk of transmitting incubating bacteria to a sexual partner as an adult would be. Children are also at no known risk of upper tract genital disease, such as pelvic inflammatory disease.

Chlamydia in Children

Chlamydia trachomatis is becoming recognized as one of the most common sexually transmitted diseases in adults and adolescents. In adults, infection with chlamydia is more common than gonorrhea, with roughly 3 million cases annually in the United States. These organisms are primarily intracellular and are not infectious outside of the host cells. For that reason, fomites transmission is extremely unlikely. In adult women, the prevalence of *C. trachomatis* infection is reported to be three to four percent of sexually active women. It may be found in up to 20% of sexually active adolescents or 30% to 50% of men with nongonococcal urethritis. The perinatal transmission of *C. trachomatis* infection has been well documented in 60% to 70% of infants born to infected mothers, placing the infant at risk for eye infection or pneumonia (Sweet & Gibbs, 1985).

Genital chlamydia infections in children have not been as thoroughly studied as infections with gonorrhea. Diagnostic tests are more expensive, less available, and the importance of this organism as a sexually transmitted disease has been only recently recognized in the pediatric age group. Rettig and Nelson (1981) first noted the concomitant infection with both *N. gonorrhea* and *C. trachomatis* in sexually abused children. Twenty seven percent of the children with positive cultures for gonorrhea also has positive cultures for chlamydia. More definite support for chlamydia as a sexually transmitted disease in the prepubertal age group was provided by a case control study by Ingram, White, and Occhiuti (1986). In 124 female children who had been sexually abused and 90 control children, they found a statistically significant difference in the incidence of vaginal chlamydia infection. Rectal and pharyngeal infections were present only in the sexually abused group of children, but these numbers were too small to be statistically significant. The authors recommended that all children suspected of being sexually abused be cultured for *C. trachomatis* and that positive cultures be considered a marker for sexual abuse.

The prevalence of *C. trachomatis* infections in sexually abused children is difficult to determine, but it appears that the number is low. Ingram found an 8% prevalence in his case control study. Hammerschlag et al. (1984) reported a 4% prevalence in her population of sexually abused children. Fuster and Neinstein (1987) reported a 17% prevalence of chlamydia in sexually abused girls who were screened for vaginal, pharyngeal, and rectal infection. These recent studies have led Rettig to conclude in an editorial in *Pediatric Infectious Disease Journal* (1984) that *C. trachomatis* infections may not be statistically significant but are of great clinical significance as a sexually transmitted disease in children.

In a group of girls evaluated for complaints of vaginal bleeding or vaginal discharge, but *not* selected for a history of sexual abuse, Bump (1985) found a 44% incidence of vaginal infection with chlamydia.

The child with a genital *C. trachomatis* infection may present much like the child described with a gonorrheal infection. Vaginitis, with complaints of vaginal pain, discharge, or vaginal bleeding, has been reported. Children may also present with symptoms of urethritis or proctitis, although the majority of infections in the rectum and pharynx will be asymptomatic. Culturing for *C. trachomatis* is clearly important in the child with vaginitis symptoms, as well as the asymptomatic child who may have been a victim of sexual abuse. *C. trachomatis* is capable of infecting the atrophic squamous epithelium of the prepubertal vagina, like *N. gonorrhea*. For this reason, vaginal culturing, rather than cervical culturing, is performed.

Once a genital infection with *C. trachomatis* has been identified in a child, determination of the source of the infection is extremely important. Although this organism is not spread by fomite transmission, the possibility of sexual abuse and perinatal transmission must be considered. In Ingram's series (1986) of patients, he found 60% of the girls with positive chlamydia cultures had no other physical evidence of sexual abuse. Included in this group were two cases where *C. trachomatis* was cultured from the urethra of the alleged perpetrator. This is certainly supportive of the concept that this infection may be acquired in the child without vaginal penetration, through genital contact with infected secretions on the hands or the genitalia of the perpetrator. Of these children, only 40% were symptomatic for genital complaints. All of the children with positive rectal and pharyngeal cultures were asymptomatic at the site of the positive culture, although some did have a vaginal discharge.

When a positive *C. trachomatis* culture is obtained in a child, the other possible source of infection to be considered is perinatal acquisition. It is well known that neonates can acquire infection with chlamydia (pharynx, eyes, rectum, or vagina) during birth through an infected maternal genital tract. Bell, Stamm, Kuo, Wang, Holmes, and Grayston (1987) followed a group of infants born to mothers with known cervical chlamydia infection. They performed serial cultures from multiple sites with treatment initiated once a positive culture was obtained from any site. They found that vaginal and rectal colonization generally presented during the third and fourth months of life. In their series, all of the positive vaginal cultures were accompanied by positive rectal cultures. Because the pharynx was the most common site of the initial positive culture in the first or second month of life, they suggested that delayed infection was due to either loss of passively acquired maternal antibodies or autoinoculation of the genital tract (Schachter, Grossman & Holt, 1979). The duration of these asymptomatic infections and the latent period from exposure to positive culture or symptoms suggests that children may present with perinatally transmitted genital chlamydia infections up to 16 to 24 months of age. The upper limit of time of this latent period between exposure at birth and positive culture is not known. Although the possibility of perinatal acquisition of infection should be considered in the younger child, especially those under 2 years of age, the possibility of sexual abuse should also be strongly considered. In these situations, careful interviewing and physical examination of the child, screening for other sexually transmitted diseases, and investigation of the social setting must be used to avoid an incorrect conclusion about the source of the infection.

Just as with *N. gonorrhea* infections, the health care professional must choose appropriate testing in children suspected of having infection with *C. trachomatis*. Culturing for *C. trachomatis* with a cell culture of McCoy cells is the gold standard. Because of misleading results with indirect methods, cell culture technique is currently recommended for the screening of children for chlamydia. These cultures are more costly and less widely available than the indirect methods, but should be used in the pediatric age group. The indirect tests, such as enzyme immunoassay (Chlamydiazyme) and direct fluorescent antibody tests (Microtrak and others) were designed for use in high prevalence adult populations with cervical or urethral infections. The sensitivity and specificity of both tests will be significantly lowered when used in a population with a low prevalence of chlamydia infection, such as sexually abused children. The Chlamydiazyme kit may cross react with fecal flora, which is often found in the vagina of a prepubertal girl, and is not recommended for use in sites other than cervix and urethra (Chlamydiazyme Diagnostic Kit, package insert, 1986). The Microtrak Direct Specimen Test is also not recommended in screening for asymptomatic rectal infections (Microtrak Direct Specimen Test, package insert). Fuster and Neinstein (1987) compared cell culture techniques and direct immunofluorescence assay (MicroTrak) in their study of 50 sexually abused prepubertal girls. Although they found 8 positive cultures for *C. trachomatis*, only 4 of the direct immunofluorescence assays were positive. These theoretical concerns were further supported by Hammerschlag, Rettig, and Shields report (1988) of false positive cases of both indirect antigen tests in children with negative cultures. Because either a false negative or a false positive test for a sexually transmitted disease in a child will have great social and legal implications, the most accurate means of testing (i.e., cell culture) should be used.

Treatment of the sexually abused children for chlamydia is reserved for those with positive cultures. The prophylactic treatment in abused children is not indicated in a disease with a low prevalence, an accurate diagnostic test, and no risk of upper genital tract disease. A number of antibiotics have demonstrated activity against chlamydia. These include tetracycline, erythromycin, and sulfonamides. Tetracycline should be avoided in the child less than 8 years of age because of the possibility of staining of the enamel of the teeth.

Condyloma (Genital Warts)

Just as sexual abuse may be first discovered because of a positive culture for gonorrhea or chlamydia, the sexually abused child may present with another sexually transmitted disease, genital condyloma, caused by the human papilloma-virus (HPV). Although this is a relatively uncommon finding during childhood, with the dramatic increase in the prevalence of this infection in the adult popula-tion (CDC, 1983) and the high recurrence rate in those infected (Stumph, 1980), the number of children with condyloma can be expected to rise.

The HPV in a double stranded DNA virus with 46 different types identified to date. Types 6, 11, 16, 18, and 31 have been associated with genital disease in adults. Although relatively few children have had DNA typing performed, HPV types 6, 11, and 16 have been recovered from genital condyloma pre-senting during childhood (Rock, Naghashfar, Barnett, Buscema, Woodruff, & Shah, 1986).

Children with genital condyloma may present because of an asymptomatic lesion noted by the parent or with complaints of bleeding, dysuria, or pruritus. The epithelium overlying the condyloma is more easily traumatized than normal skin, causing these complaints (Shelton, Jerkins, & Noe, 1986). The condyloma usually have the same typical verrucous, "warty" appearance as in adults, although the appearance in young children may be altered somewhat by the constantly moist environment of diapers. Children seem especially prone to perianal and periurethral lesions, adding additional considerations in choosing the best form of therapy.

Therapy of genital condyloma in children is guided by the goals of a safe, effective, and atraumatic treatment. The traditional therapies for condyloma are often painful and require multiple applications, making many therapies used in adults poorly suited for the pediatric population. In adults, topical caustic agents (bichloracetic acid or trichloroacetic acid) or a potent antimitotic agent such as podophyllin are often first line of therapy in patients with a small volume of disease. However, topical caustic agents are painful on application, limiting their usefulness in children, especially if several courses of therapy will be necessary. However, it may be helpful in the child with the single, small wart requiring therapy. Podophyllin has the advantage of being essentially painless, however, it must be washed off by the parent within 1 to 4 hours. Therefore, the physician must be able to count on the cooperation of the child's caretaker. Cases of severe, even fatal, toxic reactions to podophyllin have been reported. These cases have occurred where podophyllin was used over a large surface area with an occlusive dressing in pregnant patients (Slater, Rumack, & Peter-son, 1978). Physicians most accustomed to treating adults must remember that a large area covered with condyloma in a small child represents a much larger proportion of total body surface area than in an adult. Therefore, podophyllin must be used cautiously in children, especially in condyloma that are large or abraded, if parental cooperation is undependable, or if the child in still in diapers.

In a child with extensive condyloma, rapidly spreading lesions, or those which fail to respond to outpatient therapy, more aggressive treatment may be required. Usually, general anesthesia will be required for destruction of the condyloma by either electrocautery or laser. The use of the CO_2 laser has the advantage of precise control over the depth of destruction, less scarring than with electrocautery, and relatively rapid healing. (These advantages are especially important in treating periurethral and perianal condyloma.) Nevertheless, it is important for all involved to remember that there is a relatively high recurrence rate, resulting from latent virus that may remain dormant in normal appearing cells.

Clinical trials are underway to test the efficacy of interferon in the therapy of juvenile laryngeal papillomatosis. This agent is currently approved for the therapy of genital warts in adults and may eventually be useful in pediatric genital condyloma. Though interferon is not approved for this use in children, one report of two successful cases during childhood suggests that further investigation is warranted (Trofatter, English, Hughes, & Gall, 1986).

The possibility of recurrence is not only frustrating but may also be of serious consequences to the child. In adults, the HPV types 16, 18, and 31 have been associated with the development of dysplasia of the cervix and vulva. The probability of dysplastic changes developing in a child with genital condyloma is essentially unknown. However, two cases of vulvar carcinoma-in-situ in young adolescents with a history of childhood genital condyloma have been reported (Boutselia, 1972; Lister & Akinla, 1972). As well, Rock et al. (1986) have reported 1 child with a "high risk" viral type (HPV 16) out of 5 children studied with DNA typing. Presumably this child is at higher risk of developing dysplasia.

An equally difficult issue facing the physician in the evaluation of the child with genital condyloma is determining the probable source of the infection. Children have acquired genital condyloma from sexual abuse, as well as from exposure to maternal genital HPV at the time of birth. Laryngeal papillomatosis has been well documented as a perinatally acquired infection and is due generally to HPV 6 and 11. The incubation period may vary from a few months to several years, with at least 50% of the cases presenting by 3 years of age (Steinburg, Topp, Schneider, & Abramson 1983). Presumably, genital condyloma could be transmitted to a child in the same fashion, with an equally unpredictable incubation period. Typing the virus from mother and child has not been reported in the literature but could be theoretically useful. This analysis, however, may be complicated by the tendency of a single wart to contain more than one type of virus or to grow different types of virus at different times (Krzyzek, Watts, Anderson, Faras, & Pass, 1980).

The American Academy of Dermatology Task Force on Pediatric Dermatology in their statement "Genital Warts and Sexual Abuse in Children" (1984) acknowledged that at least 50% of the childhood genital condyloma may be attributed to sexual abuse. They also concluded that after careful evaluation the true incidence probably would be higher. Certainly, these children should be thoroughly evaluated for other physical findings suggestive of sexual abuse or the presence of other sexually transmitted diseases. Especially in the child beyond infancy, the possibility of sexual abuse should be strongly considered and diligently evaluated.

Other Sexually Transmitted Diseases in Children

Gonorrhea, chlamydia, and genital condyloma are the sexually transmitted diseases most commonly encountered during the evaluation of the sexually abused child. However, these are less frequent sexually transmitted diseases that have been reported and should be considered in the screening process. CDC recommendations (1985) also include screening for trichomonas, syphilis, bacterial vaginosis, and, if inflammation is present, herpes simplex.

Vaginal trichomoniasis is thought to be uncommon in the prepubertal child because the trichomonad prefers the acidic pH of an estrogenized vagina. Nevertheless, this infection has been reported in prepubertal girls. The newborn female will be frequently colonized with maternally transmitted trichomonads, with many of these infants being asymptomatic. In older girls, trichomoniasis has been reported as a cause of vaginitis and may be seen in asymptomatic girls. This infection is easily diagnosed by the presence of the motile trichomonad on a saline "wet prep" of vaginal secretions examined microscopically (Altchek, 1984). This infection may be transmitted by sexual activity, whether voluntary or involuntary, and also is thought to be transmitted via fomites. Case control studies of the presence of trichomoniasis in sexually abused girls have not been done. However, White et al. (1983) reported a 15% incidence of trichomoniasis in sexually abused girls who were screened with a wet prep. Although perinatally acquired and fomites transmitted infection is possible, sexual contact is felt to be the primary means of spread of this infection. Again, the detection of this infection in a prepubertal girl beyond the neonatal period should raise the strong possibility of sexual abuse.

Bacterial vaginosis has been reported as a sexually transmitted disease in adult women and sexually abused girls. Previously this infection has been called nonspecific vaginitis or gardenerella vaginitis. Although this is a very common cause of vaginitis in adult women (Hill, Ruparella, & Embil 1983), its existence in the pediatric age group was only recently recognized. Muram and Buxton (1984) initially reported 3 antidotal cases of bacterial vaginosis in sexually abused girls. This was further studied in several prospective studies. Hammerschlag, Cummings, Doraiswamy, Cox, and McCormack (1985) performed a prospective case control study of bacterial vaginosis in a population of girls being evaluated for sexual abuse. In their study, they found a statistically significant difference in the frequency of the diagnosis of bacterial vaginosis in girls who had been sexually abused when compared to controls. They also found that the diagnosis was often not made on the initial evaluation when a short period of time had elapsed between the abuse and the examination. Infections were often noted on follow-up visits when initial evaluations had been negative.

A number of different methods have been used to diagnose bacterial vaginosis in women and girls. From earlier studies by Hammerschlag (1978a), it is known that *Gardenerella vaginalis* may be present in the vagina of healthy, randomly selected prepubertal girls. The diagnosis of bacterial vaginosis is best made by microscopic examination of a saline wash or wet prep from the vagina. Characteristic "clue cells" (epithelial cells with a stippled appearance due to adherent bacteria) will be identified. In addition, application of KOH to the slide will produce a fishy odor. This odor may be noted clinically and can be the presenting complaint in girls and women with this form of vaginitis (Sweet & Gibbs, 1985). The presence of *Gardenerella vaginitis* on a culture from a child is alone not sufficient to diagnose bacterial vaginosis. This conclusion was confirmed by Bartley, Morgan, and Rimsza (1987) in their study of colonization with *Gardenerella vaginitis* in sexually abused girls, girls with vulvar complaints, and normal girls used as controls. They found no statistically significant difference in colonization with *G. vaginalis* among these 3 groups, again suggesting that mere colonization with this organism is not sufficient to diagnose bacterial vaginosis.

Although an infrequent sexually transmitted disease during childhood, *genital herpes* has been reported during the prepubertal years. This infection is caused by herpes simplex virus types 1 and 2 (HSV 1 and HSV 2). Although, in general, HSV 1 is responsible for oral herpetic lesions and HSV 2 causes genital lesions, either type of virus can cause genital herpes (Sweet & Gibbs, 1985). HSV 1 has been reported as a documented cause of sexually transmitted genital herpes in a prepubertal child (Hare & Mowla, 1977).

The child with genital herpes, especially a primary infection, will generally present with ulcerative lesions of the perineum or perianal area. These lesions are vesicular at first, appearing ulcerative after the vesicles are unroofed. The child may also have signs of systemic illness, such as fever or lymphadenopathy. Acute urinary retention may result from severe pain with attempts at urination. The differential diagnosis should also include severe diaper dermatitis, varicella, erythema multiform, and other sexually transmitted disease such as chancroid, granuloma inguinale, or syphilis. A viral culture should be obtained in the child with vesicular or ulcerative lesions on the perineum. Physical exam alone is generally not sufficient to diagnose or rule out genital herpes.

As recommended by the CDC, the presence of a sexually transmitted disease in a child should be considered as sign of sexual abuse until proven otherwise. Cases have been reported of autoinoculation of virus from oral lesions to the genital area (Nahamias, Dowdle, & Naib, 1986). However, in Kaplan's series (1984) of 6 prepubertal children, sexual abuse and venereal transmission of the virus was documented in 4 patients. Five of the 6 children had HSV 1 infection. Clearly, the finding of genital herpes in the prepubertal child should be considered a possible marker for sexual abuse and a thorough investigation of the social setting undertaken.

Although one of the more unusual sexually transmitted diseases during childhood, *syphilis* has been reported in this age group. The prevalence of syphilis in pediatric victims of sexual abuse is clearly low, although exact figures are not known. De Jong (1986) found 1 case of syphilis in his series of 532 sexually abused children. White, Loda, Ingram, and Pearson (1983) found only 6 cases of syphilis in 409 cases of suspected sexual abuse, although only one of these children was symptomatic.

The clinical diagnosis of syphilis in children may be difficult. There is generally a long incubation period between exposure to the organism and the development of the first symptom. The initial lesion is the syphilitic chancre, which presents as a painless, ulcerated lesion, generally on the genital or perianal area. Because this lesion is painless, the infection may not be recognized until the secondary stage. This presents with multisystem involvement; the patient may have a rash, generalized adenopathy, and lesions of the mucus membranes. This, too, may go undiagnosed. If so, the patient enters the latent stage. During this time, the patient will appear well but will have serological evidence of disease. A small number of patients will progress to the severe stage of tertiary syphilis, which may affect the skin, cardiac system, or central nervous system (Sweet & Gibbs, 1985).

Ginsburg (1983) reported on 3 children with acquired syphilis, 1 presenting during the primary stage, while the other 2 presented during the secondary stage. Diagnosis in children may be difficult. However, syphilis should be considered in the differential diagnosis of the child who presents with a genital ulcer, as well as the child with a generalized rash and adenopathy. Syphilis may be diagnosed by a darkfield microscopic examination of suspected chancres (available through local public health departments) or through serological testing. As syphilis serology is done on all neonates at birth, this information is available to help rule out the possibility of perinatal acquisition. Although syphilis is an infrequent sexually transmitted disease during childhood, children suspected of being sexually abused should be screened for syphilis. Furthermore, any child who presents with a sexually transmitted disease should be screened for all other possible sexually transmitted diseases, including syphilis.

Conclusion

The sexually abused child may present to the health care professional with behavior changes, abnormal physical findings, or a sexually transmitted disease. Regardless of the presentation, the health care professional has clear obligations and responsibilities. Legislation has been passed on the federal level making the reporting of suspected child abuse mandatory for all health care professionals. Failure to report a suspected case of child abuse is a violation of the law. This legislation requires reporting of all *suspected* cases, not only the proven cases. Often the health care professional is in the role of information gatherer. Actual proof of sexual abuse in childhood often involves the assistance of experts in other fields, such as forensic science, law enforcement, social service, and psychology/child development.

The information gathered during the course of the medical exam may later become a portion of the legal evidence in court. The health care professional may often be called on to testify during the legal proceedings. For these reasons, careful documentation is essential. The use of vague terminology, such as "hymen intact" or "hymen not intact" is best avoided. Instead, actual factual descriptions of anatomical findings, accompanied by drawings or photographs, will be more informative. The history provided by the child should be carefully recorded in the child's own words if possible. A number of months, or even longer, may elapse between the examination and the legal proceedings. Clear, accurate, and detailed records will prove invaluable as the events fade in the mind of the examiner.

Future Direction

A large number of unanswered questions remain in the medical aspects of child sexual abuse. A clearer definition of normal anatomy, and how this anatomy changes over the course of childhood, would help greatly with interpretation of abnormal findings in children. This would require careful longitudinal examinations and recordkeeping on normal children during routine pediatric care. Further studies of children with abnormal examinations, especially exploring further the value of colposcopy in the evaluation of the sexually abused child, would help to more accurately interpret the significance of these abnormal findings.

A number of unanswered questions also remain regarding sexually transmitted diseases during childhood. The possibility of perinatal transmission and long latent period between exposure and clinical disease, especially with *Chlamydia trachomatis* and *Human papillomavirus* infections, make studies regarding the natural history of these diseases during childhood important. Such studies would be of great help in determining the source of infections in young children.

Although education of the public regarding sexual abuse in children is crucial, education of physicians in training and practicing physicians is also essential. Most children will not have access to special centers dedicated to the evaluation of sexually abused children. Instead, they will be evaluated by local physicians and other health care professionals. The question of physicians' recognition of childhood sexual abuse was addressed in a recent edition of the *American Journal of Disease on Childhood*. Ladson, Johnson, and Doty (1987) conducted a survey of practicing pediatricians, family practitioners, and pediatric house staff in training. They found that the majority of the respondents believed that sexual abuse was primarily a problem of lower socioeconomic groups. They were frequently not familiar with the behavioral indicators of sexual abuse and 41 percent could not identify correctly the hymen on a photograph of a prepubertal girl. Fifty four percent of the respondents were not aware of clearly abnormal physical findings as suggestive of sexual abuse. This study raises serious questions about the quality of training of new health care professionals and the continuing education of those in practice. It also points out inadequacies in the quality of care these children receive and the ability of health care professionals to accurately diagnose and effectively deal with the sexually abused child. In an editorial in the same issue of the *American Journal of Disease of Childhood*, Britton (1987) concluded that the medical community has the responsibility of recognizing sexual abuse, as well as supporting research efforts aimed at prevention, as well as intervention.

Educating health care providers who deal with children and adolescents about sexual abuse during childhood is extremely important. However, such educational programs may miss some care providers who will be faced with the consequences of childhood sexual abuse. The impact of childhood sexual abuse may have consequences which last far beyond the childhood years. It is certainly well known that much sexual abuse goes undiagnosed and unreported during childhood. The physician who deals primarily with adult patients may be faced with an adult who has health problems related to an episode of childhood sexual abuse. Bachman (1988) surveyed her adult gynecologic practice and found that 1 in 6 reported childhood episodes of sexual abuse. Most adult gynecologists are not aware that many of the problems they face on a daily basis may be related to childhood sexual abuse. For example, Walker (1988) discovered significantly more chronic pelvic pain and sexual dysfunction in women with a history of childhood sexual abuse, compared with women in the control populations. The adolescent who has been a victim of sexual abuse is more likely to become pregnant during adolescence (Musick, 1987) or to become a runaway. Hartman, Burgess, and McCormick (1987) reported, in a study of 144 adolescent runaways, sexual victimization in 73% of the girls and 38% of the boys. Adult survivors of childhood sexual abuse are also at risk of psychopathology including suicidal behavior. A self-reported incidence of childhood sexual abuse as high as 40% has been discovered among young adult women who have attempted suicide (van Egmond, 1988).

The challenges presented to the health care professional by the sexually abused patient are great. The effects of sexual abuse are long lasting and these patients may vary greatly in their presentation. The evaluation and care of these patients cannot be left to the specialist. All health care professionals need to be familiar with basic information regarding sexual abuse; the sexually abused patient may present at any age and with a wide variety of symptoms. The training of medical learners is vitally important, as is continuing education for those who were not exposed to this information during their initial training. Research is just beginning to answer important questions about normal and abnormal anatomy, sexually transmitted diseases during childhood, and efficacy of intervention programs. We have a long way to go.

Glossary

Cystitis — Inflammation or infection of the bladder, causing frequency and pain with urination.

Dermatitis — Inflammation or infection of the skin.

Dysplasia — Premalignant condition with disordered maturation of the cell layers of epithelium.

Dysuria — Burning or pain with urination.

Erythema — Redness of the skin, usually resulting from injury, infection or irritation.

Fomites — Inanimate objects thought to be vectors in spreading infectious diseases.

Hymen/Hymenal ring — Tissue present at the vaginal opening (Figure 4.10).

Juvenile laryngeal papillomatosis — Warty growths, resulting from *human papillomavirus*, on the vocal cords. This is usually found in children delivered to mothers with active infection.

Labia — Folds of tissue surrounding the vaginal opening (Figure 4.10).

Lymphadenopathy — Swelling of lymph nodes.

Neonate — Newborn child.

Perianal — Area of skin surround the anus (Figure 4.10).

Perineum — General term describing the external genitalia.

Posterior fourchette — Area immediately below the vaginal opening (Figure 4.10).

Posterior culde sac — Pouch of tissue at the end of the vagina, behind the cervix.

Genitalia of the Prepubertal Female

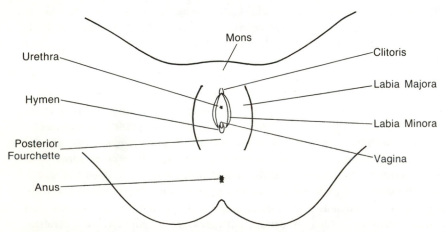

Figure 4.10 Genitalia of the prepubertal female. (Artist: Jo Taylor.)

Proctitis – Inflammation of the rectum.

Pruritus – Itching.

Salpingitis – Infection of the fallopian tubes, also known as pelvic inflammatory disease.

Squamous epithelium – A type of tissue composed of many cell layers, which composes skin and the lining of the vagina.

Tenesmus – Sensation of discomfort and urgency to defecate, usually accompanying inflammation of the rectum.

Urethritis – Inflammation of the urethra.

Vaginal mucosa – Tissue that lines the vagina, composed of squamous epithelium (Figure 4.10).

Vulvitis – Inflammation of vulvar tissue.

References

Adams, J., Ahmad, M., & Phillips, P. (1988). Anogenital findings and hymenal diameter in children referred for sexual abuse examinations. *Adolescent and Pediatric Gynecology, 1*, 123–127.

Alexander, E. (1988). Misidentification of sexually transmitted organisms in children: Medicolegal implications. *Pediatric Infectious Diseases Journal, 7*, 1–2.

Altchek, A. (1984). Pediatric vulvovaginitis. *Journal of Reproductive Medicine, 29*(6), 359–375.

AMA diagnostic and treatment guidelines concerning child abuse and neglect. (1985). *Journal of the American Medical Association, 254*(6), 796–800.

American Academy of Dermatology Task Force on Pediatric Dermatology. (1984). Genital warts and sexual abuse in children. *Journal of American Academy of Dermatology, 11*, 529–530.

Attias, R., & Goodwin, J. (1985). Knowledge and management strategies in incest cases: A survey of physician, psychologists and family counselors. *Child Abuse and Neglect, 9*, 527–533.

Bachmann, G., Moeller, T., & Bennet, J. (1988). Childhood sexual abuse and the consequences in adult women. *Obstetrics and Gynecology, 71*(4), 631–642.

Bartley, D., Morgan, L., & Rimsza, M. (1987). Gardenerella vaginalis in prepubertal girls. *American Journal of Diseases of Children, 141*, 1014–1017.

Bell, T., Stamm, W., Kuo, C., Wang, S., Holmes, K., & Grayston, J. (1987). Delayed appearance of Chlamydia trachomatous infections acquired at birth. *Pediatric Infectious Disease Journal, 6*, 928–931.

Berkowitz, C., Elvik, S., & Logan, M. (1987). Labial fusion in prepubertal girls: A marker for sexual abuse? *American Journal of Obstetrics and Gynecology, 156*, 16–20.

Boutselia, I., (1972). Intraepithelial neoplasia of the vulva. *American Journal of Obstetrics and Gynecology, 113*, 733–738.

Britton, H. (1987). Do physicians recognize sexual abuse? *American Journal of Diseases of Childhood, 141*, 402–403.

Bump, R. (1985). Chlamydia trachomatous as a cause of prepubertal vaginitis. *Obstetrics and Gynecology, 65*(3), 384–388.

Cantwell, H. (1981). Vaginal inspection as it related to child sexual abuse in girls under thirteen. *Child Abuse and Neglect, 7*, 171–176.

Centers for Disease Control: STD Treatment Guidelines. (1985). *Morbidity and Mortality Weekly Report, 34*, 1–35.

Centers for Disease Control: Condyloma acuminatum- United States- 1966–1981. (1983). *Morbidity and Mortality Weekly Report, 32*, 306–308.

Chlamydiazyme Diagnostic Kit. (1986). Abbott Laboratories, Technical Service Department, Chicago, IL.

De Jong, A., Emmett, G., & Herrada, A. (1982). Sexual abuse of children. *American Journal of Diseases of Children, 136*, 129–134.

De Jong, A. (1986). Sexually transmitted disease in sexually abused children. *Sexually Transmitted Diseases, 13*(3), 123–126.

Depaufilis, D. (1986). Literature Review of Sexual Abuse. Clearinghouse on Child Abuse and Neglect Information. US Department of Health and Human Services. U.S. Government Printing Office, 3–4.

Dodd, B. (1985). DNA fingerprinting in matters of family and crime. *Nature 1985, 318*(6046), 506–507.

Durfee, M., Heger, A., & Woodling, B. (1986). Medical evaluation in sexual abuse of young children. In K. Macfarland & J. Waterman (Eds.), *Sexual abuse of young children*, (pp. 56–61). New York: The Guilford Press.

Elkins, T. (1988). Gynecologic care of the developmentally disabled. Paper presented at the 1988 meeting of North American Society for Adolescent and Pediatric Gynecology, Houston, TX.

Emans, S., & Goldstein, D. (1980). The gynecologic examination of the prepubertal child with vulvovaginitis: Use of the knee-chest position. *Pediatrics, 65*(4), 758–760.

Emans, S., Woods, E., Flagg, N., & Freeman, A. (1987). Genital findings in sexually abused, symptomatic, and asymptomatic girls. *Pediatrics, 79*(5), 778–783.

Fuster, C., & Neinstein, L. (1987). Vaginal Chlamydia trachomatous prevalence in sexually abused prepubertal girls. *Pediatrics, 79*(2), 235–238.

Gidwani, G. (1987). Approach to evaluation of premenarchal child with a gynecological problem. *Clinical Obstetrics and Gynecology, 30*(3), 643–652.

Gill, P., Jefferys, A., & Werrett, D. (1985). Forensic application of DNA fingerpainting. *Nature 1985, 318*(6046), 506–507.

Ginsburg, C. (1983). Acquired syphilis in prepubertal children. *Pediatric Infectious Disease Journal, 12*(3), 232–234.

Gold, R., Goldschneider, I., & Lepow, M. (1978). Carriage of Neisseria meningitidis and Neisseria lactamanica in infants and young children. *Journal of Infectious Diseases, 137*, 112–121.

Groth, A., & Burgess, A. (1977). Sexual dysfunction during rape. *New England Journal of Medicine, 297*(14), 764–766.

Hammerschlag, M., Alpert, S., Rosner, I., Thurston, P., Semine, D., McComb, D., & McCormack, W. (1978a). Microbiology of the vagina in children: Normal and potentially pathogenic organisms. *Pediatrics, 62*(1), 57–62.

Hammerschlag, M., Alpert, S., Onderdonk, A., Thurston, P., Drude, E., McCormack, W., & Bartlett, J. (1978b). Anaerobic microflora of the vagina in children. *American Journal of Obstetrics and Gynecology, 131*(853), 853–856.

Hammerschlag, M., Doraiswamy, B., Alexander, E., Cox, P., Price, W., & Gleyzer, A. (1984). Are rectogenital Chlamydia infections a marker for sexual abuse in children? *Pediatric Infectious Disease Journal, 3*(2), 100–104.

Hammerschlag, M., Cummings, M., Doraiswamy, B., Cox, P., & McCormack, W. (1985). Nonspecific vaginitis following sexual abuse in children. *Pediatrics, 75*(6), 1028–1031.

Hammerschlag, M., Retting, P., & Shields, M. (1988). False positive results with the use of Chlamydia antigen detection tests in the evaluation of suspected sexual abuse in children. *Pediatric Infectious Disease Journal, 7*, 11–14.

Hare, M., & Mowla, A. (1977). Genital herpes virus infection in prepubertal girls. *British Journal of Obstetrics and Gynaecology, 84*, 141–142.

Hartman, C., Burgess, A., & McCormick, A. (1987). Pathways and cycles of runaways: A model for understanding repetitive runaway behavior. *Hospital and Community Psychiatry, 38*(3), 292.

Hayman, C., & Lanza, C. (1971). Sexual assault of women and girls. *American Journal of Obstetrics and Gynecology, 109*, 480–486.

Herman-Giddens, M., & Frothingham, T. (1987). Prepubertal female genitalia: Examinations for evidence of sexual abuse. *Pediatrics, 80*(2), 203–208.

Hill, L., Ruparella, H., & Embil, J. (1983). Nonspecific vaginitis and other genital infections in three clinic populations. *Sexually Transmitted Diseases, 10*, 114–118.

Huffman, J., Dewhurst, D., & Caparo, V. (1981a). Examination of the premenarchal child. In *The gynecology of childhood and adolescence* (2nd ed.) (pp. 76–100). Philadelphia: WB Saunders.

Huffman, J., Dewhurst, D., & Caparo, V. (1981b). Injuries of the genitalia during childhood. In *The gynecology of childhood and adolescence* (2nd ed.) (pp. 213–224). Philadelphia: WB Saunders.

Ingram, D., White, S., Durfee, M., & Pearson, A. (1982). Sexual contact in children with gonorrhea. *American Journal of Diseases of Children, 136*, 994–996.

Ingram, D., White, T., & Occhiuti, A. (1986). Childhood vaginal infections: Association of Chlamydia trachomatous with sexual contact. *Pediatric Infectious Disease Journal, 5*(2), 226–229.

Jason, J. (1982). Epidemiologic differences between sexual and physical child abuse. *Journal of the American Medical Association, 247,* 3344–3348.

Jones, M., & McQuiston, M. (1986). *Interviewing the Sexually Abused Child* (Vol. 6). Washington: C. Henry Kempe National Center for the Prevention and Treatment of Child Abuse and Neglect.

Kaplan, K., Fleischer, G., Paradise, J. & Friedman, H. (1984). Social relevance of genital herpes simplex in children. *American Journal of the Diseases of Children, 138,* 872–874.

Kramer, D., & Jason, J. (1982). Sexually abused children and sexually transmitted diseases. *Reviews of Infectious Diseases, 14,* S883–S890.

Krzyzek, R., Watts, S., Anderson, D., Faras, A., & Pass, F. (1980). Anogenital warts contain several distinct species of Human Papillomavirus. *Journal of Virology, 36*(1), 236–244.

Ladson, S., Johnson, C., & Doty, R. (1987). Do physicians recognize sexual abuse? *American Journal of Diseases of Childhood, 141,* 411–415.

Lauber, A., & Souma, G. (1982). Use of toluidine blue for documentation of traumatic intercourse. *Obstetrics and Gynecology, 60,* 644–648.

Levitt, C. (1986). Sexual abuse in children: A compassionate yet thorough approach to evaluation. *Postgraduate Medicine, 80*(2), 201–215.

Lister, U., & Akinla, O. (1972). Carcinoma of the vulva in childhood. *Obstetrics and Gynecology of the British Commonwealth, 79,* 470.

Marshall, W., Puls, T., & Davidson, C. (1988). New child abuse spectrum in an era of increased awareness. *American Journal of Diseases of Children, 142,* 664–667.

McCann, J., Voris, J., & Simon, M. (1988). Labial adhesions and posterior fourchette injuries in childhood sexual abuse. *American Journal of the Diseases of Childhood, 142,* 659–663.

McCauley, J., Gorman, R., & Guzinski, G. (1986). Toluidine blue in the detection of perineal laceration in pediatric and adolescent sexual abuse victims. *Pediatrics, 78*(6), 1039–1043.

Muram, D., & Buxton, B. (1984). Gardenerella vaginitis in children: An indicator of sexual abuse. *Pediatric and Adolescent Gynecology, 2,* 197–200.

Muram, D. (1986). Genital tract injuries in the prepubertal child. *Pediatric Annals, 15*(8), 616–620.

Muram, D. (1988a). Labial adhesions in sexually abused girls. *Journal of the American Medical Association, 259*(3), 352–353.

Muram, D. (1988b). Classification of genital findings in prepubertal girls who are victims of sexual abuse. *Adolescent and Pediatric Gynecology, 1,* 151–152.

Muram, D. (1988c). Child sexual abuse: Correlation between genital findings and sexual acts. Paper presented at the North American Society for Adolescent and Pediatric Gynecology, Houston, TX.

Musick, J. (1987). Child sexual abuse: A hidden factor in adolescent sexual behavior. Illinois Department of Children and Family Services.

Nahmias, A., Dowdle, W., & Naib, Z. (1986). Genital infection with herpesvirus homines types 1 and 2 in children. *Pediatrics, 42,* 659–666.

Nair, P., Glazer, S., Gould, C., & Ruff, E. (1986). Neisseria gonorrhoea in asymptomatic prepubertal household contacts of children with gonococcal infection. *Clinics in Pediatrics, 25*(3), 160–163.

Nelson, J., Mohs, E., Dajani, A., & Plotkin, S. (1976). Gonorrhea in preschool and school-aged children: A report of the prepubertal gonorrhea cooperative study group. *Journal of the American Medical Association, 236*(12), 1359–1364.

Orr, D. (1978). Limitations of emergency room evaluations of sexually abused children. *American Journal of the Diseases of Childhood, 132,* 125–139.

Paradise, J., Campos, J., Friedman, H., & Frishmuth, G. (1982). Vulvovaginitis in premenarcheal girls: Clinical features and diagnostic evaluations. *Pediatrics, 70*(2), 193–198.

Peters, S., Wyatt, G., & Finkelhor, D. (1986). Prevalence. In D. Finkelhor (ed.), *A sourcebook on sexual abuse* (pp. 15–59) Beverly Hills, CA: Sage Publications.

Pokorny, S, & Stromer, J. (1987). Atraumatic removal of secretions from the prepubertal vagina. *American Journal of Obstetrics and Gynecology, 156*(3), 581–582.

Pokorny, S., & Kozinetz, C. (1988). Configuration and other anatomical details of the prepubertal hymen. *Adolescent and Pediatric Gynecology, 1,* 97–108.

Polytz, F. (1984). Comparison of p30 and acid phosphotase in post-coital vaginal swabs from donor and casework studies. *Forensic Science Internal, 24,* 17–25.

Potterat, J., Markewich, G., & King, R. (1986). Child-to-child transmission of gonorrhea: Report of asymptomatic genital infection in a boy. *Pediatrics, 78*(4), 712.

Reinhart, M. (1987). Sexually abused boys. *Child Abuse and Neglect, 11,* 229–235.

Rettig, P., & Nelson, J. (1981). Genital tract infection with Chlamydia trachomatous in prepubertal children. *Journal of Pediatrics, 99,* 206.

Rettig, P. (1984). Pediatric genital infection with Chlamydia trachomatous: Statistically nonsignificant, but clinically important. *Pediatric Infectious Disease Journal, 13*(2), 95–96.

Rimsza, M., & Niggemann, E. (1982). Medical evaluation of sexually abused children: A review of 311 cases. *Pediatrics, 69,* 8–14.

Rock, B., Naghashfar, Z., Barnett, N., Buscema, J., Woodruff, J., & Shah, K. (1986). Genital tract papillomavirus infection in children. *Archives of Dermatology, 122,* 1129–1132.

Sanfilippo, J. (1987). Examining a child for suspected sexual abuse. *Clinical Practice in Sexuality, 3*(3), 9–15.

Schacter, J., Grossman, M., & Holt, J. (1979). Infections with Chlamydia trachomatis: Involvement of multiple anatomic sites in neonates. *Journal of Infectious Disease, 119,* 232–234.

Schiff, A. (1975). Sperm identification–acid phosphatase. *Medical Trial Technology Quarterly, 21,* 467.

Shelton, T., Jerkins, G., & Noe, H. (1986). Condyloma acuminata in the pediatric patient. *Journal of Urology, 135,* 548–549.

Signs and symptoms and child sexual abuse (CSA) by age and groups. Conference report at the 1985 National Summit Conference on Diagnosing Child Sexual Abuse, Los Angeles, CA.

Silber, T., & Controni, G. (1983). Clinical spectrum of pharyngeal gonorrhea in children and adolescents. *Journal of Adolescent Health Care, 4*, 51–54.

Slater, G., Rumack, B., & Peterson, R. (1978). Podophyllin poisoning: Systemic toxicity following cutaneous application. *Obstetrics and Gynecology, 52*, 94.

Soules, M., Pollard, A., Brown, K., & Verma, M. (1978). The forensic laboratory evaluation of evidence in alleged rape. *American Journal of Obstetrics and Gynecology, 130*, 142–147.

Steinburg, B., Topp, W., Schneider, P., & Abramson, A. (1983). Asymptomatic persistent infection by human papillomavirus in patients with laryngeal papillomatosis. *New England Journal of Medicine, 308*, 1261.

Stumph, P. (1980). Increasing occurence of condyloma acuminata in premenarchal children. *Obstetrics and Gynecology, 56*(2), 161–164.

Sweet, R., & Gibbs, R. (1985). Chlamydia infections. In *Infectious diseases of the female genital tract* (pp. 103–126). Baltimore: Williams and Wilkins.

Teizeira, W. (1980). Hymenal colposcopic examination in sexual offenses. *American Journal of Forensic Medicine and Pathology, 2*, 209.

Tilelli, J., Turek, D., & Jaffe, A. (1980). Sexual abuse of children: Clinical findings and implications for management. *New England Journal of Medicine, 302*(6), 319–323.

Trofatter, K., English, P., Hughes, C., & Gall, S. (1986). Human lymphoblastoid interferon (Wellferon) in primary therapy of two children with condyloma acuminata. *Obstetrics and Gynecology, 67*(1), 1937–1940.

van Egmond, M. (1988). Early sex abuse linked to repeated suicide attempts. Paper presented at the American Association of Suicidology and the International Association for Suicide Prevention, San Francisco, CA.

Wald, E., Woodward, C., & Marston, G. (1980). Gonorrheal disease among children in a university hospits. *Sexually Transmitted Disease, 7*, 41.

Wald, E., (1983). Acute sinusitis in children. *Pediatric Infectious Diseases Journal, 2*, 34–38.

Walker, E. (1988). Relationship of chronic pelvic pain to psychiatry diagnoses and childhood sexual abuse. *American Journal of Psychiatry, 145*, 75–80.

Ward, J. (1974). Fatal systemic poisoning following podophyllin treatment of condyloma acuminatum. *Southern Medical Journal, 47*, 1204.

White, S., Loda, F., Ingram, D., & Pearson, A. (1983). Sexually transmitted diseases in sexually abused children. *Pediatrics, 72*(1), 16–21.

Whittington, W., Rice, R., Biddle, J., & Knapp, J. (1988). Incorrect identification of Neisseria gonorrhoea from infants and children. *Pediatric Infectious Disease Journal, 7*, 3–10.

Woodling, B., Evans, J., & Morena, T. (1976). Rape: The Ventura County experience. Report to the Medical Research Foundation, Ventura, CA.

Woodling, B., Evans, J., & Bradbury, M. (1977). Sexual assault: Rape and molestation. *Clinical Obstetrics and Gynecology, 20*(3), 509–530.

Woodling, B., & Kossoris, P. (1981). Sexual misuse: Rape, molestation and incest. *Pediatric Clinics of North America, 28,* 481–499.

Woodling, B. & Heger, A. (1986). The use of the colposcope in the diagnosis of sexual abuse in the pediatric age group. *Child Abuse and Neglect, 10,* 111–114.

Chapter 5

Child Abuse Management: The Role of Social Work

Patsy Gemmill

Social problems and their management are the raison d'être of the profession of social work. In the global sense, anything that violates social norms, produces harm to the individual, and generates cost to the welfare of the society, is a social problem. When a social problem grows sufficiently to gain wide public recognition of the violation, harm, or cost, it then becomes a matter for negative legal sanction. In other words, it becomes criminalized. The public thinks of it in capital letters. Such is the case with child abuse.

Child abuse is not a problem of recent origin. It is not a new by-product of modern society. Child abuse, as it is currently thought of, has existed throughout history. With the development of mass education, mass media, and increased sophistication of the masses, society has begun to address such issues as the rights of minor citizens and individual human worth. For the first time, society is struggling to clarify what constitutes abuse of a minor's rights, what causes harm to the child, and what the long-term cost to society is over the long haul. At last the age-old suffering of inestimable children has graduated from being a social problem to being a negatively sanctioned social problem!

Philosophically, children in this country are viewed as belonging to the parents (especially to the father) and are the property of the parents. It is the basis for laws pertaining to children in the United States. The state sets the standards for acceptable or nonacceptable family care of children. Intervention by the state when the standards are violated or not met is a relatively new direction for the courts.

The juvenile court system was begun with the establishment of the first juvenile court in Chicago in 1899. Juvenile courts are sociolegal courts, which utilize social workers rather than attorneys as primary instruments in the process of reaching judicial decisions. Since social work as a profession seeks to humanize social systems, it is not surprising that the juvenile court system, so heavily influenced by social workers, began to consider the rights of children during the "rights decade" of the 1970s.

If the state intervenes, inevitably family integrity and family privacy are invaded and weakened by the intrusion. The child's needs are thwarted. The youthful belief in parental omniscience and power is prematurely shaken. The effect on the child's development is always detrimental. So fundamental is the importance of family integrity that it is protected by the Constitution.

155

In *Beyond the Best Interests of the Child*, Goldstein, Freud, and Solnit (1979) acknowledge the effect of external intervention into the inner world of the child as he or she develops in the family. "Physical, emotional, intellectual, social, and moral growth does not happen without causing the child internal difficulties. Smooth growth is arrested or disrupted when upheavals and changes in the external world are added to the internal ones" (p. 207).

However, to acknowledge how critical parents are for the adequate care and protection of children also leads inevitably to the knowledge that some parents fail. Some are not able and others are unwilling to provide the supports, training, and safeguards that their children require from infancy to adulthood. In some cases the element of family privacy may actually be exploited as a cover for sexual abuse in the parent-child relationship. When family privacy prevents detection of abuse, it no longer serves as a benefit to the child. Indeed, it becomes a threat to the child's well-being, safety, and life. This justifies formal state intervention.

Social Work Functions in Child Abuse and Neglect

Over the years, social work has developed specific functions for managing the widespread problem of child abuse and neglect. The primary functions are identification, investigation, intervention, and prevention. In addition, as all professions must, social work also functions to establish educational requirements, professional ethics, and standards of practice for its members. The first three functions are more directly applied to the problem of child abuse and neglect by social workers employed in Child Protective Services (CPS) through state departments of health and welfare. The prevention and training functions are carried out through child protective agencies but are also generalized throughout the profession in all the various areas of social work services.

Identification Function of Social Work

It is obvious that child abuse must be identified before intervention of any kind be brought to bear. Therefore, the report of abuse must reach the appropriate person. The reporting phase is dependent on the following:

1. Public awareness of what constitutes child abuse.
2. Public awareness of reporting procedures (the "how-to" of making a child abuse report).
3. The willingness and ability of the person or agency that has identified the incident of child abuse or neglect to initiate a report.
4. The availability of a qualified person to receive a report – a person who can obtain necessary information and initiate an appropriate response.

Clearly an informed public is a crucial factor in the management of child abuse and neglect. This may be one of the most inadequate elements in the scheme of things relating to the subject of management. In general, public sensitivity to the presence of and knowledge about effects of child abuse is limited. Many social workers are involved in community education efforts by various service agencies to help increase the general awareness of the public. In some areas, state CPS work directly or indirectly with a state coordinating committee to develop outreach programs, community education packages, and media releases.

Most professional groups have the basic knowledge necessary to recognize child abuse when the overt indicators are present. Additional training, however, is often necessary to gain knowledge of the less obvious indicators of abuse and neglect. The importance of providing specialized training for professionals such as physicians, teachers, law enforcement personnel, and clergy lies in the fact that these people can observe families and children on an ongoing basis. They can identify abusive or neglectful situations when they occur and make a formal report.

When the report is finally made, the CPS worker then faces the first action to be taken in a reported case of suspected abuse and neglect: give the case a priority. There are far more reports of abuse and neglect than there are caseworkers to investigate them. Each case cannot be handled with equal immediacy. In 1986, the American Association for Protecting Children, Inc. issued a report updating the statistics on the incidence of child abuse nationally through the CPS reporting. The report showed that:

> In 1984, an estimated 1,726,649 children were reported for child abuse and neglect to Child Protective Service agencies in the United States. The rate of reporting is estimated at 17.3 children per 1,000 United States child population in 1984. Similarly, an estimated 1,024,178 families were reported in 1984. The total number of families roughly correspond to the number of investigations performed (p. 2).

With numbers like these, the necessity for investigatory triage becomes imperative. Reports are classified into categories of decreasing urgency.

Priority of Reports.   The priority assigned to the child abuse and neglect report is based on two criteria: (1) the allegations in the reports and (2) the seriousness of the incident(s).

The worker must weigh the seriousness of the incident and risk of harm to the child. Priority 2 and 3 allegations may actually be moved to Priority 1, based on the seriousness or potential risk to the child.

Priority 1

- Death
- Brain damage/skull fracture
- Subdural hematoma/internal injuries

- Wounds
- Poisoning/noxious substances
- Bone or cartilage fractures
- Abandonment
- Sexually transmitted disease
- Sexual penetration
- Sexual molestation
- Sexual exploitation
- Incest
- Failure to thrive
- Burns/scalding

When children are placed temporarily, but a shelter care hearing is *not* held, Priority 1 standards are not required.

Priority 2

- Cuts/bruises/human bites
- Sprains/dislocations
- Tying/close confinement/bizarre discipline
- Substance misuse
- Substantial risk of physical injury
- Medical neglect

When any Priority 1 or 2 allegation of harm is listed on the report, the report is a Priority 1 or 2 respectively. When the incident is serious or a child has been taken into temporary protective custody, the report is a Priority 1 report, regardless of the allegations.

The following allegations are considered Priority 3 *only* when the investigative worker has determined that there is no risk of injury to the children, there is no need for temporary protective custody, and there are no Priority 1 or 2 allegations in the reports.

Priority 3

- Mental injury
- Inadequate food/malnutrition
- Inadequate shelter
- Inadequate clothing
- Educational neglect
- Inadequate supervision

Interviewing. To acquire the necessary information for a report, the social worker interviews many people involved in the child's situation. The child, of course, is interviewed. In addition, the worker must talk with the parents or caretakers, all adults in the home, witnesses, the initial reporter, and professionals (i.e., teachers, nurses, physicians, etc.) who may have had contact with the child.

However, the two interviews most demanding of the worker's sensitivity, insight, and withheld judgment are with the parents and the child. In a resource manual on the prevention and treatment of child abuse and neglect (Broadhurst, Edmunds, & MacDicken, 1979), the following suggestions were outlined to assist in doing such delicate interviewing:

When talking with the parents
Do:
- Select interviewer(s) appropriate to the situation.
- Conduct the interview in private.
- Tell the parent(s) why the interview is taking place.
- Be direct, honest, and professional.
- Tell the parent(s) the interview is confidential.
- Reassure the parents of the support of the program.
- Tell the parents if a report has been made or will be made.
- Advise the parent(s) of the program's legal responsibilities to report.

Don't:
- Try to prove abuse or neglect by accusations or demands.
- Display horror, anger, or disapproval of parents(s), child, or situation.
- Pry into family matters unrelated to the specific situation.
- Place blame or make judgments about the parent(s) or child.

When talking with the child
Do:
- Make sure the interviewer is someone the child trusts.
- Conduct the interview in private.
- Sit next to the child, not across the table or desk.
- Tell the child that the interview is confidential.
- Conduct the interview in language the child understands.
- Ask the child to clarify words/terms that are not understood.
- Tell the child if any future action will be required.

Don't:
- Allow the child to feel "in trouble" or "at fault."
- Disparage or criticize the child's choice of words or language.

- Suggest answers to the child.
- Probe or press for answers the child is unwilling to give.
- Display horror, shock, or disapproval of parents, child, or the situation.
- Force the child to remove clothing.
- Conduct the interview with a group of interviewers.
- Leave the child alone with a stranger (e.g., a CPS worker) (p. 28).

Assessment.   When investigation of suspected child abuse has been carried out sufficiently to file a report, the next step for the social worker is to complete an assessment of the child, the parents, and the family circumstances. Without a careful assessment, no effective treatment plan or intervention can be mounted to resolve the problem. However, child abuse and neglect cases require assessment that meets the case management needs of three diverse agencies – the CPS, the court, and the mental health agency. Diagnostic formulations and recommendations must be tailored in such a way as to be meaningful to all three. This requires translating information into the languages of these professions. In other words, a social worker must be cognizant of the different objectives of each as well as the concepts and terminology that each agency uses to view the problem.

The primary role of the CPS and the court is the direct protection of the child from further harm. A knowledge of family dynamics, human development, and environmental factors are necessary for making decisions regarding treatment/intervention objectives.

In addition to the agency consideration in making an assessment, each type of abuse – physical, sexual, psychological, and neglect – has its own different character and dynamic pattern. A case of sexual abuse would be handled very differently than a neglect case. A case involving an infant would require different information than one involving a 14-year-old. Consequently, the issues to explore regarding the child, the parent, and the environment will be discussed from a general perspective.

Parent Assessment.   In assessing the abusive parent, the social worker must try to determine what degree of risk to the child lies in allowing the child to remain with the parent(s). Certain special consideration must be taken into account to make a decision.

In the case of physically abusive parents, the major emphasis is on the parents' reaction to the injuries incurred. The family's attitude toward corporal punishment and the role this may have played in the injury are important. Some evaluation should be made as to the ease with which the parent(s) lose control of their behavior plus the amount of stress required to trigger this. Also important to know is what role the nonabusive spouse had in the abuse.

In cases of neglect, the social worker first needs to know what caused the parents to neglect their children. The social worker must try to discover which needs of the parents caused them to turn away from the child. Second, it is important to know which needs of the parent interfere with nurturing the child. Last of all, a distinction between environmental stress and psychological stress must be made.

Because emotional abuse is a difficult concept to define, most professionals agree that there must be an action, or series of actions or omissions, by the parents that can be shown to have caused emotional harm or injury. The cause and extent of injury can only be determined by a qualified mental health professional.

Sexual abuse is a problem which is very different in scope and etiology. It involves numerous special considerations, which cannot be adequately addressed so briefly. An assessment of sexually abusive parents must evolve from considerations of very complex issues of both parents.

Child Assessment. Questions most commonly asked in assessing an abused child focus on the child's role in the parent/child interaction that resulted in abusive or neglectful actions and on the extent of harm to the child. This data is basic for treatment planning. Individual variations in data obtained generally reflect the age of the child. With the age factor in mind, the social worker surveys the psychosocial functioning of the children relative to their own development, to their family, and to the particular abusive incident. There are several core issues when assessing children as well as special issues relevant to particular age groups.

Some of the special issues of infancy are the degree of attachment between parent or parent surrogate and the child and developmental delays. Physically abused infants as well as neglected infants often demonstrate failure to thrive and developmental delays. Most of the referrals of abused infants are neglect cases where effects on development are at stake.

In evaluating the preschool child, it is important to note whether the child is a problem child (i.e., a child whose developmental delay manifests in provocative behavior such as rigidity, negativism, and hyperactivity). These children often become targets of abuse or neglect. Normal developmental tasks of this period such as separation and toilet training can overstress the inadequate parent, resulting in abuse. Precocious separation or hypermaturity is sometimes secondary to abuse and neglect and may mask a significant lack of depth in interpersonal relations.

Latency or school age children who presented developmental delays or personality traits such as difficult toilet training and negativity in their preschool period may now manifest enuresis and refusal to attend school. This is rarely overlooked by parents. At this stage problems such as school failure, poor peer relations, and cranky, obstreperous behavior at home play a role in abuse. Childhood depression is another prevalent result of abuse and neglect. The social worker is dealing with children at this age who may defend the parent out of fear or loyalty and may be guarded.

Adolescents are more likely to report abuse or neglect than younger children, and they may report directly to school, police, protective service agencies, and counselors. But they are more subject to guilt feelings about the effect of the report on their parents. They want help but not at the expense of alienating parents or destroying the family. This ambivalence is manifested by changing their minds or their stories. The adolescent may be out of control and actually be of an age to victimize the parents, but whatever the provocation for parental abuse, the abusing parent is also out of control.

A complete assessment will sometimes require certain psychological testing to understand the level of functioning of the client. In addition, a family assessment should be part of the overall evaluation. Whatever the individual assessment of the parent and the child, the role of a parent of child viewed in isolation will present a partial and misleading picture of the situation leading to abuse. Adequate protective measures and appropriate treatment planning based on such a misleading picture may well be destructive.

Intervention Function of Social Work

It is not sufficient to define the bounds beyond which child treatment becomes child maltreatment. Although nothing can be brought to bear on a problem that lacks definition, the purpose of defining is so that intervention can be set in motion.

Identifying, reporting, and assessing socially unacceptable treatment of children are only the first steps in a systematic process that is set into motion. If this process were linear, the next steps would be judicial decision, protection, and treatment. However, social problems — and very assuredly child abuse — are dynamic problems and, therefore, the social solutions must be dynamic to be effective. Therefore, the particular incidence of child abuse dictates the sequence of interventive actions. It also dictates whether some or all of the established resources are brought to bear, singly or simultaneously.

If, for example, a child is neglected by a mother who is caught in the depths of a clinical depression following desertion by a spouse, failure in job seeking, impending notice of eviction, and monthly bills piled up unpaid, the process of intervention will address the material and emotional needs of mother and child. It well might not be in the child's best interests to remove her from the mother's custody.

By the same token, a mother who forces a 13-year-old daughter into prostitution may have great financial and emotional needs that should be addressed. But the primary issue would be protection of the child from further harm. In the first case it might be workable to address the child's needs indirectly by helping the mother. In the second case, the child must be helped directly and the mother secondarily. Yet, the dynamic view must always be held. The mother should not be ignored because one of the child's needs is for the mother. However, the child abuse protection and treatment will be examined as isolated elements of a dynamic system for clarity sake.

Protection.   CPS agencies differ from most human service provider agencies in that it provides an involuntary social service. It has the legally mandated responsibility for an endangered child until an appropriate placement can be arranged. In serious, but less urgent situations, an assessment of protective needs is made. The child is taken into protective custody if necessary and temporarily cared for in group housing or in short-term foster homes until court action is completed for longer-range treatment, such as foster placement or adoption.

Treatment.   Protection of the child from further abuse takes the form of treatment. The term *treatment* is also used to denote a form of problem solution, which is a curative or therapeutic approach in healing the illness within the family that manifests as child abuse.

The "illness" referred to is often a family heritage. Nadia Ehrlich Finkelstein (1980) captured the essence of illness in her article, "Children in Limbo." In Finkelstein's words, abused, neglected, and abandoned children are often:

> . . . the product of parents whose life experiences provided them with minimal nurturance and inadequate modeling of parenting. Members of these families have difficulty communicating their own needs or hearing the needs of others. These parents find themselves ill-equipped to face the responsibilities and stresses of adult living. They lack judgment in decisionmaking and their attempts to cope are impulsive. Overwhelming feelings of helplessness and subsequent rage are inevitable by-products. The parents themselves were the victims of abuse and abandonment by their families. In turn, they choose abuse and abandonment of their own spouses and children as a problem-solving method when experiencing more stress than they can handle.
>
> Without positive intervention, this cycle of human self-destruction will continue into the next generation (p. 100).

The treatment plan is designed to deal with all of the family's needs and problems and ideally the family should be involved in the planning along with the workers. In doing this, the caseworker assigns power to parents and children. By the time most abused children and abusive parents come to the attention of the CPS, they no longer experience themselves as having any control over their lives. The worker can plant the first seeds of personal power and help erase the punitive feel of outside intervention by making treatment planning and follow through as much the family's decisions for itself as possible.

Some of the resources that might be selected include public welfare, the state employment agency, legal aid, public health nurses, emergency shelters, emergency homemakers, parent aid programs, counselors, and mental health clinics. These organized health, and social service resources are described from the CPS manual by Jenkins, Salus, and Schultze (1979). These suggestions are designed to meet the kind of needs that are characteristic of abusive families and to help the worker to develop a comprehensive approach to treatment:

Need to develop self-esteem and self-nurturance

• Structured activity in which to build a sense of mastery and success in various work tasks, for example, instruction in recreational activities.

- Group experiences in which to identify with others experiencing the same problems and needs and to begin to understand similarities rather than differences between one's self and others.
- Work or volunteer activities in which to experience a sense of contribution and self-esteem.
- One-to-one treatment relationship with a professional to begin to understand personal needs and desires and their validity, and to deal with personal problems of anger, frustration, fear, and depression.
- One-to-one or group treatment in which to learn to ask for and receive constructive attention and validation of personal needs and desires.

Need to overcome isolation and fear of relationships

- A professional or paraprofessional to act as a friend, to be interested in the parent's needs, to take the parent to lunch, to babysit with the children, to model for the parent what a friendship can consist of.
- Structured social activity through which the parent can test out and begin to build relationships with peers.
- Respite from child care to enable parents to pursue their own interests and friendships more freely.
- Professional and nonprofessional relationships in which to learn to trust others and be willing to ask for and receive support from others.

Need for support systems

- A professional or paraprofessional available on a daily basis to deal with routine daily activities.
- A professional or paraprofessional to model housekeeping and/or childrearing.
- A professional or paraprofessional available to the parents by phone 24 hours a day to talk to in time of stress.
- A professional or paraprofessional available as a friend to visit weekly or biweekly who might also be available by phone in time of crisis.
- A group of parents to socialize with, through which to begin to develop personal support systems.
- A friend, neighbor, or paraprofessional to talk with from time to time to be sure everything is going smoothly and who also might be available in time of crisis.

Need for help with marital problems

- Marital counseling or family therapy to begin to deal with problems in the marriage or family unit.

- Structured group or one-to-one experiences in which to learn to ask for and receive nurturing and support from spouse.
- Help in solving environmental and life crisis.

Need for help with life crisis

- One-to-one and/or group counseling to learn what role the child plays in the parent's life, or what the child means to the parent.
- Counseling or role modeling in how to deal with the special child – the child who is handicapped, retarded, or hyperactive.
- Counseling or parent group participation to learn alternative methods of discipline that avoid corporal punishment.
- Counseling or parent group participation to learn alternative methods of receiving nurturance and feelings of self-esteem that do not include burdening the child with these needs.
- Giving the child up for adoption or temporary placement to make necessary changes for longterm stability.

Child's need for support and nurturing

- Structured experiences – daycare, school, play group – for the child, with other children and adults, to learn other systems of relationships; to learn to get support and nurturing from others besides the parents; and for socialization with peers.
- One-to-one or group therapy for the child to deal with fears, anger, frustration, or offensive behaviors – therapeutic daycare, play therapy, or traditional psychotherapy.
- Experiences that stimulate the development of motor skills or intellectual skills for those children who are lagging behind developmentally.
- Play groups for the child to alleviate isolation and promote development of peer-interaction skills.
- Foster grandparent or lay therapist to relate to the child while in a hospital, to provide support and nurturance and opportunity for the child to build trust in others.
- Foster care to protect the child, at least temporarily, until some presolution is achieved concerning his/her family or home situation.

Psychotherapeutic Treatment.   Social workers in the field of mental health function to provide treatment for the unhealthy psychosocial dynamics of abused children and abusing parents. Their involvement is more focused and specific in scope than social workers in the child protective services. They are dealing with the complexities of value systems, belief systems, family custom, cultural custom, and personality traits in dynamic with socioeconomic and psychological factors. The specific approach to treatment is chosen as a "best fit" for the individual parent, child, or family.

Many types of therapy are available. Most can be classified in four basic groups of therapeutic approaches: psychodynamic, behavioral/cognitive, interpersonal/group/family, and humanist/existential. The theory, goal, and method of the groups are different, but the purpose is commonly shared. All attempt to improve the quality of life and function of the client(s).

The psychodynamic therapies evolved from Freudian psychoanalysis. More focused techniques of this genre are practiced today than in the classical years long before psychoanalysis of Freud's era. They are based on the theory that problems are rooted in experiences — many of which are submerged in the unconscious. The goal is to discover why problems exist (what experience generated the problem) and, thereby, gain insight with which to better control one's life. The method used is analyzing dreams, random thoughts, earliest memories, and current experiences.

For instance, an abusive parent, in therapy because he beats his young son, recalls an early childhood memory of being afraid of the dark. The client's parent responded to being awakened by a crying child by yelling at him to be quiet (which increased the level of fear and volume of crying). Ultimately the client recalls his parent rising from bed and striking him in frustrated rage. Analyzing this early memory may result in the client gradually realizing that he strikes his own crying child because the child is a reminder of his own early feelings of fear and helplessness.

A behavioral/cognitive approach to treatment, on the other hand, theorizes that problems (i.e., undesirable behaviors, aversive feelings, and dysfunctional thinking patterns) are bad habits. Since habits are learned, the goal is to change problems by relearning, and the methods of relearning are desensitization, implosion, biofeedback, relaxation training, and homework assignments.

Using the previous example of the father who beat his son whenever the child cried, the behavioral/cognitive approach would focus on designing homework assignments to put new, acceptable behaviors into practice and to reward the new behavior. The client might be instructed to:

1. Punch a pillow several times in succession, as hard as possible, to discharge angry energy.
2. Pick the boy up and hold him while patting his back gently.
3. Reward oneself immediately following the parenting action with some small treat or activity that is pleasant for the parent.

In this way, this therapy modality attempts to redirect habitual emotional responses into healthier actions and improve interpersonal skills.

These first two approaches deal with the individual processes. Psychodynamic approaches are well suited to introspective, articulate people. Behavior/cognitive therapies are often better suited to solution-oriented, pragmatic people who require measurable, clearly defined success.

The interpersonal/group/family therapies are based on the theoretical assumption that problems develop from faulty interaction with others. These seek to resolve problems by improving the ability to build and maintain healthy relationships. The method is observing and discussing how the individual related to other members of a group, a family, or a couple.

The father who strikes his crying son would most likely be seen by a therapist of the interpersonal approach with the client's whole family. He would be observed by the therapist and coached in self-observation of how he responds and behaves in relation to other family members and their responses and behaviors. ("It seems, Mr. Smith, as though you feel tense when your son is tearful. You snapped the pencil in your hand when Johnny cried a minute ago. What do you feel like doing? Would that be a good thing? What else could you do instead?")

The fourth category of therapies, the humanist/existentialist, assumes that everyone possesses the inner resources for psychological healing and personal growth. Problems arise from a lack of awareness of these resources and lack of skills in utilizing them. The goal is to expand this awareness of one's true situation and choices. The primary methods are understanding the client, accepting the client's emotions as expressed, with heavy emphasis on role playing and defining choices. This is best suited for those who seek new possibilities in the future rather than explanations of the past.

The father of the crying child would not be directed toward understanding why he acted as he did. Nor would a healthier behavior program be the focus. Instead he would spend time in a humanist/existentialist therapy, role playing his son as well as other significant people in his life. He would examine his options for responding to the child's cries, and he would experience being treated with acceptance while relating unacceptable feelings and actions. The needs of the abusive person for self-esteem, security, and hope would be directly addressed. Amelioration of the child's situation would be indirectly approached through direct intervention with the abuser. The theoretical assumption is that if the parent would change sufficiently to fill his own dependency needs, the abuse would cease and the child would no longer be an abused child.

Before the social worker chooses a best-fit treatment method, the personality functioning of the abusive parent is considered. Generally the personality characteristics commonly associated with abusive parents can be loosely grouped in four categories according to Fanshel (1966). The first is the hostile and aggressive parent. These people seem to experience a near constant state of anger at someone or something. Their expressive mode is impulsive and uncontrolled. This type of parent is closer to the public's stereotype of a child abuser.

A second group of parents exhibit compulsiveness, lack of warmth, and generalized rigidity of personality. These parents do not appear to experience empathy for or identification with other people – to include their children. The pain, need, or sensibilities of others exist outside their inner world of experience, where these individuals maintain their primary focus of attention. In addition, they feel a compelling need for order, exactitude, and regimen. These qualities are not the normal traits exhibited by children. Any childhood behavior that is perceived by these parents as a threat to their carefully balanced inner world or lifestyle can result in abuse or deprivation. The parent is likely to be emotionally detached and controlling. The child who is late for dinner, for instance, might be denied food for several days, yet required to arrive at the dinner table on time to observe the family meal taking.

A third group of parents has strong feelings of passivity and dependence. They appear to relate to their children as though they and the children had reversed roles. These parents are more typically seen in cases involving neglect, although they are capable of enraged violence if the child-parent fails to keep the parent feeling secure. These parents often exhibit an air of self-pity, apathy, and pervasive depression.

The fourth and last group has a heavy representation of abusive fathers who, because of physical disabilities, are unable to adequately support their families. The characteristic attitude associated with this group is one of resentfulness, hopelessness, and negativity. Their abusive treatment of the child is more likely to be the culmination of a slow burning frustration which, although likely to be sudden action such as the first group of parents display, is less impulsive in origin.

Another consideration the mental health social worker makes is an evaluation of the parents' verbal skills and ability to introspect. Certain therapies are so dependent on the client's ability to mentally observe his/her own inner experience and thought process, plus the vocabulary to describe these observations, that it is useless to use those approaches with certain concrete thinking or nonverbal individuals.

Other Treatment Options.   Once the abusive parent is involved in treatment with a mental health worker, the learning in therapy is (ideally) reinforced by the child protective worker and a parent assistant (if parenting education services are available).

Parenting education, available through some state departments of health and welfare, is another valuable treatment intervention. The premise that a child's best interests are served when his home life can be preserved led to the development of services designed to help parents learn healthy ways to take care of their children and overcome abusive behavior. Parenting education attempts to utilize the sharing of information within a relationship between parent and parent assistant to increase the abusive parents' self-awareness, self-esteem, social connectedness, and appropriate coping skills.

Elements of education for parents are classes in parenting as well as home visits. The special needs of the parents and child are assessed before the individualized training begins. The workers and the parenting assistants observe the parents. Such things as regularity of attendance, degree of participation, attitude, cooperation, and description of home conditions provide a means of assessing the probability (or reduced probability) that child abuse is likely to be repeated.

The abused child is also served by the mental health social worker. A variety of therapeutic approaches have been developed in recent years which are used to supplement casework services. The purpose is to support the child's expression of feelings, to meet the child's emotional needs, and to offer direct treatment (Lauer, Lowie, Salus, & Broadhurst, 1979).

One modality of treatment is play therapy. Since children are less capable of expressing themselves verbally than adults, the use of play materials in a safe setting allows the child to learn to express and resolve conflicts and fears. Children as young as three and four can benefit from intensive one-to-one contact with a skilled play therapist. Play therapy is also useful as a diagnostic tool.

Most abused and neglected children can benefit from play therapy, but it is especially indicated for those whose conflicts are so intense that a group experience will not be enough to resolve their problems. Children who exhibit low self-esteem, depression, or extreme aggressiveness toward others, or who have other severe behavior problems, should be seen in play therapy.

Preadolescents and adolescents who have experienced abuse and/or neglect can benefit from group therapy. This provides experiences that help with socialization, self-awareness, and sensitivity to others.

Homogeneous groups for sexually abused children and adolescents are useful in dealing with the distortion in the parent-child relationship. There are also other benefits, such as helping the children to develop healthy attitudes toward sex, to gain support from others, and to gain self-acceptance.

Where they are available, therapeutic play schools are a third valuable tool for healing. The basic structure and format of the therapeutic play school is designed to meet the treatment needs of abused children. Provision of a safe environment, acceptance, and positive feedback help children develop trust in others and positive self-images. Consistent routines and staff predictability allow these children to test feelings and actions. With the open expression of fear and anger, these children are able to recognize and deal with these forbidden feelings and channel them appropriately.

Preventive Functions of Social Work

Naturally the prevention of all child abuse and neglect is the ideal. Realistically we can hope to significantly reduce the incidence. The public health model is the design of the prevention system, with intervention divided into three levels: primary, secondary, and tertiary. *Primary prevention* concerns itself with reducing the incidence of new cases of child abuse. *Secondary prevention* efforts attempt to reduce the duration and severity of abuse by identifying and treating child mistreatment as early as possible. Finally, *tertiary prevention* is intended to reduce the damage that abuse produces.

Primary Prevention.   Because abuse has a very complex etiology with the inter-play of many variables, primary prevention has been successful in a very limited way. The funding for child abuse prevention services is grossly inadequate, making implementation of effective primary prevention more hope than reality.

The most current primary approach has been to target specific segments of the general population. Good examples of this are programs that increase aware-ness and provide information on pregnancy and birth and provide school chil-dren some education regarding child sexual abuse.

Since it is so costly to mount prevention programs, clinicians and researchers are devoting more time and resources to high-risk populations. The following are high-risk factors for child abuse and neglect:

- Low birthweight preterm infants
- Children of adolescent parents
- Handicapped and special needs children
- Children of mentally retarded parents
- Children of substance abusers
- Children of parents who were abused as children
- Children of parents with few or inadequate support systems (i.e., family, friends, neighbors).

Some children belong to more than one of these population groups. The risk factor increases as group membership increases. But the likelihood of an earlier identification also increases earlier intervention.

Secondary Prevention.   This includes public education programs and the train-ing of professionals. In training professionals to work in the field of child abuse prevention, a basic understanding of state law, family dynamics, child abuse and neglect definitions, indicators of abuse and neglect, and reporting proce-dures are provided. Also attention is given to such concerns as treatment alterna-tives, encouragement of parental self-help, and community response to abuse and neglect.

Specific information and necessary skill training is provided for interview-ing parents and children. Learning the proper procedures and preparation for testifying in court is also covered. Treatment methods for abusive parents, treat-ment methods for abused children, and differential diagnosis are emphasized. However, training in specific therapeutic methods requires considerable time and effort. It necessitates the completion of a clinical apprenticeship experience and is beyond the range of most child protective in-service training.

Tertiary prevention.   This is the rebuilding of human lives by means of the support, assistance, and resource coordination provided to children and their parents by the CPS agencies around the country. The prevention referred to here is prevention of recurrence of abusive behavior in families which have a pattern of prior abuse.

Child Protection Service Agencies

Many services that the state departments of public health and welfare provide may be labeled as protective services in a broad general sense. The Aid to Dependent Children Program (Title 4A of the Social Security Act of 1935) was originally intended, and indeed has succeeded, in allowing children to remain in the homes of a parent or relative. Otherwise these children would have been, in many cases, destined to fill orphan's homes (as they were then referred to). Orphanages at one time appeared to be a feasible alternative to the family but actually proved to be a poor solution for the uprooted child. Although orphanages offered physical care and survival, they failed to provide the children with the kind of relationships that are necessary for the development of self-esteem, of internal mechanisms for impulse control, and for the capacity to maintain meaningful personal relationships. Consequently the foster care and group home programs have replaced orphanages.

The Food Stamp Program was originally designed to protect children from hunger and dietary deficiencies that can result from poverty and neglect. Other programs and services designed to protect children from poor care, neglect, and abuse, are adoption services and, in some states, licensure and supervision of daycare centers and other child care institutions through the Department of Health and Welfare.

To implement all of these service programs, the number of social workers involved in child welfare and CPS is impressive. The caseworker, however, is historically overworked. No child receives ideal casework because there are still too few workers for cases reported. The CPS worker must spread him/herself very thin just to do the initial investigation and assessment for all the reports of abuse.

The special demands on social workers who are employed in child protective services have had some deleterious effects on worker function. In an early study of role performance of social workers in CPS contrasted with social workers in a family service agency, Billingsley (1964) found that CPS workers:

1. Spend less time in client-centered activity and more time in collateral contacts.
2. Report less work satisfaction than family service workers.
3. Show a significantly higher personnel turnover.
4. Use a service style more attuned to the sociocultural aspects of a client's situation than to the psychodynamic.

Since 1964, the demands on CPS workers have escalated to unprecedented levels. Between 1976 and 1984, the first period for which information is available, child abuse and neglect reporting increased 158% (Harris, 1987)! However, the resources of CPS agencies have not kept pace. The overburdened CPS agencies are caught in a spiral of need that is progressing geometrically.

To grasp what is happening to America's child population, consider the general effect of stress on the individual. A person under stress no longer experiences the familiarity of homeostasis. The human system is in a state of alert arousal. The inner experience is of a demand for action. Appropriate actions (coping mechanisms, problem-solving strategies, etc.) are precisely what the abusive parent has the least ability to produce. In a large representative sample of American parents, it was shown that the stressful events have a direct positive correlation with the incidence of child abuse. The greater the number of stressful events occurring in the year surveyed, the higher the incidents of child abuse (Straus & Steinmetz, 1980).

The America of today is a society of ever-increasing stress as the climate of economics, politics, technology, and social mores continues to evolve and change faster and faster. Social problems swell as the population urbanizes and grows.

One example of a relatively new, and extremely stressful, social problem was described by Doris J. Harris (1987) in her paper, "The Emotional Traumatization of Child Victims of Parental Abuse."

> New York City's Queensboro Society for the Prevention of Cruelty to Children started receiving child protective service cases with allegations of neglect due to CRACK abuse in large numbers during the summer of 1986. One hundred and nineteen reports of abuse were received in a six month period and in 41 of those cases, the allegations involved substance abuse, mainly cocaine and CRACK, a deadly form of cocaine. This substance takes complete control of its users. Many mothers would leave their children unsupervised without food and other necessities. The number of children reported to be born addicted to drugs more than doubled between a six-month period in 1985 and the same period in 1986. The number of court cases charging abuse and neglect of children rose 48 percent in 1986 and in two thirds of the cases, drug abuse was involved. Overall, the number of reports of child abuse in 1986 in New York City jumped from 36,300 to 45,000 (p. 44).

These recent statistics reflect what is happening in only one city, related to only one social problem. Children are being victimized by the social system as well as the families. These children will become the abusing parents of tomorrow's children. As the problem spirals, CPS systems become more overloaded. The social and health care agencies are caught in the middle of a socioeconomic, politically determined method of service delivery that precludes effective large-scale, long-range programs of prevention.

These problems will continue to grow, unless the American society gives serious heed to individual human need, formally sanctions a priority of human needs, and accepts the cost for realistic programs of intervention and prevention. Until this is accomplished, there is always, at all times, somewhere in this country, a child being abused.

Conclusion

As documented in this book, the problem of children being abused and neglected is a widespread and growing problem. It is most forcibly coming to the attention of more citizens and human service professionals than ever before, demanding to be addressed. Wherever this problem surfaces – in the schools, the hospital emergency rooms, family courts, neighborhoods, or police stations – social workers will be the professionals who are always going to be involved at some point in dealing with it. If people genuinely want to build a world where children are safe to live and grow, social service programs must be expanded and more programs must be funded.

However, child abuse and neglect must compete with the demands of other social problems for the time, money, and manpower which society has available. Unless and until the problem of child abuse achieves a priority rating greater than the problem of commodity transport, we as a nation will continue to devote more of our resources to the development of highway systems than to the development of our children's welfare.

Glossary

Behavior disorder – A term used to refer to observable general and social behavior abnormalities; impaired or abnormal development of internalized controls or mechanisms with which the individual can effectively cope with the natural and social demands of his environment.

Counseling – Professional guidance on the basis of knowledge of human behavior and the use of special interviewing skills to achieve specified goals which are beneficial to the individual and mutually accepted by counselor and client.

Cultural deprivation – See environmental deprivation.

Daycare program – Extended care services provided on an ongoing basis for individuals residing in the community and not eligible for school programs or workshops; daycare programs involve social, physical, recreational, and personal care training and activity.

Environmental deprivation – Insufficient quantity, variability, redundancy, or discriminability of stimulation in the environment. This includes cultural deprivation, a condition in which the general total environment surrounding the child is markedly inappropriate for teaching skills needed for coping with the general environment, even though appropriate for the subculture.

Evaluation — The application of techniques for the systematic appraisal of physical, mental, social, economic, and intellectual resources of an individual and his family, for the purpose of devising an individualized program of action to be followed by periodic reappraisals as appropriate; it determines the extent to which the presenting problem limits, or can be expected to limit, the individual's daily living and working activities, and will be expected to be removed, corrected, or minimized by specific intervention services.

Foster care — A program or constellation of community services provided (i.e., as in a family through a recognized agency) to an individual requiring at least residential care and supervision on a short-term basis when it is impractical or impossible for the individual to live independently or with his or her natural family.

Group therapy — Treatment of psychosocial problems using the interacting forces within a small unit of individuals who may have similar or differing characteristics under trained leadership.

Parenting education — Didactic, interactional, and experiential presentation of knowledge regarding the effective actions of a caregiving person in provision of guidance, protection, and need-filling for children.

Play therapy — A type of psychotherapy for children utilizing play fantasy construction.

Prevention — The process of the rearrangement of forces in the society against those negative factors in the life of a child.

Psychosocial assessment — The overall appraisal of physical, mental, social, economic, and intellectual resources of the individual and his/her family to assist in determining how limiting the presenting problem is regarding daily living and work functions, as well as planning appropriate interventions.

Shelter care — Extended care services providing at least residential care and supervision on a temporary basis for children while assessment of long-term needs and determination of placement appropriate to those needs is made.

Worker — Most often used to refer to social workers whose job entails a great deal of work in the field or direct service as contrasted with social workers whose job relates primarily to administration or education.

References

American Association for Protecting Children, Inc. (1986). *Highlights of official child neglect and abuse reporting.* Denver: American Humane Association.

Billingsley, A. (1964). The role of the social worker in a child protective agency. *Child Welfare, 43*(9), 472–479.

Broadhurst, D., Edmunds, M., & MacDicken, R. (1979). *Early childhood programs and the prevention and treatment of child abuse and neglect.* (OHDS) 79–30198. Washington, D.C.

Fanshel, D. (1966). Child welfare. In H. Maas (Ed.), *Five fields of social service: Reviews of research* (pp. 85–143). New York: National Association of Social Workers.

Finkelstein, N. (1980). Children in limbo. *Social Work, 25*(2), 100–105.

Goldstein, J., Freud, A., & Solnit, A. (1979). *Beyond the best interests of the child.* New York: Free Press.

Harris, D. (1987). The emotional traumatization of the child abuse victim of parental abuse. In *Proceedings: Implementing a forward plan: A public health social work challenge* (pp. 33–44). Pittsburgh, PA Bureau of Maternal and Child Health and Resource Development.

Jenkins, J., Salus, M., & Schultze, G. (1979). *Child protective services: A guide for workers.* (OHDS 79-30203). Washington, D.C.

Lauer, J., Lowie, I., Salus, M., & Broadhurst, D. (1979). *The role of the mental health professional in the prevention and treatment of child abuse and neglect.* (OHDS 79-30194). Washington, D.C.

Straus, M. & Steinmetz, S. (1980). *Behind closed doors: Violence in the American family.* New York: Doubleday.

Chapter 6

Combatting Child Abuse Through Community Organizations

Molly C. McGregor

Importance of Community Development

Community organizations, whether they are public, private, or not-for-profit are started for a purpose – to meet a community need. Individuals have banned together to fill a funding gap for nonprofits (United Way), to educate the public on environmental issues (Nader's Raiders), or to protect the welfare of animals (Humane Society). Community organizations are as old as mankind. When we first raised our clubs against our fellow man, there was probably a group who banded together to prevent this violence by their attempts at negotiation, education, or programs for peace.

The importance of community development cannot be stressed strongly enough as a positive means of combatting the inequities of society. In fact, community organizations are one of the reasons why our democratic society, with all of its seeming inequalities, has survived so well. Yet, in reverse, community organizations, and the power they wield, either singly or combined, would not be possible to the extent they are in America if it were not for our democracy.

In the United States one can virtually organize for anything. However, many organizations, developed for the altruistic goal of meeting community needs, have fallen by the wayside for the lack of a sound organizational plan.

The physical or sexual abuse of children is a critical social problem that needs to be addressed. It is a difficult community issue that can be addressed effectively through the development of community organizations. If they are designed to be a supportive system to combatting child abuse by joining with the other disciplines related to alleviating the problem, a community organization of this type can be quite effective. A community organization developed to combat child abuse can be a coordinating body for social services, a clearinghouse on information, or an educational union. It would need to be an organized body composed of individuals (volunteers, agency representatives, educators, parents, etc.) working as a unit to achieve one goal — alleviating child abuse in the community.

That one ideal goal cannot be achieved without a community response to it. It cannot be accomplished without some kind of drawing together of forces that can make a difference.

This chapter will identify how to start such an organization, maintain it through comprehensive planning, and identify some of the pitfalls of negative group dynamics. Additionally, the chapter will look at some brief case studies of ineffective and effective community development attempts related to alleviating child abuse.

Getting a community organization started can be difficult at best. Child abuse, sexual or physical, although it has been high profile in recent years, is not an issue around which many people from the general public rally. Primarily, they are uncomfortable with the issue, they have difficulty accepting its frequency of occurrence, or they do not care. There are many reasons for the blockages to getting such an organization off the ground.

This chapter will attempt to ease the process by identifying seven steps necessary for starting a community organization. And, in this case, the steps are designed for starting a *nonprofit* organization. The step-by-step procedure will include the initial involvement of a small group of people who would be charged with the early organization, mission identification, and data collection. Later steps will involve bringing in community leaders, establishing the appropriate incorporation, and developing the planning aspects to the organization.

These planning phases of nonprofit organizations will be discussed in detail following standard guidelines for corporate planning in nonprofit organizations.

This planning process is critical to the success of any organization. The chapter will identify the characteristics of corporate planning, the benefits of planning, terminology, and suggested degrees of planning for a newly formed organization. It will also outline ongoing steps that will include appraisal of the organization's effectiveness in meeting its goals.

In probing the dynamics of group process, the chapter will identify how interpersonal relationships throughout an organization affect the general climate and how the attitudes of the organization affect interpersonal relations, that is, how the parts and the whole influence each other.

The level of group maturity, growth, and ability to achieve the ultimate goal will depend a great deal on the dependence and interdependence of individual members. Likewise, physical, structural and process factors will either inhibit or encourage group development, and ultimately the successful completion of organizational objectives.

Finally, the chapter will explore the successes and failures of five different organizations whose ultimate goal is the elimination of child abuse.

Seven Steps to Getting Organized

Seven steps should be used in starting a nonprofit organization. The anticipated size and complexity of the organization, its ultimate mission, the receptiveness of the community, and the scope of the social problem on which the organization will focus will determine whether or not all seven steps should be followed. It may be appropriate for the initial organizer to combine a few steps or eliminate one or two entirely. However, all of these steps in one form or another are recommended to ensure successful organization of the group. Ultimate performance of the group will depend on not only the group's and leader's capacity for organization, but also on other factors primarily related to group dynamics.

Initial Organization

Every community organization starts with an idea originating with one person. The outrage of child abuse can stir some individuals to restrained anger that is unproductive unless channeled into a positive means to fight this societal illness. Community organization is an effective weapon, yet only one answer.

The desire to solve a societal problem in a local community and actually solving that problem relies first on that initial person. An appropriate leader is a key factor in the first steps and is the motivating force to starting an organization. This individual must be a capable leader and fueled with the indignation resulting from discovering the extent of child abuse in our society. Motivation, intent, and ability to organize must be some characteristics of the leader.

The individual (hereby known as the leader) must be able to verbalize perceived community need for an organization. The mission of any community group should be based on filling a need, one that is readily identifiable.

The leader should outline briefly and with as much clarity as possible the purpose or mission of the proposed organization. Unless this purpose is clear, further organization will be difficult if not impossible.

Imagining the kinds of programs the organization would develop once on its feet will assist future group members in visualizing how the mission will be carried out. The programs would become tools through which the mission is accomplished. For instance, in response to the problem of child abuse in a community, an initial organizer may determine the mission or the organization to be education of the public. The form that education takes could be varied and extensive. Much of this depends on the size and resources of the organization. However, philosophy of the organization will set the tone and methodology of the programs. And that philosophy can be a determining factor in the success or failure of the organization.

The leader should develop a listing of initial objectives both for development of the organization and potential objectives to be met once the group gets off the ground. These objectives or goals would become a working base for future planning that would be conducted by the group.

In addition, the leader needs to determine if there are organizations currently providing these services. It would be counterproductive to duplicate community services if those services are being effective. Duplication of community services also generates competition for funding. And funding is crucial to a successful organization, particularly when it is new.

Once the community needs are clear in the leader's mind and potential programs have been identified, the leader should investigate the possibility of collaborating with agencies or organizations that are currently relating to, whether effectively or not, the problem. Naturally, this collaboration could eliminate the need for another organization. It would also identify that the need is indeed not being met.

Once the purpose, programs, and philosophy have become clear in the leader's mind, then a committee of four to six people is necessary to continue. Now the leader would need to bring together four to six persons who have a personal interest in the development of such a community organization. This interest would need to be backed by a strong commitment to pursuing the necessary steps for development and the skill to do that. Of course, their commiseration for the victims of child abuse would be a key motivating factor.

One characteristic of the group's makeup could be that they have only one thing in common, that being the desire to solve this social malady. However, it is recommended that these four to six individuals constitute a representation from disciplines involved in combatting child abuse or have experience in areas that will prove useful to the group in the future.

Backing Up Ideas

There would be a variety of tasks for this initial group. First, the group would be charged with assembling community data. This information would be used as background materials supporting the case for development of a community organization.

Assembling community data is a formidable task, one that will require the cooperation of all members of the initial four to six group. Therefore, the leader must assign tasks for gathering data, including all group members.

The group would need to produce demographic data describing, in general, the existing community. This is important in that community boundaries, population statistics, income, age breakdown, education, and household makeup would establish a foundation for comparison of demographic data relating to the social problem.

Second, demographic data directly related to the social problem should be drawn from a variety of sources. For instance, the Department of Human Resources (DHR) would be a veritable resource of information. DHR records could identify frequency of occurrence of child abuse and, the form it took (i.e., sexual, physical, or mental). Sex and ages of the victims as well as statistics on the perpetrators could also be gleaned from DHR. Of course, much child abuse is not even reported. Studies have been done that draw conclusions from existing data regarding the frequency and type of abuse.

Police reports and court records can be valuable resources for gathering evidence supporting the case for community development. Information regarding the disposition of individual cases can show rates of conviction, acquittal, and dismissal.

Since many cases are reported through the school systems, boards of education, education associations, and even PTAs may have statistical data confirming the prevalence of child abuse in school-age children.

Interviews should be conducted by members of the initial group with individuals related to the previously named disciplines. Although statistical data may be sufficient, personal opinions will be extremely valuable in supporting the cause. Statistical information alone is not as potent emotionally as private conclusions from professionals who deal with child abuse regularly. A strong emotional case, in addition to a well-thought out plan for development will go a long way to securing the future of the organization.

Besides these resources, previous research articles or studies should be included in the case for development. Child abuse studies conducted by universities, physicians, sociologists, and other individuals or professional groups would lend tremendous credence to the need for community development.

Anonymous community surveys would provide additional data that may be unattainable from public sources. Also, people tend to be more candid in responding to anonymous surveys. These surveys should be conducted at random taking in a cross section of the population identified by the demographic data.

Once the information has been gathered, the group needs to evaluate the data for its dependability. Some demographic data (interviews, surveys, etc.) can be somewhat unreliable because of the method by which they were attained and the accuracy of the information.

Drawing appropriate conclusions around the pervasiveness of the problem that would back up the need for developing a community organization is crucial. These conclusions will become the foundation for further development of the group's mission and objectives.

The group leader will then need to assign the task of writing a summary of the group's findings. This summary will later become a case for support of the organization. Rather than disseminating statistical information in a formal fashion, the author should create the summary as a written verbalization of the statistics, outlining the group's conclusions.

Initial Recommendations

By invitation the group would bid 20 to 25 key community leaders to review the materials, data, and summary in an effort to generate support for starting an organization. These leaders should be influential members of the community.

They should have the means available to them to support such an organization or be able to generate support from within the community.

Such individuals may be educators in the area of child abuse, business leaders, foundation directors, politicians, ministers, and in some cases, victims who have the ability to spawn support. There are certainly others to consider, but the group invited to review the materials needs to have the capacity to generate funds, volunteers, and public cooperation. In addition, they must have the fore-sight and experience for planning the proposed organization.

The primary focus of the initial group, by getting the key community leaders to review the materials, is to recommend the establishment of an organization designed to combat child abuse. Besides ensconcing the need in the minds of the leaders, the organization's preliminary mission statement and potential pro-gram areas should be identified to this group.

The materials, the case for support, the outline for the new organization, and the invitation to become part of the early phase of the organization should be discussed in person, if possible, by members of the initial group. This one-on-one method can be very effective in developing personal commitment to the cause. It will be much easier to fill leadership positions later on if the commit-ment to the mission is there.

Once the key leaders have acquiesced to the need for such an organization designed to help eliminate child abuse in the community, a temporary board of directors should be selected. The method for selecting this temporary board is unimportant. The significant factor would be assuring that those selected under-stand the social problem, the need for community development, and what is expected of them as a temporary board.

Initial Functioning

Although it may seem to some that establishing a temporary board of directors may be unnecessary, it needs to be made clear that there is no official organiza-tion at this point. An interim group of leaders is extremely important to the fledgling organization. The individual board members will have particular respon-sibilities related to their posts.

This small body will have the authority, extended by the community leaders, to conduct business for the organization. And, the next few steps the group takes will establish the pattern of leadership roles as well as facilitating the group's functioning for the future.

The first responsibility the temporary board will have is to elect officers. These posts can be anything that seems to be necessary for the effective opera-tion of the organization: chairman, vice-chairman, treasurer, and secretary. There are many excellent civic club models from which to choose when determining officers. One office is recommended, however. A membership chairman will become a pivotal leader as new members are sought early on. Maintaining that membership, including records, will be important to future recruitment and fund-raising efforts.

The board of directors would need to appoint various committees. These committees would more than likely act as permanent committees after a permanent board is elected. Committee members can be recruited from the group of community leaders drawn together in step three. They can also be generated from the community, which may be necessary to fill particular committee chairs that require a certain skill.

The first committee to begin functioning would be the membership committee. Their primary responsibility would be to recruit new, committed members. Under the leadership of the membership chairman and working with the finance committee, the membership committee would need to set dues. The membership dues generated during such a membership drive would subsequently become the base from which the finance committee would develop a preliminary budget for the organizational operations. Initial expense funds will be needed to accomplish recruitment goals.

This first priority of the membership drive should include a charter membership enrollment. The charter membership dues should be set a little higher than regular dues. This would be done for two reasons: to generate more funds and to give evidence of strong community support. A charter membership list is usually published for use in recruitment and fund raising. Charter memberships should be limited and invitations to become a charter member should be made first to the body of community leaders and then to the general public.

An organizational option to having a membership base is to have straight fund raising. The important point is to get a solid base of support for future operations, both for financial support and voluntary support.

Making It Official

Following the membership-enrollment or fund-raising drive, the temporary board would need to approve a revised budget based on the level of success seen by the drive. Nonprofit organizations must be keenly aware of the need to monitor finances constantly. Deficit spending is inappropriate and only puts more burdens on the frail makeup of a new organization. High budget controls on both sides of the balance sheet are necessary for a sound organization.

The health of the organization is also dependent on having an adequate constitution and bylaws. These tools will steer the organization as it begins the planning phases of its operation. Agonizing over the development of such a document is unnecessary. Many suitable models are available. Keeping it simple should also be a rule of thumb because adjusting the constitution and bylaws is always a future possibility.

The job of preparing a constitution and bylaws will be significantly easier if three things occur. First, the board of directors needs to identify any policies that should be adopted. These may need to become a part of the bylaws. Second, the board should investigate what is necessary for articles of incorporation and achieving nonprofit status. Finally, legal advice is needed. Finding an attorney who understands the legal issues and the nature of the organization will save the group a tremendous amount of time and trouble.

Next the temporary board of directors needs to guarantee the election of a permanent board of directors. This should be done through a ballot format soliciting votes from the membership. The usual method is for a nominating committee to present a slate of directors with a listing of officers. The constitution and bylaws should spell out for the group exactly how the election should be conducted.

Nothing at this point is official. There is only a temporary board of directors and proposed constitution and bylaws. The election by the membership of the directors and officers will begin to give the organization a sense of permanency.

Getting Started

The permanent board of directors can now get started with the business of the organization. They will be charged with leading the organization and its members in pursuing the proposed mission.

The first concern will be adoption of the proposed constitution and bylaws by the general membership. Next, the board of directors will need to apply for the articles of incorporation that are necessary for establishment of the organization as a nonprofit corporate entity. Finally, the board will need to obtain tax-exempt status from the state and federal governments and local if necessary. These last three steps are very important to the organization and legal assistance may be necessary.

To assure the smooth processing of the organization's business and make a fluid transition, the board will find it necessary to appoint permanent committee chairs and committees from within the board and then from the general membership. Again, this course may only be a formality. The board may choose to appoint those who have already held positions on the temporary committees.

Beginning A Corporate Planning Process

All the official elements should be in place at this time. Now it is time to begin the work of the organization. Planning processes should be put in place. Emphasis on the word *process* is important. There needs to be a plan for planning. Having goals and objectives is of significant concern for any organization; knowing what the mission is and how to achieve it is the key.

A major concern is having a plan for achieving the mission. Following a corporate planning procedure will not only assure the group of a higher potential of meeting the community need, but also it will also give future direction and vigor to the organization that will be needed to sustain it.

A corporate planning process is a systems approach to planning. It will become a continuous, methodical yet flexible process. Every level of the organization needs to become involved in planning for their own areas of responsibility. Joined into one integral unit, the plans will move the organization to achieving its goals.

The process identified in the next section should only be applied where needed for a new organization. Again, keeping it simple is the key. The emphasis needs to be on adapting the concepts and suggestions to the needs of the new organization.

Keeping the planning informal, using only those concepts that will apply, and collecting and retaining only data needed for continuing the process will cause the process to be much more effective.

The planning process is a tool that should be used to assure accomplishment of the organization's mission. It should not become a superficial exercise and the leadership should not allow the process to become overwhelming in detail and focus. It needs to be a motivating tool for the organization's volunteers.

Corporate Planning – A Systematic Approach

All of the concepts in this next section have been taken and adopted from work developed over many years by Dr. James M. Hardy. Fondly known as "Bo" by many who have worked with him in the nonprofit sector, Dr. Hardy has developed an intensive corporate planning process for nonprofit organizations for use as an organizational tool in meeting their missions. Nonprofit organizations have had a tremendous impact on all of us. They have become an essential element in our lives and will become even more important in our futures.

Hardy (1984) states that nonprofit organizations are here to provide or facilitate human care services which will contribute to the improvement of the quality of life in our society. Hardy feels that management of a nonprofit organization is complex due in part to the volunteer nature of the organization. Although Hardy sees the voluntary character of nonprofits as a strength, he also believes that management practices in nonprofit organizations need to be planned for and will become more complex as the organization increases in size.

This chapter up to this point has dealt with development of nonprofit organizations that are totally voluntary in nature. Growth of the organization and the range of activities and programs the organization has will determine whether or not a paid management staff will be needed. The following concepts can be utilized in the planning process by voluntary leaders, paid staff, or a combination. In a voluntary organization, management of the planning process should be a shared responsibility on both levels.

Planning is a systematic arrangement for determining in advance what an organization is going to do, when and how it will be done, and who is to do it. Corporate planning for nonprofit organizations is a method for identifying ahead of time the programs and services as well as organizational maintenance tasks that will effect the accomplishment of the mission.

Hardy, who has developed the corporate planning process for nonprofits by working with hundreds of organizations over the years, has given 10 characteristics to corporate planning. They will assist in defining the purpose and necessity for nonprofit organizations, particularly new organizations, to conduct organizational planning.

According to Hardy in his book *Managing for Impact in Nonprofit Organizations* (1984), the elements that combine to make corporate planning unique are:

- *Comprehensive* — All levels of the organization are involved in the process — all partake in determining how their individual units (i.e., committees) will accomplish their plans for programs, finances, volunteers, etc.
- *Integrated* — Each committee's plans become integrated into one plan for the whole organization giving definitive direction.
- *Long-range dimension* — It can give an organization a plan that can last up to 5 years. It is based on where the organization wants to go rather than focusing on past or present operating pressures.
- *Process totality* — It includes long-range goals with short-range objectives and takes into account resources available and past successes or failures, while making sure all organizational levels, regardless of function, are included.
- *Maximizes collaboration* — Internal cooperation between organizational levels and working with outside agencies will put an emphasis on utilizing resources to the fullest.
- *Enhances ownership* — The corporate planning process will rely on involvement and participation at all levels. Volunteers develop ownership of the organization's goals and objectives if they are part of their establishment.
- *Ongoing, dynamic management process* — Not only does corporate planning give the organization direction, it also gives management a step-by-step plan by which to lead the group. It is an ongoing tool for the administrative leaders.
- *Differentiates between volunteer and staff responsibilities* — Cooperation and partnership between volunteers and staff are critical and will be facilitated as corporate planning delineates specific responsibilities owned by each.
- *Effects a congruence between personal and organizational goals* — Individual influence in selecting the organization's goals, which is facilitated by the corporate planning process, allows for personal and organizational goals to be achieved.
- *Flexible and action oriented* — Because of its flexible nature and because it requires a set course of action, corporate planning encourages participation that is creative, committed, and open to change.

Corporate planning is not problem solving. Rather, it avoids organizational pitfalls by planning for their elimination. However, according to Hardy, "...It is important to recognize the differences between planning and problem solving in order to further clarify the nature of corporate planning and in order to use the skills of problem solving in a comprehensive planning effort" (1984, pp. 7–8).

A new organization, particularly if it is small in size, may not realize the rewards offered by adapting a corporate planning process. The organization's members may view a corporate planning process as a burden and prefer to set goals less methodically or formally. But the dividends that can be received will show the true benefit of the time invested in implementing such a process.

The advantages that Hardy found were most often identified by executives of nonprofits that have incorporated such a process. The advantages identified by his years of consulting with a variety of nonprofit organizations are summarized in the following discussion.

Corporate planning gives direction to the organization, gives it a road map to follow with a destination in mind. In providing coordination to the organization it, therefore, increases the impact of resources that are usually limited to nonprofits while at the same time giving the organization a tool for measuring progress.

Because goals are definitive, the ability for members of the organization to interpret the purpose to the public is expedited. As the corporate plan identifies specific roles and tasks for volunteers and staff, personal involvement is enriched and enthusiasm for the mission is enhanced. Staff members ease into the tasks of management and have the ability to make judgments as to the overall impact the organization is having on the social problem. This, in turn, affects the organization's ability to determine how to go about meeting the future societal needs. Corporate planning allows the group to focus on its potential, redirecting energies from crisis management to meeting prospective goals.

A real advantage is that evidence of sound planning can position the organization in a very positive light with contributors and potential volunteers. However, evidence of practicing the plan needs to be clear. This will be seen as an attribute in the eyes of funding institutions.

There can be some traps to corporate planning. One is that the leadership will create too much paperwork in an effort to keep all levels informed of the process. This can become encumbering and unproductive. The leaders would need to control the flow of paper, limiting information to individuals, based on what their planning needs are. Also, too many goals can overwhelm an organization. Goals need to be set based on available volunteers to carry out the tasks and resources to meet the physical and financial needs. A new organization should set small goals initially and build on successes for the future.

Five Levels to the Planning Process

There are many ways to go about determining a planning process. Keeping it simple will produce benefits for the organization and individuals involved in it.

Ideal Goals.   Setting the ideal goal of the organization is the mission or reason for being. Elimination of child abuse is the chief ideal this book is addressing. In developing an organization that would deal with the elimination of child abuse, it may be necessary to be more specific in defining the ideal goal. For instance, the "education of the public" on the issues surrounding the child could be an ideal goal.

According to Hardy (1984), "an organization's purpose, mission, ideals, beliefs and philosophies represent a critical base for effective corporate planning. An ideal goal that clearly expresses the organization's reason for being provides general direction and a unification of effort within which definitive planning can be accomplished" (p. 67).

In the first of the step to getting organized, the original leaders identified the potential purpose and mission of the organization. The formulation of the actual ideal goal should include others both inside and outside the organization, if desired.

This goal needs to be based on community needs that have gone unmet and the ability and potential of the organization to meet those needs. Relying on past experiences will be impossible if the organization is new, but relying on the experiences of similar organizations may be helpful in formulating the goal.

The amount of time and energy devoted to establishing an ideal goal depends on the size of the organization and how well defined its prestated purpose is.

Ideal goals are generally broad in scope and set a general philosophical tone for the organization. Hardy (1984) outlines five criteria for ideal goals. In summary, he says that the statement should identify the essential reason for being; be community rather than organizationally oriented; be stable, not requiring future adjustment; describe the ultimate result; and reflect values and philosophy that will hold true for today and in the future (p. 60).

Once the ideal goal had been stated, the development of corporate or operational goals would be the next step.

Corporate or Operational Goals.   Corporate goals become the road map for the organization, which should be followed by all of the established committees. The corporate goals should each have a set of expected outcomes or a description of what will happen when the goal is achieved. These expected outcomes give further direction to the committees required to carry out the goals.

For a new organization, corporate goals should be limited in their set time span for achievement. Usually, in a well-established organization, 5-year goals are the norm. However, 2- to 3-year goals would be recommended for the first few years of operation of a newly formed organization.

Corporate goals need to be formulated very carefully, as they comprise the essential plan of the organization. However, they should not be drafted without first retrieving certain information.

Since a new organization has no data base of previous internal operation, determining its strengths or weaknesses could not be based on experience. Rather, it would need to be based on three things.

First, the organization's leaders would need to determine what its financial prospects would be to fund the work of the group. This could be determined by the amount of funds generated by the initial membership campaign and from the potential of outside funding. Second, the number of volunteers that have been recruited to conduct the organization's business should be considered; filling positions of leadership would be the key to determining the organization's strengths. Finally, the opinions of key people will be very helpful in gauging the organization's strengths and weaknesses as well as identifying potential corporate goals.

The retrieval of external data and the evaluation of societal trends and opportunities have already been done in step two. This information and the preliminary goals the group developed will be invaluable in establishing corporate goals.

Once internal and external data have been recovered, the board of directors and key volunteers need to draft the corporate goals. After they have been tested on the group and reworked, expected outcomes should be developed to give more clarification to each goal.

Objectives.   Meeting the goals requires a third level of planning, which is setting objectives. Following the outcomes identified by the corporate goals, objectives become individual statements that show how the goal will be accomplished. Each objective will have a date by which it will be achieved. Who will provide primary leadership for the particular objective and how important the objective is to achieving the goal will also be identified. Also, the objective will give clear measurement indices for determining when an objective has been realized.

Each corporate goal may have numerous objectives or just a few. The complexity of the goal will determine the number of objectives required to fulfill it. Certain goals can be achieved in a variety of ways. For instance, a new organization designed to combat child abuse may designate a corporate goal to educate all the kindergartners, in a given school district, on child abuse.

The organization's method for achieving this goal could be accomplished through numerous objectives, limited only by the imagination and resources available. For instance, developing or conducting theatrical plays, age-appropriate publications, use of video productions, and even group storytelling events could become objectives or means to achieve the goal of educating kindergartners. Objectives can contribute to the accomplishment of one or more goals but the associations between the goals and the objectives need to be well formulated and direct.

According to Hardy, there should be two kind of objectives for the organization: operational objectives and effectiveness objectives. Operational objectives would relate to maintaining the organization, helping it to operate more efficiently or expanding its scope. Effectiveness objectives would relate specifically to the activities the organization would carry out, improving on what is being done.

Hardy (1984) recommends that when formulating objectives certain criteria should be met for each objective. The following are those that would apply to a small, totally volunteer nonprofit organization.

- Is the objective designed to contribute to the achievement of one or more corporate goals?
- Is the objective feasible in light of internal and external constraints?
- Is the objective measurable? Are results observable?
- Were those who will be affected by the objective involved in the process of formulation?
- Does the objective have "reach" and challenge to it? (pp. 129–130).

Objectives should not be duplicated in more than one committee within the organization. In other words, objectives should be brought into accord with the entire organization's efforts. Committees should not be working against each other. The step-by-step procedure for accomplishing the objective is known as the action steps.

Action Steps.   Critical to the achievement of objectives, action steps are very specific in nature, identifying activities to be conducted. Additionally, they mark which individuals within the organization will be responsible for attaining each action step. Also, dates for attainment should be identified for each action step. The time span for action steps is usually very short, depending on the activity, and is often under 12 months.

When developing action steps, it is necessary to understand what financial and physical resources are available, the amount of time needed to accomplish the task, and the availability of volunteers to accomplish it.

Reviewing Performance.   The corporate planning process is one that should involve continual renewal giving closure to the five-step cycle and making the goals and objectives concrete rather than just ideas.

Going through a methodical, yet simple, process of review on each objective, on an ongoing basis, is important to charting the progress of achievement of the organization's goals. This performance review will enhance the probability of success for each objective.

Situations can change, personnel can turn over, financial resources can vanish, all creating conditions that can alter the attainability of an objective or eliminate it entirely. The review process facilitates the organization's ability to stay on top of any changes that can affect it.

However, key to the review process is the measurability of each objective and the involvement of the leadership in their formulation and the corresponding action steps.

The review process should be conducted by a key board member, committee chairperson, and the person or persons responsible for each objective. The process should be positive and helpful in nature and should provide an opportunity or adjustment of the objective. Timely appraisal of objectives' progress will further enhance the organization's chances for success.

Dynamics of Group Process

Interpersonal relationships throughout an organization affect the general psychological climate of that organization. Likewise, the attitudes of the organization, and its structural makeup, can affect the interpersonal relations of the group members.

Problems of Content and Process

Content is the literal task, what the group is working on at a particular time. For instance, members could be developing a new budget of determining a way to promote an educational program. The way the organization is structured, how that structure affects the member's ability to work on the content of the organization, and the indirect problems that can affect the group's ability to function involve process.

The success of the corporate planning process and the ultimate success of the organization are dependent on the human dimensions involved. Blending the two elements, content and process, is a function of leadership. Following the clearcut corporate planning process may not be as easy a task as it seems. Interpersonal relationships and how the leadership harmonizes the interworkings of group members will be a major factor in the group's ability to accomplish outlined tasks.

The behavior of the key leaders, their belief in the group members' ability to accomplish the task, through acknowledgment and delegation, will create a climate for success. Group members will perform as they are expected to perform.

However, as interpersonal problems emerge and group dynamics take hold, the leadership's ability to act as quarterback, recognizing how the group is operating, and taking appropriate action is critical. Having the technical skills and being able to conceptualize the function and purpose of the organization are ineffective without the leader's ability to apply human skills to the group process.

Group Mind

The leader's ability and the perceptions and consequent actions of other group members to affect the group mind or atmosphere will have an effect on the group functioning. The personality of the group, its cohesiveness, the outside pressures, and the group's ability to conform to the corporate plan will all be elements the leader will need to take into account.

In a newly established group, situations can become ambiguous or the process of organization can become too complex for those involved only on the periphery of leadership. When people do not understand what's happening, they tend to yield their own judgment to others, becoming dependent. In an organization devoted to eliminating child abuse, knowledge of the social problem is critical to avoiding ambiguous situations and voids of understanding.

People also tend to become too independent, relying on their own judgment, feelings, and impressions as a guide to action and participation. A void in the leadership can cause this independence. And, like dependency, it is a situation that is nonproductive.

A mature group, which is often the exception rather than the rule, has a good mixture of both. There is a certain level of interdependence among group members. Synergy and collaboration begin to become the group mind with a high level of independent thinking and action present. This only occurs when group and personal differences are resolved. Interdependence occurs at certain moments during the life of an organization. Keeping the frequency of those moments and thereby increasing the productivity of the group is dependent on the complexity of the task and the ability of the leadership.

Group Maturity and Growth

Resolving the group and personal differences and the ability to meet conflict depends significantly on the communication skills of the group members. As in one-on-one personal relationships, effective group functioning and the level of group maturity depends on group members' ability to sort through the difficulties a group, particularly a new one, may face.

Group maturity and growth will also depend on its ability to adapt to the external and internal pressures. It will depend on its capacity to remain focused on the goals set and its ability to integrate the different committees within the organization, while maintaining unity. Group maturity and growth is also contingent on the group's ability to absorb new members, conveying the group's goals and modes of operations.

Individual vs. Group Productivity

Many other issues will influence individual productivity and thereby group productivity. The group size, makeup of group membership, the basis for participation, the time for personal involvement, time allotted for the accomplishment of tasks, and the compatibility of personal and group goals are all components in group productivity. Naturally, group productivity will increase or decrease depending on all of these factors. In most groups it is unusual to see high levels of productivity sustained for long periods of time from the group as a whole. High individual productivity needs to be a frequent occurrence among members for the group to have a high level of productivity.

This high level of individual productivity is enhanced when individual and group goals compliment each other. The tasks at hand seem to become just as important as the individual's reason for participation. Keeping group members motivated is very difficult and depends on the leader's ability to identify what motivates members.

Structure

When a group is highly structured, group members become more concerned with the task than with group process. When this happens, the group moves more quickly toward the goal. This only allows for surface communication and relationships. The main leaders maintain more power over the group in a highly structured organization.

When a group has low structure, there is a greater deference to the group process and members' feelings. The task becomes secondary.

A median level of structure would be more productive for the group. The focus on the task would still be evident but the inclusion of the opinions and feelings of all members of the group would be more possible.

Conflict

Conflict within a group is handled in a variety of ways. Eliminating any opposition or ganging up against opposition can be counterproductive. Working within the structure of the group to come to compromises or integrating adverse ideas into new methods would be the most efficient way to handle conflict. The leadership plays a key role in bringing the group to compromise positions on issues or adapting opposing ideas.

Role/Morale/Communication

Individuals within a small group will take on natural roles that produce characteristic patterns of behavior, giving an individual a set place in a group. It is likely that unless the group makeup changes drastically the individual roles will carry over to each task the group pursues. Group morale will depend on the level of effectiveness the group has in achieving its goals and will emulate how members feel about belonging to the group. High morale is the key to the group's success.

Communication, as discussed earlier, can affect the group's success. There is both verbal and nonverbal communication within a group. Listening to each member of the group and overcoming questions of power and influence, making every member's participation count, is a function not only of the leadership but also of each member as well. The leadership of the group and the use of power that leadership exerts can be the "make-it or break-it" factor to the group's success in achieving its goals.

Case Studies

This chapter has primarily dealt with, up to this point, getting a community organization started. Nonprofit organizations have been the focus of the seven steps to getting organized. The corporate planning process for nonprofit organizations, as outlined primarily by Dr. James M. Hardy, has been presented in an adapted version. And, group dynamics has been discussed as an issue of effective group functioning.

Nonprofit organizations and community programs designed to alleviate child abuse have been popping up all over the country. Prevention and intervention programs have begun to be seen in growing numbers and strength as more and more groups recognize the very real, largely unmet need for programs of this type.

My experience with antichild abuse organizations has been limited on a personal level. Having been actively involved in one unsuccessful organizational effort, it has come to my attention that there needs to be more systematic approaches to community organization development, particularly in this area. As a result of further study, I have become aware of four organizations that have exhibited a high degree of success. In addition to identifying the negative components of the group with which I was personally involved, I will give brief summaries of three of the four organizations identified in the rest of the chapter. Learning from experience can prove to be very beneficial, but identifying role models early on will assist a fledgling organization in adopting positive characteristics of organizations. Each organization identified has positive qualities for emulation. There are, however, many other positive models across the nation that are doing an excellent job of organizing to combat child abuse.

Help Now

The name of the first group, Help Now, is fictitious to protect the organization. The group is still functioning, although in a limited capacity, and under completely different leadership than when I was associated with it. Hopefully the organization's leaders are incorporating better techniques in mobilizing their resources and in operating to meet their goals.

My experience with the group was brief, about 1 year, and became a very frustrating experience, indeed. The group, Help Now, was started by two women. One had an incredible amount of energy and enthusiasm for meeting the community need for alleviating child abuse. However, her lack of organizational skills, her ineffective leadership style, and her inability to motivate volunteers assisted in bringing about the near demise of the organization. One lone volunteer, who was a student in the field of social work, concentrating on child abuse, rescued the remains of the organization that still exists today.

The other organizer was the mother of two victims of child sexual abuse. Her motivations, although entirely pure, were based solely on personal experience. That type of motivation can be extremely helpful in starting an organization. However, her skill lay in her ability to act as a counselor to victims and their families. Like the other leader, her organizational experience was not evident, and she often deferred to her peers in organizational matters. Her skill in counseling brought to the group numerous volunteers who wanted primarily to meet personal needs centered around counseling and telling their own horror-stories. This was unproductive for the group, as it was difficult for the leadership to set aside feelings to focus on the group's purpose.

Unfortunately, the purpose of the group was very broad in scope. And the purpose had never been accurately articulated. The group's mission seemed to be to fight child abuse. It focused on starting education programs but began to overextend itself both in financial and human resources, which were very limited. Even their focus on education was ill defined. The group seemed to want to educate everyone in the community — school children, parents, educators, businessmen, and so on.

If the organization had been able to adopt a corporate plan and work to define their mission and goals, it may have been more successful. An attempt was made, but too late. By the time the corporate planning process was started, many of the volunteers had lost their commitment. Certainly, the community receptivity for such an organization was very positive in light of the recent awakening of awareness of the problems surrounding child abuse. Focusing on a few goals at a time, set within the group's limitations, would have been helpful to the organization's success.

The Prescott House — Birmingham, Alabama
Child Advocacy Center — Huntsville, Alabama

The Prescott House was started as an effort to pull together the various disciplines related to the prosecution of child abuse cases. The program was modeled after the Child Advocacy Center in Huntsville, Alabama, which, along with the Prescott House, now stands as a positive example of community development.

The Jefferson County District Attorney's Office in Birmingham, Alabama, undertook the task of establishing a center under one roof where child victims and their families and the child protection professionals could come together. The Prescott House, which is a nonprofit organization with a board of directors and a staff, is more than just a house. The house operates under the Jefferson County Child Abuse Prosecution Project, started by Jefferson County District Attorney, David Barber. The house provides a warm, friendly, and nonthreatening environment and services that address the very special needs of children who have been abused.

Its main mission or purpose is to simplify the process a child victim goes through, easing him or her into the criminal justice systems. One goal is that the Prescott House will alter the child victims's and family's perceptions of the criminal justice system. Another goal is to gain the cooperation of various law enforcement agencies and child protection professionals in the community in providing a variety of services to the victims and their families.

The expected outcome of these goals is the maximization of the chances for effective prosecution and serve the best interests of the child victims. Prescott House provides the following services:

- Coordinating efforts in preparing the child victims and their families for the criminal prosecution process, preventing further victimization.
- Providing the child with consistency and support.
- Providing immediate therapy interventions for victims and their families, early on, when the chances of success are highest.
- Coordinating investigations with all involved professionals from an initial screening to final disposition.
- Mobilizing and training community resources and health care providers to better identify the child abuse victim and to work with the criminal justice system.
- Assuring the child adequate protection and well-being through ongoing monitoring (McGregor, 1987).

A community effort, the Prescott House is jointly funded by a grant from the Alabama Department of Economic and Community Affairs, the Jefferson County District Attorney's office, and local community support through donations and in-kind services. The grant and funding by the DA's office will eventually subside causing the Prescott House to be self-sufficient.

The actual house itself was purchased by a volunteer and is leased back to the organization. Hundreds of volunteer hours and thousands of dollars of in-kind services were donated to ready the house for its mission. The level of cooperation from within the organization and from the community leaders has been high and somewhat unprecedented. The leadership in both the Prescott House and the Huntsville Child Advocacy Center seems to have been the predominate factor in each organization's success.

Establishing a mission, which was generated from statistical data derived from child abuse cases, was the first step. This was articulated by the primary leadership well in advance to generating community support and cooperation from the various child protection professionals. The data showed the inability to adequately prosecute a majority of child abuse cases because of a variety of factors. One factor was the unstructured approach and often confusing method of handling cases on the part of the agencies involved. There was no centralized coordination preparing the victims for the prosecution because the court system further traumatized the child. Another factor was that because of a lack of training and understanding of the problems of child abuse on the part of officials, it was difficult to generate sufficient cooperation and evidence to effectively prosecute and achieve conviction. Often cases were dismissed or reduced on a plea because of the child victim's inability to testify, which can largely be traced to fear and confusion on the part of the child.

Once the mission was established, the goals and objectives of the Prescott House, as was the same in the case of the Huntsville Child Advocacy Center, became clearcut. Through hard work on the part of the staffs and boards of each center, efforts are directed toward achieving these goals. The Prescott House and the Huntsville Child Advocacy Center are models for community collaboration and a visible example of how effective a nonprofit organization can be.

Kid-Ability — Girl's Club of Omaha

Another model for effective operation of a community organization designed to combat child abuse is the Girls Club of Omaha's Kid-Ability, a program which has been adopted by the Girls Clubs of America across the country.

It is primarily a preventative education program for parents and their children ages 6 to 12. The program helps the child acquire "the knowledge and skills needed to grow up safely" (*Kid-Ability*, 1987). The Kid-Ability program has three components:

- Information for parents and educators.
- Training for adult program volunteers (facilitators).
- Training for children including films, discussions, role playing, and small and large group activities.

The Kid-Ability program's main goal is to teach children the difference between normal, healthy, loving touching and that which is potentially dangerous. The program frees children from fears.

The expected outcomes for children who take part in this program are that they will:

- Build self-confidence in their ability to protect themselves.
- Identify potentially dangerous situations and learn to avoid them.
- Distinguish between appropriate and inappropriate touching.
- Identify people in their lives they could ask for help and practice doing so assertively.

Kid-Ability is a program that was modeled after the Girl's Club of Portsmouth, Virginia's program, Cat and Mouse. Out of 2,700 concept papers submitted for funding, Kid-Ability was awarded a $150,017 grant from the U.S. Department of Health and Human Services. Over a 15-month period, they developed a national training and replication project to help youth service professionals from girl's clubs and other agencies to implement their own Kid-Ability programs.

The program already has had an impressive record of success on a statewide level in Nebraska. Since the program's inception in 1982, over 10,000 school-age children have learned to protect themselves from physical and sexual abuse and to practice assertiveness techniques and responses.

Mary Kay Hockabout, director of National Kid-Ability, stated, "There is more to this program than 'Don't talk to strangers.' It is the most comprehensive program of its kind in the United States. Kid-Ability teaches self-protection rather than self-defense" (personal communication, May 1988). The Kid-Ability name alone clearly identifies the mission or purpose of the program, which is teaching kids how to use their abilities to protect themselves.

The National Exchange Club —
Centers for the Prevention of Child Abuse

In the spring of 1979, the National Exchange Club adopted the prevention of child abuse as a national project. Subsequently, the National Exchange Club Foundation for the Prevention of Child Abuse was established to diminish the tragedy of child abuse. The organization utilized the services of a private agency in Arkansas to implement an effective treatment modality based on a voluntary therapy intervention approach.

The foundation, with headquarters in Toledo, Ohio, is chartered as a non-profit corporation by the state of Ohio. It is administered by a board of trustees consisting of business and professional men selected from the membership of local exchange clubs.

The primary objective of the program is to train volunteer parent aides who enter the homes of abusive families. It is intended that the supportive relationship that develops between the volunteer parent aide and the family breaks the abusive cycle.

Volunteer parent aides are recruited, trained, and supervised by the local exchange club center staff. Parent aides are expected to visit the family a minimum of four times weekly to establish the relationship necessary for change and to confirm that abuse no longer exists.

Exchange club centers also are instrumental in establishing multidisciplinary teams, parental classes, and numerous other auxiliary programs as a part of their total effort. Naturally, this depends on the particular need and the area to be served. Each local exchange club center has an agreement with their local department of social services guaranteeing referrals and in some locations, providing funding.

The following are the goals of the Exchange Club Centers for the Prevention of Child Abuse:

• Reduce child abuse and neglect through the exchange lay therapy and other auxiliary services.
• Keep families together when possible by maximizing the potentials parents have in resolving their difficulties.

- Provide information on child care and management, modeling of effective parental techniques and support to parents to enhance parent/child relationships (National Exchange Club, 1979).

The National Exchange Club Foundation for the Prevention of Child Abuse provides the local exchange clubs with information on how to institute a center, articles of incorporation and bylaws, information and guidelines for determining a budget, and fund-raising ideas. They also provide guidelines for publicity for recruitment of volunteers, a sample interagency agreement, and a personnel policy.

Clearly, the National Exchange Club's program for combatting child abuse, on the local level, the resources that it provides to its local chapter, and the method by which it pursues its mission should be applauded. It is also an excellent example of a community organization designed to eliminate a serious social problem.

Conclusions

The formulas and suggestions identified in this chapter do not guarantee the success of a community-based organization. However, they will enhance the probability of success. Efforts will be rewarded if an organized approach is used in developing a community organization, an approach that has much forethought and that is based on real community needs.

Even the success stories I have outlined probably had many pitfalls along the way. But the essential elements must have been in place to cause these organizations to be successful:

- Appropriate, qualified, and dedicated leadership.
- A committed body of community leaders.
- Availability of financial and human resources.
- A solid case for the community need.
- A well-defined mission or purpose.
- A receptive community.
- A plan for action with continuous review.
- An atmosphere for positive group dynamics.

Developing a community organization takes much more than these elements. It requires something that cannot be quantified or organized. That element is the human compassion to right a wrong against our children to solve this outrageous social dilemma. Community organization requires people who care for the child victims of abuse. Concern for others put into action through an organization is a noble accomplishment. The maturity of our society can be gauged by the depth of accomplishments achieved through its ability and desire to organize for the betterment of its people.

Glossary

Action steps — Step-by-step procedures for accomplishing objectives specific in nature.

Case for support — Documentation and collaborative evidence showing reason for supporting an organization and its mission.

Charter membership — Those individuals who are the first to join or support an organization; a select body with a limited membership who join for the life of the organization for a premium.

Comprehensive planning — Organizational planning that is done, including all levels and functions of the organization for unified direction.

Content — The literal task on which members of a group are working at a particular time.

Corporate goals — A description of a desired future providing definitive organizational direction.

Corporate planning — Formal long-range planning conducted within a corporation, including all levels of the organization and giving futuristic direction; a process that is a systematic approach to planning for an organization.

Effectiveness objectives — Objectives that relate specifically to the activities the organization would carry out, improving on what is being done.

Group mind — Way, state, or direction of thinking or feeling a group has as one body at a particular time.

Group process — The methods by which a group functions both formally and informally.

Ideal goal — A description of the ideal or reason for an organization's existence; statement of mission.

Incorporation — To form individuals or units into a legally organized group that acts as one individual body.

Mission — An organization's purpose or reason for existing.

Mission identification — The process through which an organization goes to specifically identify and articulate its mission or purpose.

Negative group dynamics — Interpersonal and intergroup relationships and interactions that cause group dysfunction.

Nonprofits — Organization whose reason for existing is for the good of society rather than intending to earn a profit.

Objectives — Specifically measurable statements of attainable outcome that are strived for on an annual basis to meet corporate goals.

Operational objectives — Objectives that relate to maintaining the organization, helping it to operate more efficiently, or to expand its scope.

Programs — Tools an organization uses to carry out its mission.

References

General information: National exchange club foundation for the prevention of child abuse. (1979). Toledo, Ohio: National Exchange Club.

Hardy, J. (1984). *Managing for impact in nonprofit organizations*. Erwin, Tennessee: Essex Press.

Kid Ability (1978). Omaha, Nebraska: Girls' Club of Omaha.

McGregor, M. (1987). *Under one roof*. Birmingham, Alabama: The Prescott House.

Chapter 7

Child Sexual Abuse: A Review of Research

Mary de Chesnay
Debbie Stephens
Leslie West

In the other chapters of this book, attention has been paid to the topic of abuse, whether physical, emotional, or sexual. This chapter will focus only on sexual abuse because the volume of material covered on research in sexual abuse constitutes sufficient information to compose an entire chapter.

Problems in conducting research on sexual abuse were identified in the areas of design, methods, and sampling. Therefore, an analysis of the research literature can assist future investigators to design better studies.

Similar suggestions would also be made for future directions for research. These would include the need for quantitative studies to be well done – with random samples, adequate sample size, comparison groups, and thorough treatment of validity and reliability. The theory and or premise on which the study stands should be explicit. The review of the literature should support the need for the study. Qualitative studies are also needed.

The cultural taboo against talking about child sexual abuse seems to have been reversed in recent years. There are literally hundreds of articles, news items, feature stories, and films on incest and other forms of the sexual abuse of children by adults. The research literature is fast catching up with the popular literature as investigators turn their attention to the critical problem of child sexual abuse.

For this chapter, the authors reviewed nearly 100 studies from the past several years to discover the major areas of interest for researchers. The articles were identified by computer searches of the medical, social science, and education literatures. The primary limitation is that only readily accessible materials were analyzed, and there might be valuable studies conducted as dissertations or presented at research conferences that are, as yet, unpublished.

First, the authors examined the articles to determine the focus and found that the two largest categories were concerned with effects on victims and incidence/prevalence. Some work has also been done on families and offenders. No cross-cultural studies were found, but several investigators used non-U.S. samples, and these were treated as a separate group in addition to reviewing them in terms of their primary focus.

The purpose of the chapter is to articulate a position on the state of the art of the accessible, published research on child sexual abuse. With this in mind, three objectives emerged:

1. Summarize the major findings about victims, offenders, and families.
2. Present a concise statement about the level of development of research.
3. Suggest future directions for research.

It is hoped that this chapter will suggest ways in which professionals can intervene more effectively in terms of aid to victims, prosecution, and rehabilitation of offenders, development of policy, and prevention.

Findings

Impact on the Victim

The impact of child sexual abuse has been studied by many investigators in terms of initial response and long-term effects. An extensive review of the research has recently been completed by Browne and Finkelhor (1986). This section will summarize the areas of agreement and disagreement and will include a few studies not cited by Browne and Finkelhor. Our conclusions are consistent with theirs in that there are well-documented, negative initial, and long-term effects of child sexual abuse on the victim.

Most of the studies reviewed did not use standardized measures and relied on retrospective accounts; therefore, it is difficult to obtain a precise profile of common reactions. However, most survivors report negative reactions (some form of distress), but the nature of the response varied a great deal, depending on the form, duration, and frequency of the abuse.

Courtois (1980) reported that the worst severe initial effects experienced by the 30 women surveyed were related to sense of self (63%), psychological (47%), social (30%), and relations with men (30%). For long-term effects, the percentages were: sense of self (47%), social (43%), relations with men (37%), psychological (33%), and sexual (30%). Similar distributions were reported on a sample of 21 women interviewed by Brunngraber (1986).

Gold (1986) reported on 103 adult survivors and a control group of 88 nonvictims. Survivors differed significantly from the control group on level of depression, psychological distress, and self-esteem. Gold suggested that the victim's adult functioning was strongly related to her attributional style for bad events and quality of social support.

Two samples of adult survivors—a nonclinical sample and a group of outpatients—were studied by Herman, Russell, and Trocki (1986). They found that all the women reported severe initial distress, and half of the women perceived substantial lasting effects. Nearly one third believed that the abuse had some lasting impact on their lives, even if they did not believe it was severe. The most severe effects were related to abuse by a father or stepfather.

The incidence of assault-related, sexual functioning problems was striking (41%) in a study of 371 survivors (Becker, Skinner, Abel, Axelrod, & Cichon, 1984). The investigators suggested cognitive restructuring as a way of helping survivors relabel their sexual feelings.

The preceding studies used adult survivors of childhood sexual abuse and have problems inherent in any retrospective account. The following studies, however, used child and adolescent respondents, and some studies included validation measures for the self-reported symptoms.

Scott and Stone (1986) compared Minnesota Multiphasic Personality Inventory (MMPI) measures of psychological disturbance. Twenty-seven adolescents and 31 adults who had been molested by their fathers or stepfathers as children were evaluated. Both groups produced overall elevated profiles, on the MMPI, especially on the alienation scale. There was evidence of schizoid process and ego-strength deficits, as well as sexual preoccupation and concerns of inadequacy and vulnerability.

Self-destructive behaviors, such as substance abuse, suicide attempts, perfectionism, isolation, and depression, were recorded on a sample of 27 adolescent victims (Lindberg & Distad, 1985). Prostitution is a more frequent outcome also for victims of childhood sexual abuse (James & Meyerding, 1977). In some cases, children do physical harm to themselves – cutting, slashing, bruising, self-poisoning, and attempting to break bones (de Young, 1982).

Child sexual abuse has been linked to a variety of mental and psychogenic illnesses – chronic pain (Gross, Doerr, Caldirola, Guzinski, & Ripley, 1980–1981), depression (Blumberg, 1981), hysterical seizures (Goodwin, Simms, & Bergman, 1979; Gross, 1979), acting out and sexual acting out (Adams-Tucker, 1982; Emslie & Rosenfield, 1983; Friedrich, Urquiza, & Beilke, 1986; Kohan, Pothier, & Norbeck, 1987), ego deficits (Scott & Thoner, 1986), and premenstrual affective syndrome (Friedman, Hurt, Clarkin, Corn, & Aronoff, 1982).

Sexual preoccupation is also a sequel to sexual abuse. The assessment of sexual preoccupation can be an important clinical tool for diagnosis and treatment. Three studies were found that established an association between a history of sexual abuse and the presence of genitalia in children's drawings (Hibbard, Roghmann, & Hoekelman, 1987; Wohl & Kaufman, 1985; Yates, Beutler, & Crago, 1985). The investigators warned that the absence of genitalia in a child's drawing does not exclude the possibility of abuse, just as the presence does not prove abuse. However, it does seem reasonable to use children's drawings as a valid projective technique for assessing child sexual abuse.

Usually, when physical effects of sexual abuse are discussed in the literature, the effects have a related psychogenic origin (e.g., the somatizing and sleep disorders associated with anxiety and distress). It is widely noted in the theoretical literature that there is a high incidence of venereal disease and pregnancy among child victims of sexual abuse, but few studies were found that specifically addressed these conditions or the presence of trauma. This was surprising because the documentation of physical trauma is a key feature of the prosecution of offenders.

The medical literature is cited in chapter 4, so only three recent research reports will be discussed. A study was done at Johns Hopkins that helps in assessing the likelihood of sexual abuse in children who have genital tract papillomavirus infection, a disease that, in adults, is transmitted by sexual contact. The researchers demonstrated that the viral types in children were the same as in adults, but that some were not necessarily transmitted by adults to children via a venereal route, primarily in cases that infected adults who bathed with children. The investigators concluded that the presence of the infection did not necessarily indicate sexual abuse but cited literature that indicated transmission is usually venereal (Rock, Naghashfar, Barnett, Buscema, Woodruff, & Shah, 1986).

The small sample size and lack of a control group indicates the findings are not generalizable. However, it does seem reasonable to assume and rule out sexual abuse in cases of genital infections as opposed to discounting the possibility and failing to conduct further assessments.

A less common marker for sexual abuse is the presence of labial fusion or adhesions of the labia minora. Incidence and prevalence rates for these cases are uncertain, but Berkowitz, Elvik, and Logan (1987) found 10 cases in a sample of 500 medical records of patients age 2 months to 5 years referred for sexual abuse evaluations. History and other physical findings were consistent with a diagnosis of sexual abuse in 6 cases. Grossly abnormal anal findings were consistent with anal penetration in 5 patients.

In a prospective study, McCauley, Gorman, and Guzinsky (1986) established that the use of toluidine blue dye in pediatric patients can help in detecting perineal lacerations. The presence of lacerations in the posterior fourchette region of the perineum strongly suggests sexual abuse. In a 1-year study, 49 cases were identified in the emergency room, and all participated in the study. Of the 49 victims, 24 were 6 months to 10 years old, with an average age of 5, 11 were younger than age 4, and 25 were adolescents.

The findings of these studies have implications not only for clinicians but also for others who participate in the assessment and treatment of sexual abuse because the physical findings might be neglected in the overall assessment. Children who engage in masturbation or who report irritation on urination or defecation should be referred for medical evaluation. Too often the concern is with obtaining evidence and not with treating the condition to prevent chronic physical problems that may result from sexual abuse.

Finally, despite many theoretical articles on how to treat child sexual abuse, only two studies were found that examined treatment outcomes and these only spoke to the need for conducting follow-up (Byrne & Valdiserri, 1982; Vitulano, Lewis, Doran, Nordhaus, & Adnopoz, 1986).

Verleur, Hughes, and de Rios (1986) studied enhancement of self-esteem in adolescent incest victims. They conducted group therapy and sex education with 15 adolescent females and a matched control group. Results indicated a significant difference between groups on the self-esteem measures and knowledge about human sexuality, birth control, and venereal disease.

Kroth (1979) evaluated a family therapy treatment program by using a cross-sectional longitudinal design. In general, results indicated positive outcomes, but the authors discussed methodological limitations that limit the generalizability of the findings.

Both studies suggest that the impact on the victim can be minimized, but it is clear that much more needs to be done in the way of developing and evaluating effective treatments. Perhaps one barrier is the fact that most people who are among the first contacts for disclosure (friends, teachers, school counselors, emergency room nurses, and social workers) do not conduct research. Most clinicians who treat sexual abuse are not primarily researchers – even if they have been trained in graduate schools to conduct research. So, it is natural that the people conducting the research are interested in other questions. Collaboration and consultation among professionals would help to expand the body of research-based theory on child sexual abuse.

In summary, there seems to be a large enough body of research literature to make some definitive statements about the impact of child sexual abuse. In clinical and nonclinical populations, victims or survivors report that the experience was, at the least, distressing and often resulted in symptoms that required treatment.

A legitimate criticism of the existing research is that, even though some studies used control or comparison groups, no studies were found that examined the potential for presenting symptoms of adult distress to result from stressors other than child sexual abuse (i.e., would the woman have become depressed had she not been a victim?). The absence of such studies could be cited as evidence to support the claim that the effects are not really all that bad.

At least three things are wrong with this argument. First, failure to show direct linear causality between child sexual abuse and various forms of adult distress does not mean that being abused as a child was not a bad experience and that it did not contribute, even in a small way, to adult problems. Second, all of the studies used self-reports, either alone or in combination with other measures, such as the MMPI. Even if we assume a degree of fabricating or blaming the experience for one's current problems, it is clear that adult women perceived the experience as having an adverse effect on their lives. Finally, adverse effects can be assessed by objective measures in nonclinical populations of survivors, even when the woman claims that the experience was not harmful. For example, one such survivor indignantly insisted to the senior author that she was not harmed in any way by having her grandfather molest her as a child. In further conversation, the individual confided that she had had a very satisfying sex life with her husband. After having two children, she informed him they would no longer have a sexual relationship, but she loved him deeply and did not want a divorce. She reported no stressors in her life except being molested by her grandfather as a 4-year-old, but saw no connection between the assaults and her sexual anorexia with her husband. The woman denied having ever sought help, but she exhibited many negative signs of depression.

There is agreement that the victim's distress is exacerbated by a combinaton of relationship of the offender, genital contact, negative response of the person to whom the secret is disclosed, and institutionalized messages that blame the victim. A common clinical observation is that offenders threaten to kill the victim if he or she tells, but this is probably a contributing factor more to disclosure than to impact.

The role of duration as a contributing factor to trauma is controversial. In Browne and Finkelhor's review (1986), some studies found a direct relationship, some found no relationship, and one found an inverse relationship.

An area of consensus seems to be that adult survivors experience some form of self-image distortion that they usually, but not always, attribute to child sexual abuse. The degree and extent, however, to which this interferes with normal functioning have yet to be established.

With rare exceptions, the studies reviewed used quantitative designs. These are helpful in generalizing and establishing incidence and prevalence rates, but they are extremely limited in helping the people who work with these children and their families — teachers, counselors, clinicians, and health care providers. People who do the primary assessments and treatments need to understand the experience from the point of view of all the actors — victims, offenders, and families. Only qualitative designs can elicit this kind of data in any depth.

The major disagreements in the literature center around issues related to incidence and prevalence. Although these rates are important to examine, particularly because of their policy implications, it is much more valuable practically to examine the victim's experience in as many contexts as possible. Qualitative designs need to include ways to understand the victim's experience and her or his interpretation of each response. This work should be done before developing more treatments since treatment that is not framed in ways that are understandable to the client is not accepted and, consequently, is not effective.

Incidence and Prevalence

A meaningful study was conducted by Russell (1983). The incidence and prevalence of both intrafamilial and extrafamilial sexual abuse of female children were calculated based on the responses of 930 randomly selected adult women. It was found that 16% of these women reported at least 1 intrafamilial sexual assault, and 31% reported extrafamilial sexual abuse before the age of 18. Fifteen percent of the cases were committed by an unknown assailant, and only 8% of the total cases were ever reported to the police.

Russell's research design was clear and thorough. Randomly selected women were interviewed by highly trained and competent female interviewers using a carefully designed questionnaire. Russell not only elicited useful demographic data concerning sexual abuse but also offered possible interpretations of the data, in contrast to many others who examined incidence and prevalence. Russell's study is the only study that used a random sample from the general population. The remainder of the studies reviewed were limited to specific populations, and the results cannot be generalized to the general public.

Mims and Chang (1984) administered a questionnaire concerning unwanted sexual experiences occurring during childhood, adolescence, or adulthood to three different groups (i.e., military women, college women, and a group of women involved in a community service organization). Fifty-four percent of the women reported an unwanted sexual experience. Assault by a stranger accounted for only 12% of all the cases, abuse by a relative accounted for 22%, and 66% of the offenders were either husbands or friends. Two hundred sixteen incidences of sexual abuse occurred before the age of 18, and 180 after the age of 18. This study also reported whether or not the person ever disclosed the incident and to whom they turned as a source of help.

Gordon and O'Keefe (1984) studied frequencies of incest, as well as characteristics of both victims and offenders, in a historical review of social-service agencies' case records between 1880 and 1960. Using a mixed design, they found that (a) 10% of the randomly selected case records contained cases of incest, (b) the majority of the victims were female (93 of 97), (c) 38% of all cases lasted over 3 years, (d) fathers accounted for 48% of all sexual abuse, and (e) stepfathers were involved in 29% of the cases. Other factors, such as characteristics of the mother, alcoholism, and other stress factors, were also examined.

Two studies on prevalence rates among psychiatric populations were conducted by Kohan, Pothier, and Norbeck (1987) and Husain and Ahmad (1982). Kohan et al. (1987) used questionnaires with 110 inpatient child psychiatric units and found that 16% of the male patients and 48% of the female patients had a history of sexual abuse. Intrafamilial sexual abuse accounted for 72% of all cases, extrafamilial abuse for 35%, and pornography was involved in 5% of the cases. These figures indicate that some children were victimized by both relatives and nonrelatives. The study also examined behavioral characteristics of the children, clinical care issues, and staff-patient relationships.

Husain and Ahmad (1982) surveyed 437 adolescent females admitted to a psychiatric facility about possible sexual abuse and found that 23% reported a history of sexual abuse. Sixty-one percent of the offenders were relatives, 19% were friends of the family, and only 20% were strangers.

Finally, Simari and Baskin (1982) examined incidence, frequency rates, and effects of incest within the homosexual population. Gay organizations referred 29 female and 54 male homosexuals to complete a 16-page questionnaire. It was found that 38% of the females and 46% of the males had participated in an incestuous relationship at some point in their lives. In the majority of cases, the partner was an extended family member, most often a cousin, and in several cases the respondent was the initiator. In looking at attitudes toward the experience, the authors found that 77% of the males considered the incestuous experience positive. Females considered homosexual incestuous experiences positive, but all heterosexual incest was experienced negatively. Sexual preferences before the incident and family characteristics of the respondents were also explored.

Questionnaires mailed to physicians were used in two foreign studies – one conducted in Ireland and the other in the United Kingdom. The Ireland study (O'Rourke & Sweeney, 1983) had a return rate of 35%, representing 20 physicians in a particular county. Of the total 11 incest cases, 6 involved fathers and daughters (the article did not state whether natural father or stepfather). The United Kingdom study sampled a larger population with 1,599 doctors and child psychiatrists asked to complete questionnaires. From the 622 respondents, it was found that at least 3 per 1,000 children were being recognized as sexually abused. Intrafamilial abuse accounted for 43% of the total cases, and strangers were involved in only 26% of the cases. Females were the victims in 158 of the 183 cases, which detailed the sex (Mrazek, Lynch, & Bentovim, 1983).

In addition to these prevalence studies, six research reports that reviewed emergency room records of children with a history of sexual abuse were examined. Although neither prevalence nor incidence investigations, the data regarding characteristics of the victim and offender and their relationship is very helpful in studying the problem.

De Jong, Emmett, and Herrada (1982) reviewed emergency room records of 416 alleged cases of sexual abuse of children under the age of 16. They found that the majority of the victims were female (84%), 24% of the offenders were relatives, 23% of the offenders were friends or acquaintances of the family, and strangers were involved in 54% of the of the cases. Males were found to be at risk between the ages of 6 and 7 years, whereas girls had two ages of greater risk, 5–6 years old, and 14–15 years of age.

An additional study, which found a high number of strangers involved in the sexual abuse, was conducted by Enos, Conrath, and Byer (1986). They examined 162 emergency room records in which the sexual abuse victim was examined by a forensic specialist and found that abuse by strangers accounted for 41% of the cases. Intrafamilial sexual abuse was involved in 19% of the incidents. In 50% of these cases, the offender was the natural father, and in 33% of the episodes the offender was the stepfather. Females were the victims in 82%, and males were involved in 18% of the cases. Enos and colleagues also found that boys tended to be more at risk between the ages of 10 and 12, whereas females were more at risk at the age of 6 years and again at 12 years of age.

Shah, Holloway, and Valkil (1982) examined emergency room records of alleged sexual abuse cases. These Canadian researchers also found females comprising the majority of the victim group (90%). Intrafamilial sexual abuse accounted for 28% of the total cases, whereas strangers were involved in an additional 28%.

Grant (1984) conducted a retrospective review of the medical records of 157 cases of alleged sexual abuse and found that the victims were predominantly female (136 cases). Intrafamilial sexual abuse was present in 46% of the cases with the biological fathers accounting for 16% of the offenses and stepfathers involved in 11%. The remaining 19% accounted for other relatives. Only 12% of the offenders were strangers.

A fifth study by Khan and Sexton (1983) collected data on 113 alleged cases of child sexual abuse by examining emergency room records and the medical social worker's interview. Seventy-five percent of the victims were female, 53% of the victims were under 6 years of age, and 44% of the offenders were relatives. Strangers made up only 7% of the offender group.

Scherzer and Lala (1980) descriptively analyzed 73 cases of child sexual abuse as reported on emergency room records. Findings concluded that females represented 83% of the victim group, 83% of the offenders were known to the victim, and 75% of the families of the victims were receiving public aid.

Jason, Williams, Burton, and Rochat (1982) conducted a unique study that examined both confirmed cases of sexual and physical abuse comparing 735 cases of child sexual abuse with 3,486 cases of physical abuse confirmed by the Georgia Department of Protective Services. Cases were compared with regard to age, sex, socioeconomic characteristics, and morbidity and mortality rates. In sexual abuse cases, the victims were predominantly female (91%); offenders were predominantly male (91%). Male victims were found to be younger than female victims and incidence rates increased after the age of 2. In physical abuse cases, there was no significant difference between the sex of the victims. Only slightly more than half (56%) of the abusers were male, and peak incidence rates occurred in children under 2 and then again in the late teens. Both the morbidity rate and mortality rate were higher for physically abused children.

A review of the current research examining incidence rates of child sexual abuse and characteristics of both victims and abusers provides limited conclusive evidence. The variations in research design, methodology, population sampled, and definitions of terms make comparison of the results difficult. Table 7.1 presents a summary of the studies on incidence and prevalence.

Overwhelmingly, females constituted a large percentage of the victim group. Males accounted for only 9% to 30% of the sexual abuse victims included in the previously cited research studies. In contrast, males almost exclusively constituted the offender group. In only a few cases were females involved as offenders in sexual assault and, in most of those instances, they were accomplices to males.

A common belief is that adults must protect their children from strangers that are lurking around every corner ready to assault them; however, statistics show that strangers account for less than 20% of the reported sexual abuse

Table 7.1 Studies on Incidence and Prevalence

Study/date	Source of sample	N	Gender of sample	Design	Control group	Respondents
De Jong et al. (1982)	Emergency room records	416	344 female 72 male	Quantitative	No	Child victims
Enos et al. (1986)	Forensic records	162	132 female 30 male	Quantitative	No	Child victims
Gordon & O'Keefe (1984)	Case records	97	93 female 4 male	Mixed	No	Child victims
Grant (1984)	Medical records	157	136 female 21 male	Quantitative	No	Child victims
Husain & Ahmed (1982)	Psychiatric unit	100	100 female	Quantitative	No	Adolescent victims
Jason et al. (1982)	Protective service agencies	4218	2382 female 1836 male	Quantitative	Yes	Child victims
Khan & Sexton (1983)	Emergency room records	113	84 female 29 males	Quantitative	No	Child victims
Kohan et al. (1987)	Psychiatric inpatient unit	110	Not available	Quantitative	No	Staff
Mims & Chang (1984)	Military, colleges, and community	404	404 female	Quantitative	Yes	Nonclinical adult women

Table 7.1 Continued

Study/date	Source of sample	N	Gender of sample	Design	Control group	Respondents
Russell (1983)	Community	930	930 female	Quantitative: structured interview	No	Random sample nonclinical adult women
Scherzer & Lala (1980)	Emergency room records	73	61 female 12 male	Quantitative	No	Child victims
Shah et al. (1982)	Emergency room records	843	750 female 93 male	Quantitative	No	Child victims
Simari & Baskin (1982)	Gay organizations	83	29 female 54 male	Quantitative	Yes	Adult homosexuals

cases. Of the studies that reported extrafamilial sexual abuse, only three reported percentages higher than 20. Most of the offenders are known to the victim. They are either friends of the family or family members. Incestuous experiences ranged from a low of 19% to a high of 72%, with most studies leaning toward the lower end. In the six studies in which the relationship was further examined between natural father and step/foster/adoptive father, it was found that the natural father accounted for more sexual abuse than stepfathers. However, probably more biological fathers are reported. As Russell (1983) pointed out, this supports the idea that stepfathers are proportionately more likely to abuse. Although many more biological fathers have access to their children, the majority of biological fathers do not abuse them.

Ages of greatest risk for sexual abuse cannot be determined from the research reviewed. Two studies (De Jong et al., 1982; Jason et al., 1982) reported that male victims tend to be younger than female victims, whereas Khan and Sexton (1983) contradicted and reported boys tend to be older. Enos et al. (1986) found females had a higher incidence rate at age 6 and again at age 12, and De Jong et al. (1982) reported peaks at ages 5 to 6 years and again at 14 to 15 years. Khan and Sexton (1983), however, reported that females were at a higher risk before 6 years of age. Discrepancies in reported age of risk is due in part to the age limits of each study and, possibly, because it is not always clear whether the age reported is the age upon disclosure or the age of initial occurrence.

Several studies included statistics on the age of the offender but, again, conclusive data is not available. De Jong et al. (1982) reported that 50% of the offenders were under 20 years of age in contrast to the Scherzer and Lala (1980) finding of 73% of the offenders over the age of 20 years.

Two studies reported percentages of child offenders. De Jong et al. (1982) found 10% of offenders were under 10 years of age and, similarly, Khan and Sexton reported 15% of the offenders were under 13 years of age. Questions must be raised, however, concerning the nature of these offenses. Is the 7-year-old a sexual abuser or merely a child exploring sexually? What were the sexual acts? Who were the "victims"?

Several studies attempted to identify the prevalence of specific activities involved in child sexual abuse. Because of the differing definitions and use of terms, comparisons or conclusive information on types of acts that predominate are impossible to draw.

Limitations

The major limitation encountered in reviewing the research on incidence and prevalence is the lack of random samples drawn from the general population. Russell's study (1983) is the only one to date that used this technique, and she only interviewed females. Since the majority of the research has been conducted with specific populations, the results of these quantitative studies can only be generalized to that particular population.

A further limitation is the lack of agreement among definitions of terms. For example, some researchers used the term "incest" to refer to only blood relatives, whereas others included persons occupying kinship roles such as a stepfather or adoptive father. The definition of sexual abuse also differs among various researchers. It is imperative that researchers clarify the terms they use, and in several studies this was not done.

An obvious limitation of the current research using clinical populations is that the findings are only characteristic of those cases actually reported. It is safe to say that many cases of child sexual abuse never are reported for a variety of reasons, such as the nonverbal child, the mentally retarded child, or the child who is too terrified to disclose. Thus, the findings cannot be taken as conclusive because they might, in fact, be ignoring a substantial population with differing ages and characteristics.

In addition to these limitations, there were several specific to the group of studies reviewed. Every study reviewed used differing upper ages to define the sample (the range was from 12 years to adult), but in doing so, raises questions concerning their findings on victims' age of risk. For example, De Jong et al. (1982) found that girls were at greater risk at age 12–14, whereas another using the upper age limit of 12 found girls to be at greater risk before the age of 6 (Khan & Sexton, 1983).

Another problem is that the use of retrospective review of medical or agency files introduces two potential problems:

1. That data is missing or is not recorded in a way the researchers can use.
2. There is no way of knowing if the original recorder was biased when writing the files.

A common problem encountered in this review was the lack of technical skill in writing and reporting the research. Several of the research reports were not well organized or clear in describing their design or findings, nor did they discuss their findings in light of previous research or offer any possible interpretations or conclusions of the data.

Families

Maternal Distance

The available research literature on incest families gives clues to several family characteristics that are apparent in cases of father-daughter incest. The most frequently cited characteristic is maternal distance. Some therapists have used maternal distance as a way to allocate blame to mothers for allowing fathers to abuse their daughters (Poznansky & Blos, 1975). Byles (1980) noted a high incidence of physical violence of fathers toward mothers and alcohol use by mothers and suggested that mothers have little emotional energy available for involvement with their children.

Maternal distance was also a key finding in a study by Browning and Boatman (1977) in which 14 cases of incest were examined for prevailing family characteristics. They found a high incidence of chronic depression among the mothers in the sample and an eldest daughter forced to assume parental responsibilities.

Anderson and Shafer (1979) noted that the victim is often the primary caretaker of younger siblings, implying some abdication of maternal responsibilities. A similar pattern was found in a study of mother-daughter role reversal in which it was observed that mothers reversed roles in child-rearing tasks and that incest fathers referred to the victim as "my little sweetheart," "my baby," and "my little wife." Many nonabusive fathers also use these terms, but what is noteworthy here is that the incest fathers used terms of endearment to their victims that they previously had used in relation to their wives (de Chesnay, 1984).

In a brief report, La Barbera (1983) reported an investigation into a related dimension of mother-daughter role reversal. He administered questionnaires to 80 women from 17–24 years old. Mother replacement (extent to which the daughter felt compelled to adopt the maternal role) was positively associated with the victim's need to be held by a man and negatively associated with sexual responsivity of the victims. La Barbera concluded that, although more work needs to be done, variables that ordinarily characterize incest families may also be measured in nonincest families.

Scott and Stone (1986) administered the MMPI to four groups of family members, including 44 mothers of victims of father-daughter incest. They reported surprise at the finding of a normal group profile for the mothers. There was little indication of high levels of depression or anxiety in the group. However, consistent with the previous reports, the mothers showed a marked tendency toward dissociative phenomena.

Finally, in a study of 52 incest families, de Chesnay, Marshall, and Clements (1988) found an overwhelming majority of families (96%) in which a high degree of maternal distance was present. This finding is consistent with both theoretical and research literature that mothers of incest victims are often emotionally, or even geographically, distant from their daughters. However, since no prospective studies were found, the precise pattern cannot be clearly stated. Therefore, it is not legitimate to specify a direct, linear relationship between maternal distance and incest, and it is unfair to blame mothers for encouraging incest.

The available studies on maternal distance suggest new directions for research in this area. First, prospective studies should be done in order to identify the patterns of family functioning that precede incest. Although it seems certain that maternal distance is a factor, it is important to look deeper into the antecedents of the mother's distancing.

Bowen's family systems theory (1978) suggests explanations for incest. The theory suggests a pattern of movements in triadic relationships. The mother distances from both the child and husband; the father might move toward the child, even becoming the primary caretaker. Or, the father involves himself in the child's care to the point of pushing the mother into a distant relationship. Either pattern could produce a sexualized father-child relationship. Evidence in support of this pattern of paternal overinvolvement comes from a study by Parker and Parker (1986) of 56 abusive fathers and a control group, in which they found that fathers who were involved in the early socialization of their daughters tended to be incestuous.

Families should be observed in their naturalistic settings to obtain more rich detail. All of the cited studies were quantitative and relied on self-report to some extent. The de Chesnay et al. (1985) study made an attempt to go beyond self-report by using therapists' impressions, but this creates a different kind of risk of error.

Comparison groups with normal subjects were lacking in the cited studies. Consequently, though maternal distance is clearly established as a factor in incest families, the extent to which maternal distance is a factor in nonincest populations is unknown. Might there be something different about the ways in which mothers of incest victims distance? Or, is maternal distance more accurately viewed within the context of the entire family system?

Family Structure

Byles (1980) studied 120 adolescent girls in need of protective services for sexual abuse and found two distinct family classifications. Disorganized families (35%) were characterized by continuous change in family structure, parental promiscuity, parental separation, and common-law unions. In contrast, organized families (41%) seemed to be nuclear, regained stability after a major crisis, and were not characterized by parental promiscuity.

Anderson and Shafer (1979) reported that 60% of the 62 families they studied involved incest between natural father and daughter and 39% between stepfather and stepdaughter. In a comparative study of 32 adolescent runaway girls and a nonrunaway control group, it was found that 14 of the 18 (78%) runaways who lived in nuclear, intact families had sexual contacts with their fathers, and 4 of the 20 (2%) nonrunaways who lived in intact nuclear families had sexual contacts with their fathers. Sexual contacts with stepfathers for both samples were negligible (de Chesnay, 1980).

Gordon and O'Keefe (1984) also found a greater frequency of biological father incest than stepfather abuse (48% and 29%, respectively) in their study of 50 case records from three Boston agencies. However, when examined in view of the proportion of their numbers, stepfathers were more likely than natural fathers to be sexual assailants. This finding was similar to the results of Gruber and Jones (1983).

In the previously cited study by de Chesnay et al. (1985), a significant relationship was found between family structure and severity of incest. Although distributions of natural and stepfather offenders were similar, natural fathers tended to be more severe in form, duration, and frequency of sexual abuse than did stepfathers. In the same study, family structure was negatively associated with marital power, with stepfather families tending to be more patriarchal than nuclear, intact families. This finding suggests that mothers may be willing to abdicate more control to second husbands and might be less accepting of abuse by natural fathers or less willing to acknowledge abuse by stepfathers to whom they are committed.

Marital Power

Marital power as a variable was found in only two studies. In a study of 52 families, marital power was significantly related to severity of abuse (de Chesnay et al., 1988). Patriarchal families demonstrated more severe abuse occurring more frequently than egalitarian families. No families characterized by maternal power were found.

This finding is consistent with work done by Herman and Hirschman (1981) in a landmark study in which they discovered that patriarchal distributions were associated with father-daughter incest. From this, Herman (1981) developed a theory in which she stated that father-daughter incest is a logical consequence of patriarchy. Herman's theory was supported by de Chesnay (1985), comparing ethical reasoning patterns of incest fathers and two comparison groups. Incest fathers demonstrated an ethical decision-making style in accordance with conceptions of their own rights toward their daughters rather than their duties to daughters and daughters' rights.

There are several problems with the literature on family structure and marital power, in addition to the scarcity of studies. A major problem is that the two constructs are often operationalized to mean marital decision making. Therefore, when the concept of family structure appears, it might have either of two meanings.

Another problem is that more valid and reliable measures of marital power are needed. In the Herman and Hirschman study, the determination was made from the victim's report. Therapists' assessments provided an external review in the de Chesnay et al. (1988) study, but neither allowed for direct assessment by the investigator. Both were quantitative studies, so more elucidating measures could not be performed. Naturalistic designs might help to clarify the extent of marital power differences.

A third problem is that accurate incidence and prevalence rates are not available for these two constructs. Although many researchers happened to report type of family structure, they did not stratify the sample so their percentages of natural father and stepfather offenders do not necessarily reflect the general population. For example, we do not know whether victims report incest by natural fathers more frequently than by stepfathers. The de Chesnay et al. (1988) study had a sample representative of geographic regions in the United States. We can infer that such a high frequency (about half) of biological fathers who abused their children indicate that clinicians can legitimately operate on the assumption that biological fathers do abuse and leave the problem of determining accurate proportions to the demographics.

Alcohol

Paternal alcohol consumption was a significant factor in the studies by Anderson and Shafer (1979), Byles (1980), de Chesnay (1980, 1985), Martin and Walters (1982), and Herman (1981). However, Gordon and O'Keefe (1984) found a relatively low association between alcohol abuse and incest in contrast to alcohol and other forms of child abuse. Drunkenness at the time of abuse was reported in most of the cases of child abuse, neglect, and incest they studied, with alcohol a stress factor in 31% of the incest cases. Parker and Parker (1986) found that alcohol was not significant.

The importance of alcohol as a stress factor deserves study in itself because clinicians often hear stories from offenders that they never would have touched their children had they not been drunk at the time. This becomes a seductive argument to gloss over the episode and minimize attempts to hold the offender accountable because "he couldn't help it." Overworked mental health professionals and social service agencies can then devote their time to "more serious" cases. The cultural norms about alcohol use allow the offender much latitude before social sanctions are applied. Tracking patterns of alcohol use might establish whether the offender premeditates incest and drinks to obtain courage — a cycle that would indicate very different treatment strategies.

Summary

Table 7.2 summarizes studies on families and family characteristics. There is a great deal of support in the literature for specific family characteristics. Among these, maternal distance plays a pivotal role. However, much work needs to be done to clarify patterns, as it is not at all clear from the literature why mothers distance, the relationship between father's closeness to the child and mother's distancing, antecedents of maternal distance, and the role of alcohol use by mothers.

Alcohol use by offenders, at least in terms of drunkenness at the time of sexual contact, continues to be an unknown variable, with some researchers reporting significance and others not. Only one study was found that systematically examined alcohol use as a major variable, but this study did not go far enough in explaining the phenomenon and did not use a control group.

Table 7.2 Studies on Families and Family Characteristics

Study/date	Source of sample	N	Gender of sample	Design	Control group	Respondents
Anderson & Shafer (1979)	Child abuse team	62	N/A	Quantitative	No	Families
Byles (1980)	Child protective services	120	120 female	Mixed	No	Adolescent victims
Browning & Boatman (1977)	Case records	14	13 female 1 male	Quantitative	No	Child victims
de Chesnay (1980)	Family court	42	42 female	Mixed	Yes	Adolescent victims
de Chesnay (1984)	Therapy referrals			Mixed	No	Adult women victims
de Chesnay et al. (1985)	Community mental health centers	52	Families	Mixed	No	Therapists
Gordon & O'Keefe (1984)	Case records: social agencies	50	49 male offenders 1 female offender 4 male victims 90 female victims	Quantitative	No	Adult offenders Child victims
Gruber & Stone (1983)	Delinquency program	20	Not available	Quantitative	Yes	Adult women victims

Table 7.2 Continued

Study/date	Source of sample	N	Gender of sample	Design	Control group	Respondents
Herman & Hirschman (1981)	Psychotherapy outpatients	40	40 female	Mixed	Yes	Adult women victims
LaBarbera (1983)	Not available	80	80 female	Quantitative	No	Adult and adolescent female victims
Martin & Walters (1986)	Case records	489	Not available	Mixed	No	Adult offenders
Parker & Parker (1986)	Penal and social service agencies	56	56 male	Quantitative	Yes	Adult offenders
Scott & Stone (1986)	Psychotherapy groups of incest families	128	62 female 66 male	Quantitative	Yes	Adult offenders adolescent victims

There is a high degree of consensus in the literature that marital power distributions in incest families are skewed in favor of patriarchal prerogatives, albeit the number of researchers who investigated marital power was small. Much more could be accomplished by examining patterns of decision making, conditions under which mothers have their say, and situations in which mothers break the patriarchal rules. The latter would be especially important in establishing parameters of mothers' overall involvement or lack of involvement in the sexual abuse of their daughters.

Finally, though the relative distributions of biological and stepfather offenders are still uncertain, it is clear that biological fathers account for a significant amount of child sexual abuse. Therefore, clinicians and policy makers should not be distracted from this problem by statistics that indicate children are at greater risk of sexual abuse by their stepfathers.

Offenders

Adult

In contrast to studies that include data on offenders discussed under other sections of this chapter, the following group has, as the major focus, examination of offender behavior, characteristics, and traits. Groth, Burgess, Birnbaum, and Gary (1978) descriptively studied 148 convicted child molesters and derived a substantial volume of detailed information, much of which refutes societal myths regarding child molesters. The design and methodology appear sound with one limitation – the sample was not randomized. This convenience sample consisted of incarcerated offenders who had actual physical contact with their victim, thereby limiting generalizability to nonincarcerated populations. Groth et al. (1978) concluded that the profile of a child molester is one of a young, heterosexual male who is neither sexually frustrated, insane, nor mentally retarded. He is not a stranger to the child, as 71% are known – at least casually – by their victims. His compulsive sexual behavior is thought to be motivated by an effort to control the child or to have personal affiliation and belonging needs met.

Several authors have investigated the psychological profiles of offenders. Panton (1979) analyzed the MMPI profiles of convicted incestuous and non-incestuous offenders. The conceptualization of incestuous assault was comparable to that of other researchers. This historical study lacked randomization and consisted of a relatively small sample (35 incest offenders and 28 child molesters). Only the Social Introversion (SI) Scale proved to be statistically significant, with the incestuous sample revealing a greater degree of social introversion. Interestingly, both samples revealed elevated means Lie (L) Scale, intended to aid in assessing validity, thereby limiting the reliability of the results.

In a similar study, with contrasting findings, Kirkland and Bauer (1982) randomly selected 10 cases of incarcerated incest offenders and compared their MMPI profiles with a matched comparison group. In contrast to Panton (1979), these researchers found the incest sample to have statistically significant elevated means in the areas of psychopathic deviate, psychoasthesia, and schizophrenia. The Groth et al. (1978) sample was 95% nonpsychotic, yet it is likely that frankly psychotic offenders would be incarcerated in a facility for the criminally insane instead of a corrections institution and thereby escape the Groth et al. (1978) sample.

A correlational study conducted by Famularo, Stone, Barnum, and Wharton (1986) compared a randomized sample of parents whose children had been removed from their home by protective services because of abuse with a self-selected control group. The primary variable of interest was alcoholism, which was operationalized in a fashion resembling other measures of alcoholism, although reliability was not established. It was found that 30% of the court-referred mothers and 50% of the court-referred fathers were alcoholics, compared with 9% and 6% respectively in the comparison group. Given the fact that these parents were seeking custody of their children, it would be understandable for parents to lessen their self-reported alcoholic behaviors, and thus there may be an even greater incidence of alcoholism than revealed in this study. It would have been valuable to analyze the prevalence of alcoholism according to the specific type of child abuse as these researchers group sexual assault, physical abuse, and neglect cases together into their sample, thereby clouding this study's relevance to child sexual assault. In contrast, one third of the Groth et al. (1978) sample reported alcohol dependency. Finkelhor's analysis (1984) also failed to reveal any association between victimization and alcoholism in either parent.

Investigating paternal perceptions of rights and duties regarding their daughters, de Chesnay (1985) randomly selected subjects to comprise three groups: an incestuous father-daughter group who had participated in family therapy, a nonincestuous father-daughter group who had undergone family therapy for other difficulties, and a control group of nonincestuous, nontherapy pairs. As hypothesized, incestuous fathers and daughters held perceptions of different rights and duties in the parent-child relationship when compared with nonincestuous subjects. Both of the therapy groups were 6 months post-termination, and since it is possible that parental and child perceptions of rights and duties may be altered as a result of therapy sessions, the values obtained may be even less severe than perceived originally, before therapeutic intervention. Assessment of these variables in a pre- and postintervention design would offer additional information. The advantage of the study was that the sample consisted of nonincarcerated offenders, but a larger sample from diverse populations would have increased generalizability of the findings.

Finkelhor (1984) offered substantial descriptive information based on a sample of 796 college students and proposed a model of predictive factors found to predispose a child to sexual assault. Finkelhor included exhibitionism in his conceptualization of sexual assault, unlike other studies, some of which included only physical contact between offender and victim. Although much of Finkelhor's findings pertain to victims, stepfathers were found to be five times more likely to victimize their daughters than natural fathers. Finkelhor has also devised a multifactoral model that attempted to operationalize child molestation.

Overholser and Beck (1986) investigated heterosocial skills, social anxiety, hostility, impulsivity, and sexual attitudes of incarcerated rapists and child molesters who were matched demographically with two comparison groups — imprisoned nonsex offenders and nonimprisoned males. A third comparison group of male college students was not matched. Multiple measurements were chosen, but reliability information for the self-report measures was not provided. Reliable physiologic measurement and behavioral measures of anxiety were used. Overholser and Beck reported their investigation revealed that child molesters and rapists have poor heterosocial skills, and that child molesters held highly stereotyped views of sex roles when compared with controls. Measures of hostility and compulsivity were found to be insignificant. The multimethod assessment may increase the strength of the results obtained, but without information regarding the reliability of the eight self-reported measures utilized, results must be viewed with caution.

Traver (1978) attempted to propose a model to explain the outcome of child molester and incestuous abuser cases based on an analysis of case variables such as the use of a public defender versus a private counsel and recommendations of probation officers. Although a sample of 268 was obtained, the gender of subjects was not identified, and some of the subjects were categorized as incurable sexual psychopaths, although the process of labeling a subject as such was not disclosed. Instead of analyzing the incest and child molestation cases separately, the authors chose to combine the groups and so lost potentially valuable statistics. Therefore, the findings are suspect.

Freund, Scher, Chan, and Ben-Aron (1982) attempted to compare the prevalence of bisexuality in pedophiles with subjects who preferred mature partners. The researchers chose three experimental groups, yet included subjects who only reported being sexually attracted to children and who had not necessarily acted on their attractions with individuals who had acted, thus contaminating these groups. The researchers excluded incestuous offenders from their sampling. The authors also chose one group of psychiatric patients to serve as a control and a group of volunteers recruited from a homosexual bar as the second control group. It was hypothesized that pedophiles would exhibit a higher incidence of bisexuality than the comparison groups. Although the authors stated the hypothesis was supported, they failed to reveal data to support or discredit the stated hypothesis; therefore, the findings must be interpreted with caution.

Adolescent Offenders

Research of adolescent offenders is limited, for reasons that may become clear in the final discussion. Groth (1979) found that 20% of his adult offender sample had a juvenile sexual assault history, and an even greater percentage reported committing sexual assaults during adolescence. He also stated that there were more antisocial sexual behaviors known to the adolescents' parents, neighbors, and the police than was revealed in their criminal records. He also noted that in 75% of cases, the offender had committed prior sexual assaults that were dismissed without referral. It appears that adolescent sexual assault may not be considered a serious offense or a sufficient rationale for referral and evaluation of the adolescent.

Tarter, Hegedus, Alterman, and Katz-Garris (1983) measured the cognitive capacities of juvenile violent, nonviolent, and sex offenders and found no systematic group differences on measures of intelligence, learning, and neuropsychological functioning.

Research in all areas related to the adolescent offender would prove valuable in gaining insight into this specific population.

Female Offenders

As with adolescent offenders, the volume of research material available on female offenders is limited. Groth (1979) cited experience with only three female offenders as compared with 250 male offenders and described two of these cases qualitatively.

The most extensive study of female offenders described childhood, adulthood, and parenting of 26 mothers who had committed incest (McCartey, 1986). All findings were self-reported and, as such, subject to the inherent weaknesses therein. Interestingly, 78% of the mother offenders had been victimized sexually as a child. There was a higher incidence of drug abuse (46%) in this sample than in the Groth et al. (1978) male sample (30%). Emotional disturbance was also a prevalent variable, occurring in 50% of McCartey's (1986) sample, but since the determination of this label was not explained in the study, it is unclear whether this label reflected psychopathology or a more benign condition. As with most research regarding sexual offenders, the sample was one of convenience — imprisoned offenders — and this influences generalizability of the findings. Table 7.3 summarizes the studies on offenders.

There are a few areas of disagreement and consensus in the literature on offenders. First, there appears to be disagreement regarding the relationship of alcoholism and sexual victimization. Repeat studies with various samples are needed to aid in clarifying the relationship between these two variables. There is a relative disagreement regarding the mental health of the imprisoned offender based on MMPI profiles, past history, and the presence of psychosis; therefore, repeat studies with nonimprisoned subjects are needed. All studies reviewed

Table 7.3 Studies on Offenders

Study/date	Source of sample	N	Gender of sample	Design	Control group	Respondents
de Chesnay (1985)	Therapist case load	60	30 female 30 male	Mixed	Yes	Adult male offenders child victims
Famularo et al. (1986)	Psychiatric clinic	50	Not available	Quantitative	Yes	Court referred abusive parents
Finkelhor (1984)	Random community survey	521	Not available	Quantitative: structural interviews	No	Parents of children age 6–14
Freund et al. (1982)	Psychiatric institute	82	82 male	Quantitative	Yes	Adult offenders
Groth et al. (1978)	Court referrals	148	148 male	Mixed	No	Adult offenders
Kirkland & Bauer (1982)	Social service referrals	10	10 male	Quantitative	Yes	Adult offenders
McCartey (1986)	Case records	26	26 female	Case study	No	Adult offenders
Overholser & Beck (1986)	Medium-security prison	72	72 male	Quantitative	Yes	Adult offenders

Table 7.3 Continued

Study/date	Source of sample	N	Gender of sample	Design	Control group	Respondents
Panton (1979)	State prison	63	63 male	Quantitative	No	Adult offenders
Tarter et al. (1983)	Psychiatric clinic	73	73 male	Quantitative	No	Adolescent offenders
Traver (1978)	Court referrals	268	Not available	Quantitative	No	Adult offenders

revealed no significant difference among offenders with regard to religion or ethnicity. The literature also revealed that most offenders are heterosexual. Most of the research at present is based on imprisoned offenders, and authors have proposed that incarcerated offenders may have behaved in a more compulsive or blatant fashion, which contributed to their entering the criminal justice system. Nonimprisoned offenders may differ dramatically from incarcerated offenders and, therefore, much of the present research must be interpreted conservatively.

The literature suggests that mental health professionals may never evaluate most adolescent offenders because of undetected or dismissed cases. Given the finding that many offenders have a history of victimization, intervention with adolescent offenders could be imperative in resolving victim issues and/or altering the likelihood of future offenses. Given their developmental status, intervention could rehabilitate the adolescent before sexual behaviors become ingrained. Longitudinal studies of adolescent offenders are also needed and might reveal factors that contribute to the development of adult offenders.

Clear definitions of what actually constitutes an assault are needed. Authors vary widely — from including only physical contact to calling exhibitionistic behavior an assault. Explicit operationalization in the research report and the theoretical framework would provide better information.

Groth (1979) reported that 49% of his sample of offenders responded exclusively to children who had not yet developed secondary sex characteristics. He proposed that pedophiles seek affiliation and a sense of belonging from these children, yet fulfill these needs through sexually assaultive behavior. If child sexual assault is not sexually motivated, then why are the offenders' needs being expressed through sexually assaultive behavior rather than another form of interaction? Further research of the motivational dynamics of offenders is needed to aid understanding and facilitate development of interventions. Therapy for offenders has been described in the literature, yet, not researched. Studies comparing the outcome of offenders participating in various treatment modalities and offenders imprisoned without therapy are needed.

One of the few findings consistently supported by the literature is that women sexually assault children less often than men. Yet, studies have also revealed that girls report being victimized more frequently than boys. Whether these self-reports are reliable may be related to socialization factors that foster reporting by girls and deter reporting by boys. However, given that many offenders were themselves sexually victimized as children, it would be reasonable to hypothesize that there may be even larger numbers of female offenders and male victims than available statistics show. Given that the largest group of offenders is male, investigations that compare groups by gender and more controlled predictive studies on offenders need to be done. If women offenders are truly a minor group, more studies need to be done on why women do not tend to be abusers. A study by Simari and Baskin (1982) found that homosexual incest was the only reported type of abuse among male homosexuals and that heterosexual incest was predominant among female homosexuals. They reaffirmed the notion that women tend not to seek incestuous experiences, but the reasons need to be explored. Also in their study, Simari and Baskin found that all women, who reported that the perpetrators were male, experience incest as negative, but none of the women with female perpetrators experienced the incest as negative.

Replication studies are desperately needed as are longitudinal studies of victims and offenders. Explanatory models that have been developed need to be tested empirically. Research in all areas of child sexual assault must become a priority to aid in understanding and development of treatment modalities, not only for offenders, but for all affected.

Attribution of Blame

Five studies were found in which studies about incest or attribution of blame were examined. Jackson and Ferguson (1983) administered the Jackson Incest Blame Scale to 201 male and 211 female college students. Most subjects attributed blame to the offender, followed by situational and societal factors. Relatively few blamed the victim. However, males tended to blame the victim more than did females. There were no significant differences between males and females on any of the other categories.

Dietz and Craft (1980) surveyed 200 caseworkers in the Iowa Department of Social Services to test the pervasive attitude that mothers are to blame. Of the respondents, 78% perceived mothers as a victim of abuse by husbands, but they did not accept submissiveness and despair as reasonable grounds for not reporting incest. Consistent with prevailing attitudes of blame, 87% of the workers believed the mother gives unconscious consent, and 65% believed she is equally responsible with the father. Dietz and Craft found that a significant factor in the formation of these attitudes was familiarity with the incest literature. Possibly, workers do not read the literature critically or, perhaps, they operate from a position of helplessness with regard to offenders.

Evidence that the attitudes of Dietz and Craft's professionals is reflective of a more inclusive cultural response comes from a study by Adams and Roddey (1981). A community action group organized to protect sexually abused children revealed the existence of a pro-incest lobby which denied or obscured the problem of father-daughter incest. The investigators analyzed language patterns that served to protect incest fathers and to impugn the child victim. The lexicon developed by Adams and Roddey consisted of nine categories that include terms and phrases used by the pro-incest lobby. They warn child-care professionals to attend to their own language patterns that might unconsciously reflect the same attitudes.

Sagatun (1982) evaluated the effects of the self-help program, Parents United, on family members. Blame was attributed first to fathers, then to mothers, and least to victims. Fathers were significantly more likely than mothers to blame themselves. The finding of fathers accepting responsibility is not surprising for this sample. Presumably, fathers in a self-help group would be more willing to accept responsibility than the general population of incest fathers.

Finally, a team of Australian researchers surveyed 193 general practitioners, 80% of whom were male and who practiced in the Adelaide metropolitan area. Forty-one percent of the comments to an open-ended question broadly denied the scope of the problem of child sexual abuse. Reasons given by respondents included that the media exaggerated the problem and/or that when it does occur, it is not an important problem. Seventeen percent said they did not believe the child's report (Winefield & Castell-McGregor, 1986).

This small, but important, group of studies indicates that much more needs to be done to educate the professionals who work in the area of child sexual abuse. Primarily, the problems seem to center around societal mobilization to protect offenders, not victims. Some communities are developing innovative programs to help the child victim, but are meeting either active or passive resistance to firm attempts to hold the victim accountable.

No studies were found showing survey attitudes among school personnel or criminal justice workers — two primary groups who deal with disclosure. Often, the first person to whom a child discloses is the teacher or school counselor. Police are also involved extensively, both by referrals from protective services agencies and directly by the child or family. It would be valuable to ascertain whether recent efforts to educate these groups have been successful.

Prevention

Only three studies were found that examined prevention of child sexual abuse, a surprising finding in view of the many nonresearch articles that speak to prevention. Muller, Shaw, and Towner (1987) asked London nurses to compare two video programs and found that the more effective one was shorter and explicitly stated that sexual abuse can be committed by someone the child knows. Both programs discussed ways in which children could recognize signals and how to say "no." The authors concluded that both programs accomplished the objective and might be useful to health care professionals in prevention programs.

The other two studies also involved films, but the respondents were children. Saslowsky and Wurtele (1986) evaluated the effectiveness of an Illusion Theater film on 67 elementary school children. Children who saw the film tested more knowledgable about sexual abuse and aware of personal safety than the control group.

In a similar study, a combination of the film and a personal safety skills training program produced the best results of making children aware of the potential problem and how they might deal with it (Wurtele, Saslowsky, Miller, Marrs, & Britcher, 1986).

No studies were found that focused on ways to prevent the offenders from abusing, although it is hoped that some of the work on rapists might apply to this group. Also, given that there does seem to be evidence that mothers receive a share of the blame for not protecting their children, it is curious that no studies were found that tested ways to help mothers. The focus on teaching children to cope with the problem and to prevent abuse by learning to defend themselves obscures the major factor that it is the offender who commits the crime. Clearly, studies are needed that provide direction for primary prevention with the group at risk for offending. Until cultural attitudes toward this powerful group change, though, there are not likely to be significant studies in this area.

Incestuous Contact in Nonclinical Population

Of significance to those who work with clinical populations is a study conducted on 576 upper-middle-class children to determine how children are socialized around bathing practices. Sometimes, clinicians and attorneys hear reports about deviant sexual behavior by one spouse, as a concern about healthy behavior or as part of a custody battle. Therefore, the authors wanted to examine what happens in normal or healthy families when parents and children bathe together. They surveyed the parents of 324 boys and 252 girls who were 2 to 10 years old. Mothers completed most of the questionnaires. Generally, children bathed alone after age 8 to 9, and by that age, it was uncommon for parents to bathe with the opposite-sex child. Though sometimes children touch the parents' genitals, this is seen by the parent as normal curiosity and a low-anxiety behavior (Rosenfeld, Bailey, Siegel, & Bailey, 1986; Rosenfeld, Siegel, & Bailey, 1987).

More work on healthy families and nonclinical control groups needs to be done to establish norms of healthy behavior. Priorities have been directed at solving difficult problems, but prevention efforts need to be expanded, too. More work like the Rosenfeld et al. (1986 and 1987) studies will point the way to identifying high-risk groups. Researchers who elect to do quantitative studies might do well to construct conceptual frameworks around health promotion constructs.

Fatal Sexual Assaults

Only two studies were found that examined forensic evidence. Perhaps more specialized journals in pathology have published studies that include data on fatalities. The Enos et al. (1986) study was analyzed in the incidence and prevalence section of this chapter. The other study is discussed here.

Case files of 41 female victims of fatal sexual assault were examined. Victims ranged in age from 10 to 88, with 6 cases younger than 20 years old. Assailants ranged in age from 15 to 54 years old. Most deaths were caused by mechanical asphyxiation, usually strangling, and younger women tended to be found in isolated areas rather than in their homes (Deming, Mittleman, & Wetli, 1983).

The investigators did not report data separately for child victims, but the study is worth citing to emphasize that, not only is the problem of child sexual abuse serious, but also it can be fatal. This would seem to contradict prevailing attitudes that minimize the importance of child sexual abuse.

Studies Conducted Outside the United States

No cross-cultural or cross-national studies were found, but there is evidence that investigators outside the United States are turning their attention to the problem of child sexual abuse. Twelve studies conducted in five countries were identified. Though the computer search included foreign language journals, the only research articles were found in English-language journals.

Several of the research articles were concerned with incidence and prevalence. Mrazek, Lynch, and Bentovim (1983) circulated questionnaires to 1,599 physicians in the United Kingdom, and 622 responded. They found that this group of respondents could identify at least 3 cases per 1,000. Most cases involved actual or attempted intercourse by a perpetrator known to the child (74%) and about 43% of the cases resulted in criminal prosecution. The all-physician sample does not accurately reflect the incidence and may not even reflect the incidence of reported cases, and the investigators rightly recommended acknowledging the problem as the first step in improving services.

General practitioners were also surveyed in Australia (Winefield & Castell-McGregor, 1986) and Ireland (O'Rourke & Sweeney, 1983) with similar results. Incidence figures are likely to be too low because of underreporting and failure of physicians to diagnose the problem.

Two Canadian studies by Shah et al. (1982) and Grant (1984) have been discussed in the section on incidence and prevalence, but it is worth noting here that the authors considered their figures to be a conservative estimate, consistent with the Australian and United Kingdom investigators.

In Northern Ireland, Lukianowicz (1972) reported a case study review of 26 cases of father-daughter incest. Findings were consistent with other studies in which family characteristics were identified in that (1) no offenders were psychotic or clinically neurotic; (2) mother-daughter role reversal was observed; (3) maternal distance was a factor; and (4) most of the victims had negative effects, but some showed no apparent negative effects, a finding surprising in that all were therapy patients.

Other studies conducted outside the United States focused on offenders (Freund et al., 1982), prevention (Muller et al., 1987), attitudes (Lewin, 1983), long-term effects (Gold, 1986), and incestuous motifs of psychosomatic patients (Levitan, 1982). These have been discussed elsewhere in this chapter. Table 7.4 summarizes the studies conducted outside the United States.

A high priority should be placed on conducting cross-national studies and improving the treatment of ethnicity variables in one-country studies. Many of the studies included frequencies of abuse by race of victim and race of assailant, but there were no statistical treatments to identify whether differences were significant. Also, there was no attempt to stratify samples – at least in the reports. Frequency counts are certainly legitimate, but the use of simple measures of association would add much to designs that include demographic data collected to describe the sample.

Cross-cultural studies and more sharing of information by investigators in diverse societies would greatly improve our understanding of the phenomenon of child sexual abuse because by identifying universals, we can better understand what is healthy. This would facilitate not only health promotion but also would help spot potential high-risk groups.

State of the Art

Issues

Conceptualization. The prevailing paradigm was overwhemingly rationalistic or scientific reductionist. That is, studies were quantitative, and subjects were asked to fit their responses into the investigator's frame of reference (etic perspective). These studies are needed to test theory and to generalize beyond the sample. However, most of the studies we reviewed did not specify either the assumptions or theoretical underpinnings of the study. Even in situations in which editorial space limitations preclude a thorough discussion, it seems reasonable that authors should at least state the theory tested.

That qualitative methods were lacking in the studies reviewed reflect their general underutilization in social science research. In child sexual abuse, though, it is crucial to document the experience from the victim's perspective. Questions about the meaning of the experience, patterns of response, coping mechanisms, factors in disclosure, and health promotion remain unanswered because most researchers have focused on narrow aspects, such as behavior traits, long-term changes, incidence and prevalence rates, use of alcohol, and demographic characteristics. These questions are important, particularly for developing policy, but inadequate in addressing the needs of children from the perspective of those who deal with them most – teachers, counselors, clinicians, and criminal justice personnel.

Table 7.4 Studies Conducted Outside the United States

Study/date	Source of sample	County	N	Gender of sample	Design	Control group	Respondents
Finkel (1984)	Workshop participants	Canada	177	50 male 127 female	Quantitative	No	Middle-class professionals
Freund et al. (1982)	Inpatients: psychiatric facility	Canada	72	72 male	Quantitative	Yes	Adult pedophiles
Grant (1984)	Case records: Child Protection Center	Canada	157	21 male 136 female	Quantitative	No	Child victims
Gold (1986)	"Ads," therapy referrals, and college students	Canada	103	103 female	Quantitative	Yes	Adult women
Levitan (1982)	Chart review: author's case file	Canada	62	Not available	Mixed	Yes	Adult patients
Lewin (1983)	Schools	Sweden	381	291 female 90 male	Quantitative	No	Adolescents in school nonclinical population

Table 7.4 Continued

Study/date	Source of sample	County	N	Gender of sample	Design	Control group	Respondents
Lukianowicz (1972)	Therapy records: case review	North Ireland	26	26 female	Qualitative	No	Cases of father-daughter incest
Mrazek et al. (1983)	Mailing lists	United Kingdom	622	Not available	Quantitative	No	Family, physicians, police, surgeons, child psychiatrists, and pediatricians
Muller et al. (1987)	Training program	Great Britain	28	Not available	Quantitative	No	Health professionals— mostly nurses
O'Rourke & Sweeney (1983)	Mailing lists	Ireland	20	Not available	Quantitative	No	General practitioners
Shah et al. (1982)	Case records: emergency department	Canada	843	754 female 89 male	Quantitative	No	Child victims

No qualitative studies were found, although we noted that several investigators used mixed designs (i.e., they included open-ended questions that were content analyzed for themes and patterns). It would be helpful in mixed-design studies if authors clearly stated their interest in obtaining emic data (from the subject's perspective) because the assumptions for interpreting this type of data are different from the assumptions about etic data. For example, generalizability is not a concern in qualitative analysis, because the purpose is not to find out if many others perform the same, but rather how do these particular subjects view their world.

Finally, definitions were not always specified, though they could usually be inferred from the instrumentation. The major term that needs to be defined clearly and consistently is sexual abuse. Some authors included exposing and fondling in definitions that also included penetration and force.

Definitions on childhood need to be specified. Age ranges varied widely and were often buried in other detail. Authors who used adolescent subjects usually stated so in the title, but, even then, the subjects were sometimes recalling abuse that happened in childhood for some and in early adolescence for others. The question of age is especially important because we do not have accurate data on preverbal children. Furthermore, when children abused as infants or toddlers enter school, they might exhibit behavior problems that are associated with sexual abuse, yet do not have the verbal skills or frame of reference to disclose — a fact of which teachers and pediatric staff particularly need to be aware.

Measurement.   Neither theoretical nor operational definitions were stated in most studies, but this may be a problem with editorial policy. In some cases, statements about definitional problems were presented as limitations in the methods section or discussed in the general summary section.

Statistical procedures were critiqued according to design, the level of measurement of the data, and the presentation of results. A strength of the available literature as a whole was that the use of statistics seemed adequate, and tests were appropriately selected and clearly presented.

Validity and reliability assessments seemed adequate when presented, but the majority of reports did not include discussion of validity and reliability. Even in studies that included reports of validity and reliability measures, the authors did not always acknowledge methodological limitations that might have affected their results. Also, recommendations for further research rarely included direct statements about how replication studies might improve validity and reliability.

Limitations were most often addressed in terms of how generalizable the findings would be, probably because most investigators used samples of convenience instead of random samples. The type of research, the limitations on time and money, and the problems with access to sample all contribute to the need to use convenience samples. However, it does seem reasonable that we should take advantage of the willingness of some subjects to talk to us and obtain rich detail about their experience. This means more support for qualitative methods and emic perspective. There is a need for some researchers to conduct quantitative studies using random sampling and tight controls. However, others can do much in the way of valuable work on child sexual abuse by treating the limitation of nongeneralizability as a nonproblem; that is, we should concern ourselves not with generalizing, but with thoroughly describing the experience of those subjects generous enough to tell us about their lives.

Interpretation.   Conclusions were generally clear and presented in a straightforward way. For a few descriptive studies, authors could have said more about their findings, but, for the most part, they stated whether or not they found what they expected to find. Space constraints in professional journals are always a factor.

Another strength was that authors seemed aware of the need to make specific recommendations for further research. Only in a few cases did they commit the grave sin of leaving the reader hanging with the vague statement that more research is needed.

With a few exceptions, most authors did not do nearly as much as they could have with implications for practice or education, either professional or public education. It is not clear whether they do not consider it their job to say how their research should be used, whether editors delete this information, or whether no one thinks to ask. It seems legitimate to us, as professionals who deal with children who are sexually abused (two nurses and one teacher), that authors should tell us how we might use their work to improve what we do with these children. However, we cannot be too hard on the people who study child sexual abuse, because research utilization is a problem in all the professions.

Trends and Recommendations

In summary, the major trends in child sexual abuse research seem to be the following. Overwhelmingly, investigators are selecting scientific reductionist designs and quantitative methods. Although these are important studies, their value depends on adequate conceptualization and measurement. Many problems with both can be seen, particularly in the area of measurement. Therefore, two priorities are indicated. First, if quantitative studies are to be done, they should be done well – with random samples, comparison groups, adequate sample size, and thorough treatment of validity and reliability. The theoretical framework should be made explicit and the review of literature should support the need for the study.

The second priority is that there is a crucial need for qualitative studies on child sexual abuse: phenomenological studies on the meaning of the experience, grounded theory studies to generate typologies and theories, field studies, and so on. With at least two exceptions of Groth's research program on offenders and Herman's work on adult survivors, research on child sexual abuse does not generate enough theory that can be tested and applied in practice settings such as schools and treatment centers.

Victims or survivors are the most frequently studied group, but studies are also needed on prevention — from the point of view of victims, offenders, and, in cases of incest, mothers. We know a lot about characteristics of these groups, but we know little about what the experience is like for them.

It is significant to note that there is a tendency to use clinical populations of victims and incarcerated offenders, both easily obtained subjects. But we must know more about those who do not come for treatment and those who do not disclose. How do offenders get away with it? How do victims cope successfully on their own? How is it that some mothers blame their children and others race to protect them?

Few treatment outcome studies have been done, and the ones that are available demonstrate the effectiveness of therapy. Exactly what, though, is effective about therapy? When is therapy not effective? What harm can come of therapy? Under what conditions?

No cross-cultural or cross-national studies were found, so we cannot assume that patterns true of Anglo middle-class families in the United States are also true for ethnically diverse populations. Many authors reported ethnic breakdowns, but the small sample size and the use of a convenience sample resulted in cell sizes too small to make meaningful comparisons about ethnicity. The two priorities here would be to conduct cross-national studies (and federal-funding agencies often encourage collaborative research) and to stratify samples or, at least, increase cell sizes of ethnically diverse subjects so that tests of significance can be performed.

Conclusion

This chapter has been an attempt to describe the state of art of the research in a variety of disciplines about child sexual abuse. The primary gap in the literature is in understanding the problem from the point of view of the actors. For this reason, the case was made for incorporating more qualitative designs into future studies. Specific suggestions were also made for improving quantitative designs.

Glossary

Emic view — The subject's perspective on his or her own experience.

Etic view — The researcher's perspective on the subject's experience as defined through objective measures.

Incidence — The frequency of a condition over time in a population.

Mixed designs — Studies that incorporate elements of quantitative and qualitative methods.

Prevalence — The number of cases in a population at a given point in time.

Prospective studies — Studies that allow for measurements of conditions as they occur, as in longitudinal studies.

Qualitative designs — Studies developed primarily to generate theory by subjective data.

Quantitative designs — Studies developed to test existing theories by objective measures.

Retrospective studies — Studies that rely on recall of the past by respondents or the interpretation of collected data as in case record reviews.

References

Adams, P., & Roddey, G. (1981). Language patterns of opponents to a child protection program. *Child Psychiatry and Human Development, 11,* 135–157.

Adams-Tucker, C. (1982). Proximate effects of sexual abuse in childhood: A report on 28 children. *American Journal of Psychiatry, 139,* 1252–1256.

Anderson, L., & Shafer, G. (1979). The character-disordered family: A community treatment model for family sexual abuse. *American Journal of Orthopsychiatry, 49,* 436–445.

Becker, J., Skinner, L., Abel, G., Axelrod, R., & Cichon, J. (1984). *Women and Health, 9,* 5–20.

Berkowitz, C., Elvik, S., & Logan, M. (1987). Labial fusion in prepubescent girls: A marker for sexual abuse. *American Journal of Obstetrics and Gynecology, 156,* 16–20.

Blumberg, M. L. (1981). Depression in abused and neglected children. *American Journal of Psychotherapy, 35*(3), 342–355.

Bowen, M. (1978). *Family therapy in clinical practice.* New York: Jason Aronson.

Browne, A., & Finkelhor, D. (1986). Impact of child sexual abuse: A review of the research. *Psychological Bulletin, 99,* 66–77.

Browning, D., & Boatman, B. (1977). Incest: Children at risk. *American Journal of Psychiatry, 134,* 69–72.

Brunngraber, L. (1986). Father-daughter incest: Immediate and long-term effects of sexual abuse. *Advances in Nursing Science, 8,* 15–35.

Byles, J. (1980). Adolescent girls in need of protection. *American Journal of Orthopsychiatry, 50,* 264–278.

Byrne, J., & Valdiserri, E. (1982). Victims of childhood sexual abuse: A follow-up study of a non-compliant population. *Hospital and Community Psychiatry, 33,* 938–940.

Courtois, C. (1980). Studying and counseling women with past incest experience. *Victimology, 5,* 322–334.

de Chesnay, M. (1980). Incestuous behavior as an antecedent stressor in female adolescent runaways. Poster session at Nation League for Nursing, "Responding to Stress in the 80's," New Orleans, LA.

de Chesnay, M. (1984). Incest and mother — mother-daughter role reversal. *The Journal of the Alabama Academy of Science, 55*(3): 223–224.

de Chesnay, M. (1985). Father-daughter incest: Who owns the child? In A. Carmi & S. Schneider (Eds.), *Nursing Law and Ethics* (pp. 75–81). Berlin: Springer Verlag.

de Chesnay, M., Marshall, E., & Clements, C. (1988). Prediction of incest from family structure, marital power, maternal distance, and paternal alcohol consumption. *Family Systems Medicine, 6*(4), 57–65.

De Jong, A., Emmett, G., & Herrada, A. (1982). Sexual abuse of children: Sex-, race-, and age-dependent variations. *American Journal of Disease of Children, 136,* 129–134.

de Young, M. (1982). Self-injurious behavior in incest victims: A research note. *Child Welfare, 60,* 577–584.

Deming, J., Mittleman, R., & Wetli, C. (1983). Forensic science aspects of fatal sexual assaults on women. *Journal of Forensic Sciences, 28,* 572–576.

Dietz, C., & Craft, J. (1980). Family dynamics of incest: A new perspective. *Social Casework, 61,* 602–609.

Enos, W., Conrath, T., & Byer, J. (1986). Forensic evaluation of the sexually abused child. *Pediatrics, 76,* 385–398.

Emslie, G., & Rosenfeld, A. (1983). Incest reported by children and adolescents hospitalized for severe psychiatric problems. *American Journal of Psychiatry, 140,* 708–711.

Famularo, R., Stone, K., Barnum, R., & Wharton, R. (1986). Alcoholism and severe child maltreatment. *American Journal of Orthopsychiatry, 56,* 481–485.

Finkel, K. (1984). Sexual abuse of children in Canada. *Canadian Medical Association Journal, 130,* 345–346.

Finkelhor, D. (1984). *Child sexual abuse: New theory and research.* New York: Free Press.

Freund, K., Scher, H., Chan, S., & Ben-Aron, M. (1982). Experimental analysis of pedophilia. *Behavioral Research and Therapy, 20,* 105–112.

Friedman, R., Hurt, S., Clarkin, J., Corn, R., & Aronoff, M. (1982). Sexual histories and premenstrual affective syndrome in psychiatric inpatients. *American Journal of Psychiatry, 139,* 1484–1486.

Friedrich, W., Urquiza, A., & Beilke, R. (1986). Behavior problems in sexually abused young children. *Journal of Pediatric Psychology, 11,* 47–57.

Gold, E. (1986). Long-term effects of sexual victimization in childhood: An attributional approach. *Journal of Consulting and Clinical Psychology, 54,* 471–475.

Goodwin, J., Simms, M., & Bergman, R. (1979). Hysterical seizures: A sequel to incest. *American Journal of Orthopsychiatry, 49,* 698–703.

Gordon, L., & O'Keefe, P. (1984). Incest as a form of family violence: Evidence from historical case records. *Journal of Marriage and the Family, 46,* 27–34.

Grant, L. J. (1984). Assessment of child sexual abuse: Eighteen months' experience at the Child Protection Center. *American Journal of Obstetrics and Gynecology, 148,* 617–620.

Gross, M. (1979). Incestuous rape: A cause for hysterical seizures in four adolescent girls. *American Journal of Orthopsychiatry, 49,* 704–708.

Gross, R., Doerr, H., Caldirola, D., Guzinski, G., & Ripley, H. (1980–81). *International Journal of Psychiatry in Medicine, 10,* 79–96.

Groth, N. (1979). Men who rape: *The psychology of the offender.* New York: Plenum Press.

Groth, N., Burgess, A., Birnbaum, H., & Gary, T. (1978). A study of the child molester: Myths and realities. *Journal of the American Criminal Justice Association, 41,* 17–22.

Gruber, K., & Jones, R. (1983). Identifying determinants of risk of sexual victimization of youth: A multivariate approach. *Child Abuse and Neglect, 7,* 17–24.

Herman, J. (1981). *Father-daughter incest.* Cambridge: Harvard University Press.

Herman, J., & Hirschman, L. (1981). Families at risk for father-daughter incest. *American Journal of Psychiatry, 138,* 967–970.

Herman, J., Russell, D., & Trocki, K. (1986). Long-term effects of incestuous abuse in childhood. *American Journal of Psychiatry, 143,* 1293–1296.

Hibbard, R., Roghmann, K., & Hoekelman, R. (1987). Genitalia in children's drawings: An association with sexual abuse. *Pediatrics, 79,* 129–137.

Husain, A., & Ahmad, A. (1982). Sexual abuse of children: Diagnosis and treatment. *Missouri Medicine, 79,* 331–334.

Jackson, T., & Ferguson, W. (1983). Attribution of blame in incest. *American Journal of Community Psychology, 11,* 313–321.

James, J., & Meyerding, J. (1977). Early sexual experience as a factor in prostitution. *Archives of Sexual Behavior, 7,* 31–42.

Jason, J., Williams, S., Burton, A., & Rochat, R. (1982). Epidemiologic differences between sexual and physical child abuse. *Journal of the American Medical Association, 247,* 3344–3348.

Khan, M., & Sexton, M. (1983). Sexual abuse of young children. *Clinical Pediatrics, 22,* 369–372.

Kirkland, K., & Bauer, C. (1982). MMPI traits of incestuous fathers. *Journal of Clinical Psychology, 38,* 645–649.

Kohan, M., Pothier, P., & Norbeck, J. (1987). Hospitalized children with history of sexual abuse: Incidence and care issues. *American Journal of Orthopsychiatry, 57,* 258–264.

Kroth, J. (1979). Family therapy impact on intrafamilial child sexual abuse. *Child Abuse and Neglect, 3,* 297–302.

La Barbera, J. (1983). Correlates of seductive father-daughter relationships. *Archives of General Psychiatry, 40,* 1344.

Lewin, B. (1983). Attitudes among adolescents in a Swedish city toward some sexual crimes. *Adolescence, 18,* 159–168.

Levitan, H. (1982). Explicit incestuous motifs in psychosomatic patients. *Psychotherapy and Psychosomatics, 37,* 22–25.

Lindberg, F., & Distad, L. (1985). Survival responses to incest: Adolescents in crisis. *Child Abuse and Neglect, 9,* 521–526.

Lukianowicz, N. (1972). Incest. *British Journal of Psychiatry, 120,* 301–313.

Martin, M., & Walters, J. (1982). Familial correlates of selected types of child abuse and neglect. *Journal of Marriage and the Family, 44,* 267–276.

McCauley, J., Gorman, R., & Guzinsky, G. (1986). Toluidine blue in the detection of perineal lacerations in pediatric and adolescent sexual abuse victims. *Pediatrics, 78,* 1039–1043.

McCartey, L. (1986). Mother-child incest: Characteristics of the offender. *Child Welfare, 65,* 447–458.

Mims, F., & Chang, A. (1984). Unwanted sexual experiences of young women. *Journal of Psychosocial Nursing, 22,* 7–14.

Mrazek, P., Lynch, M., & Bentovim, A. (1983). Sexual abuse of children in the United Kingdom. *Child Abuse and Neglect. 7,* 147–153.

Muller, D., Shaw, D., & Towner, M. (1987). Preventing child abuse: An evaluation of two video programs. *Health Visitor, 60,* 15–16.

O'Rourke, M., & Sweeney, C. (1983). Incest in Ireland: A general practice survey. *Irish Medical Journal, 76,* 252.

Overholser, J., & Beck, S. (1986). Multimethod assessment of rapists, child molesters, and three control groups on behavioral and psychological measures. *Journal of Consulting and Clinical Psychology, 54,* 682–687.

Panton, J. (1979). MMPI profile configurations associated with incestuous and non-incestuous child molesting. *Psychological Reports, 45,* 335–338.

Paperny, D., & Deisher, R. (1983). Maltreatment of adolescents: The relationship to a predisposition toward violent behavior and delinquency. *Adolescence, 18,* 499–506.

Parker, H., & Parker, S. (1986). Father-daughter sexual abuse: An emerging perspective. *American Journal of Orthopsychiatry, 56,* 531–549.

Poznansky, E., & Blos, P. (1975). Incest. *Medical Aspects of Human Sexuality, 9,* 46–76.

Rock, B., Naghashfar, Z., Barnett, N., Buscema, J., Woodruff, D., & Shah, K. (1986). Genital tract papillomavirus infection in children. *Archives of Dermatology, 122,* 1129–1132.

Rosenfeld, A., Bailey, R., Siegel, B., & Bailey, G. (1986). Determining incestuous contact between parent and child. *Journal of the American Academy of Child Psychiatry, 25,* 481–484.

Rosenfeld, A., Siegel, B., & Bailey, R. (1987). Familial bathing patterns. *Pediatrics, 79,* 224–229.

Russell, D. (1983). The incidence and prevalence of intrafamilial and extrafamilial sexual abuse of female children. *Child abuse and neglect, 7,* 133–146.

Sagatun, I. (1982). Attributional effects of therapy with incestuous families. *Journal of Marital and Family Therapy, 8,* 99–104.

Saslowsky, D., & Wurtele, S. (1986). Educating children about sexual abuse. *Journal of Pediatric Psychology, 11,* 235–245.

Scherzer, L., & Lala, P. (1980). Sexual offenses committed against children. *Clinical Pediatrics, 19,* 679–685.

Scott, R., & Stone, D. (1986). MMPI measures of psychological disturbance in adolescent and adult victims of father-daughter incest. *Journal of Clinical Psychology, 42,* 251–259.

Scott, R., & Stone, D. (1986). MMPI profile constellations in incest families. *Journal of Consulting and Clinical Psychology, 54,* 364–368.

Scott, R., & Thoner, G. (1986). Ego deficits in anorexia nervosa patients and incest victims: An MMPI comparative analysis. *Psychological Reports, 58,* 839–846.

Shah, C., Holloway, C., & Valkil, D. (1982). Sexual abuse of children. *Annals of Emergency Medicine, 11,* 18–21.

Simari, C., & Baskin, D. (1982). Incestuous experiences within homosexual populations: A preliminary study. *Archives of Sexual Behavior, 11,* 329–344.

Tarter, R., Hegedus, A., Alterman, A., & Katz-Garris, L. (1983). Cognitive capacities of juvenile violent, nonviolent, and sexual offenders. *The Journal of Nervous and Mental Disease, 171,* 564–567.

Traver, H. (1978). Offender reaction, public opinion and sentencing. *Criminology, 16,* 403–419.

Verleur, D., Hughes, R., & de Rios, M. (1986). Enhancement of self-esteem among female adolescent incest victims: A controlled comparison. *Adolescence, 21,* 843–854.

Vitulano, L., Lewis, M., Doran, L., Nordhaus, B., & Adnopoz, J. (1986). Treatment recommendation, implementation and follow-up in child abuse. *American Journal of Orthopsychiatry, 56,* 478–480.

Winefield, H., & Castell-McGregor, S. (1986). Experiences and views of general practitioners concerning sexually abused children. *Medical Journal of Australia, 145,* 311–313.

Wohl, A., & Kaufman, B. (1985). *Silent screams and hidden cries: An interpretation of artwork by children from violent homes.* New York: Brunner/Mazel.

Wurtele, S., Saslowsky, D., Miller, C., Marrs, S., & Britcher, J. (1986). Teaching personal safety skills for potential prevention of sexual abuse: A comparison of treatments. *Journal of Consulting and Clinical Psychology, 54,* 688–692.

Yates, A., Beutler, L., & Crago, M. (1985). Drawings by child victims of incest. *Child Abuse and Neglect, 9,* 183–189.

Appendix

Child Abuse and Neglect Reporting Agencies

Each state has designated a particular agency or department to serve as the child protective service agency. It is to these offices that suspicions of child abuse and neglect are reported. The National Center for Child Abuse and Neglect has compiled the following roster of state reporting procedures.

Alabama

Alabama Department of Human
   Resources
Division of Family and Children's
   Services
Office of Protective Services
64 North Union Street
Montgomery, AL 36130-1801

During business hours, make reports to the county department of human resources child protective services unit. After business hours, make reports to local police.

Alaska

Department of Health and Social
   Services
Division of Family and Youth Services
Box H-05
Juneau, AK 99811

To make reports in-state, ask the operator for Zenith 4444. Out-of-state, add area code 907. This telephone number is toll free.

American Samoa

Government of American Samoa
Office of the Attorney General
Pago Pago, American Samoa 96799

Make reports to the department of human resources at (684) 633-4485.

Arizona

Department of Economic Security
Administration for Children, Youth,
   and Families
P.O. Box 6123
Site COE 940A
Phoenix, AZ 85005

Make reports to department of economic security local offices.

Arkansas

Arkansas Department of Human
   Services
Division of Children and Family
   Services
P.O. Box 1437
Little Rock, AR 72203

Make reports in-state to (800) 482-5964.

California

Office for Child Abuse Prevention
Department of Social Services
714-744 P Street, Room 950
Sacramento, CA 95814

Make reports to county departments of welfare and the Central Registry of Child Abuse (916) 445-7546, maintained by the Department of Justice.

Colorado

Department of Social Services
Central Registry
P.O. Box 181000
Denver, CO 80218-0899

Make reports to county departments
of social services.

Connecticut

Connecticut Department of Children
and Youth Services
Division of Children's and Protective
Services
170 Sigourney Street
Hartford, CT 06105

Make reports in-state to (800) 842-2288
or out-of-state to (203) 344-2599.

Delaware

Delaware Department of Services for
Children, Youth, and Their Families
Division of Child Protective Services
330 East 30th Street
Wilmington, DE 19802

Make reports in-state to (800) 292-9582.

District of Columbia

District of Columbia Department of
Human Services
Commission on Social Services
Family Services Administration
Child and Family Services Division
500 First Street, N.W.
Washington, DC 20001

Make reports to (202) 727-0995.

Florida

Florida Child Abuse Registry
1317 Winewood Boulevard
Tallahassee, FL 32301

Make reports in-state to (800) 342-9152
or out-of-state to (904) 487-2625.

Georgia

Georgia Department of Human
Resources
Division of Family and Children
Services
878 Peachtree Street, N.W.
Atlanta, GA 30309

Make reports to county departments
of family and children services.

Guam

Department of Public Health and
Social Services
Child Welfare Services
Child Protective Services
P.O. Box 2816
Agana, GU 96910

Reports made to the Child Protective
Services Agency at (671) 646-8417.

Hawaii

Department of Social Services and
Housing
Public Welfare Division
Family and Children's Services
P.O. Box 339
Honolulu, HI 96809

Make reports to each island's Department of Social Services and Housing
Child Protective Services Reporting
hotline.

Idaho

Department of Health and Welfare
Field Operations Bureau of Social
Services Child Protection
450 West State, 10th Floor
Boise, ID 83720

Make reports to Department of
Health and Welfare regional offices.

Illinois

Illinois Department of Children and
 Family Services
Station 75
State Administrative Offices
406 East Monroe Street
Springfield, IL 62701

Make reports in-state to (800)
25-ABUSE or out-of-state to
(217) 785-4010.

Indiana

Indiana Department of Public
 Welfare-Child Abuse and Neglect
Division of Child Welfare-Social
 Services
141 South Meridian Street
Sixth Floor
Indianapolis, IN 46225

Make reports to county departments
of public welfare.

Iowa

Iowa Department of Human Services
Division of Social Services
Central Child Abuse Registry
Hoover State Office Building
Fifth Floor
Des Moines, IA 50319

Make reports in-state to (800) 362-2178
or out-of-state (during business hours)
to (515) 281-5581.

Kansas

Kansas Department of Social and
 Rehabilitation Services
Division of Social Services
Child Protection and Family Services
 Section
Smith-Wilson Building
2700 West Sixth Street
Topeka, KS 66606

Make reports to Department of Social
and Rehabilitation Service area offices.

Kentucky

Kentucky Cabinet of Human Resources
Division of Family Services
Children and Youth Services Branch
275 East Main Street
Frankfort, KY 40621

Make reports to county offices in 14
state districts.

Louisiana

Louisiana Department of Health and
 Human Resources
Office of Human Development
Division of Children, Youth, and
 Family Services
P.O. Box 3318
Baton Rouge, LA 70821

Make reports to parish protective
service units.

Maine

Maine Department of Human Services
Child Protective Services
State House, Station 11
Augusta, ME 04333

Make reports to regional office of
human services; in-state to
(800) 452-1999 or out-of-state to
(207) 289-2983. Both operate 24
hours a day.

Maryland

Maryland Department of Human
 Resources
Social Services Administration
Saratoga State Center
311 West Saratoga Street
Baltimore, MD 21201

Make reports to county departments
of social services or to local law
enforcement agencies.

Massachusetts

Massachusetts Department of Social
Services
Protective Services
150 Causeway Street, 11th Floor
Boston, MA 02114

Make reports to area offices or
protective screening unit or in-state
to (800) 792-5200.

Michigan

Michigan Department of Social Services
Office of Children and Youth Services
Protective Services Division
300 South Capitol Street
Ninth Floor
Lansing, MI 48926

Make reports to county departments
of social services.

Minnesota

Minnesota Department of Human
Services
Protective Services Division
Centennial Office Building
St. Paul, MN 55155

Make reports to county departments
of human services.

Mississippi

Mississippi Department of Public
Welfare
Bureau of Family and Children's
Services
Protection Department
P.O. Box 352
Jackson, MS 39205

Make reports in-state to (800) 222-8000
or out-of-state (during business hours)
to (601) 354-0341.

Missouri

Missouri Child Abuse and Neglect
Hotline
Department of Social Services
Division of Family Services
DFS, P.O. Box 88
Broadway Building
Jefferson City, MO 65103

Make reports in-state to
(800) 392-3738 or out-of-state
to (314) 751-3448. Both operate
24 hours a day.

Montana

Department of Family Services Child
Protective Services
P.O. Box 8005
Helena, MT 59604

Make reports to county departments
of family services.

Nebraska

Nebraska Department of Social Services
Human Services Division
301 Centennial Mall South
P.O. Box 95026
Lincoln, NE 68509

Make reports to local law enforcement
agencies or to local social services
offices or in-state to (800) 652-1999.

Nevada

Department of Human Resources
Welfare Division
2527 North Carson Street
Carson City, NV 87910

Make reports to division of welfare
local offices.

New Hampshire

New Hampshire Department of Health
and Welfare
Division for Children and Youth Services
6 Hazen Drive
Concord, NH 03301-6522

Make reports to Division for Children
and Youth Services district offices or
in-state to (800) 852-3345, ext. 4455.

New Jersey

New Jersey Division of Youth and
Family Services
P.O. Box CN717
One South Montgomery Street
Trenton, NJ 08625

Make reports in-state to
(800) 792-8610. District offices
also provide 24-hour telephone
services.

New Mexico

New Mexico Department of Human
Services
Social Services Division
P.O. Box 2348
Santa Fe, NM 87504

Make reports to county social
services offices or in-state to
(800) 432-6217.

New York

New York State Department of Social
Services
Division of Family and Children
Services
State Central Register of Child Abuse
and Maltreatment
40 North Pearl Street
Albany, NY 12243

Make reports in-state to
(800) 342-3720 or out-of-state
to (518) 474-9448.

North Carolina

North Carolina Department of Human
Resources
Division of Social Services
Child Protective Services
325 North Salisbury Street
Raleigh, NC 27611

Make reports in-state to
(800) 662-7030.

North Dakota

North Dakota Department of Human
Services
Division of Children and Family
Services
Child Abuse and Neglect Program
State Capitol
Bismarck, ND 58505

Make reports to county social
services offices.

Ohio

Ohio Department of Human Services
Bureau of Children's Protective
Services
30 East Broad Street
Columbus, OH 43266-0423

Make reports to county departments
of human services.

Oklahoma

Oklahoma Department of Human
Services
Division of Children and Youth
Services Child Abuse/Neglect
Section
P.O. B0x 25352
Oklahoma City, OK 73125

Make reports in-state to
(800) 522-3511.

Oregon

Department of Human Resources
Children's Services Division
Child Protective Services
198 Commercial Street, S.E.
Salem, OR 97310

Make reports to local children's
services division offices and to
(503) 378-4722.

Pennsylvania

Pennsylvania Department of Public
  Welfare
Office of Children, Youth, and
  Families
Lanco Lodge, P.O. Box 2675
Harrisburg, PA 17105

Make reports in-state to CHILDLINE
(800) 932-0313 or out-of-state to
(717) 783-8744.

Puerto Rico

Puerto Rico Department of Social
  Services
Services to Family With Children
P.O. Box 11398
Fernandez Juncos Station
Santurez, PR 00910

Make reports to (809) 724-1313.

Rhode Island

Rhode Island Department for Children
  and Their Families
Division of Child Protective Services
610 Mt. Pleasant Avenue
Building #9
Providence, RI 02908

Make reports in-state to
(800) RI-CHILD or 742-4433 or
out-of-state to (401) 457-4996.

South Carolina

South Carolina Department of Social
  Services
1535 Confederate Avenue
P.O. Box 1520
Columbia, SC 29202-1520

Make reports to county departments
of social services.

South Dakota

Department of Social Services
Child Protection Services
Richard F. Kneip Building
700 Governor's Drive
Pierre, SD 57501

Make reports to local social services
offices.

Tennessee

Tennessee Department of Human
  Services
Child Protective Services
Citizen Bank Plaza
400 Deadrick Street
Nashville, TN 37219

Make reports to county departments
of human services.

Texas

Texas Department of Human Services
Protective Services for Families and
  Children Branch
P.O. Box 2960, MC 537-W
Austin, TX 78769

Make reports in-state to
(800) 252-5400 or out-of-state to
(512) 450-3360.

Utah

Department of Social Services
Division of Family Services
P.O. Box 45500
Salt Lake City, UT 84110

Make reports to Division of Family
Services district offices.

Vermont

Vermont Department of Social and
  Rehabilitative Services
Division of Social Services
103 South Main Street
Waterbury, VT 05676

Make reports to district offices or to
(802) 241-2131.

Virgin Islands

Virgin Islands Department of Human
  Services
Division of Social Services
P.O. Box 550
Charlotte Amalie
St. Thomas, VI 00801

Make reports to Division of Social
Services (809) 774-9030.

Virginia

Commonwealth of Virginia Department
  of Social Services
Bureau of Child Protective Services
Blair Building
8007 Discovery Drive
Richmond, VA 23229-8699

Make reports in-state to (800) 552-7096
or out-of-state to (804) 281-9081.

Washington

Department of Social and Health
  Services
Division of Children and Family
  Services
Child Protective Services
Mail Stop OB 41-D
Olympia, WA 98504

Make reports in-state to (800) 562-5624
or local social and health services
offices.

West Virginia

West Virginia Department of Human
  Services
Division of Social Services
Child Protective Services
State Office Building
1900 Washington Street, East
Charleston, WV 25305

Make reports in-state to (800) 352-6513.

Wisconsin

Wisconsin Department of Health and
  Social Services
Division of Community Services
Bureau of Children, Youth, and
  Families
1 West Wilson Street
Madison, WI 53707

Make reports to county social services
offices.

Wyoming

Department of Health and Social
  Services
Division of Public Assistance and
  Social Services
Hathaway Building
Cheyenne, WY 82002

Make reports to county departments
of public assistance and social
services.

Author Index

A

Abel, G., 205
Abrams, M., 54
Abramson, A., 140
Adams, J., 117–118
Adams, P., 229
Adams-Tucker, C., 205
Adnopoz, J., 206
Ahmad, A., 209
Ahmad, M., 117–118
Akinla, O., 140
Alabama Department of Human Resources, 16
Alexander, E., 130, 133
Allen, R., 41
Altchek, A., 141
Alterman, A., 225
American Academy of Dermatology Task Force on Pediatric Dermatology, 140
American Association for Protecting Children, Inc., 157
American Medical Association, 111
Anderson, D., 140
Anderson, L., 216, 217, 219, 220
Aronoff, M., 205
Artemyeff, C., 25
Attias, R., 123
Axelrod, R., 205

B

Bachman, G., 145
Bailey, G., 231
Bailey, R., 231
Bakan, D., 1, 17
Baladerian, N., 44, 45
Barnett, N., 139, 206
Barnum, R., 223
Barry, R., 2, 18
Bartlett, R., 64
Bartley, D., 142

Baskin, D., 209–210, 228–229
Bauer, C., 223, 226
Beck, S., 224, 226
Becker, J., 205
Beezer, B., 57
Beezley, P., 51
Beilke, R., 205
Bell, T., 137
Ben-Aron, M., 224
Bentovim, A., 55, 210, 232
Bergman, R., 205
Berkowitz, C., 116–117, 206
Beutler, L., 205
Biddle, J., 135
Billingsley, A., 171
Birnbaum, H., 222
Bishop, I., 51
Blacher, J., 28, 51
Blick, L., 7
Blos, P., 215
Blumberg, M. L. 205
Boatman, B., 216, 220
Bourne, R., 39
Bousha, D., 28, 43
Boutselia, I., 140
Bowen, M., 217
Brandwein, H., 46, 49
Brenner, A., 7
Britcher, J., 231
Britton, H., 145
Broadhurst, D., 19, 159, 169
Browne, A., 204, 208
Browning, D., 216, 220
Brunngraber, L., 204
Buchanan, A., 48
Bump, R., 137
Burgess, A., 145, 222
Burgess, R., 45
Burton, A., 211
Buscema, J., 139, 206
Buxton, B., 141

253

Subject Index

About the Authors

MARY de CHESNAY, DSN, RN, CS, is professor and head of the Department of Research, College of Nursing at Clemson University. Her clinical and research programs have focused on child sexual abuse for the past 16 years. She assisted in founding an innovative service program for child victims in Birmingham (Prescott House) and currently serves on its board of directors. Dr. de Chesnay's mailing address is College of Nursing, Clemson University, Clemson, South Carolina 29634.

RICHARD M. GARGIULO, PhD, currently serves as professor and chair of the Department of Special Education at the University of Alabama at Birmingham. A former public school teacher of children with mental retardation, Dr. Gargiulo is also a licensed psychologist with over a decade of experience in working with victims of child abuse and their families. He is the author of a textbook on counseling parents of exceptional children and has addressed audiences both nationally and internationally on the topic of families with special needs and child abuse. Dr. Gargiulo's mailing address is Department of Special Education, School of Education, University of Alabama at Birmingham, UAB Station, Birmingham, Alabama 35294.

PATSY A. GEMMILL, MSW, serves as adjunct instructor of Social Work at the University of Alabama and as Clinical Specialist at Sparks Center for Developmental Learning Disorders, University of Alabama at Birmingham. Ms. Gemmill's 12 years of experience include training police academy cadets and crisis center volunteers to handle family violence and crisis intervention. During her years with a hospital-based psychiatric service, she worked with abusive families referred by the family court for therapy. She also provided inservice education programs for new medical staff regarding abuse and neglect of pediatric patients. Ms. Gemmill's mailing address is Department of Social Service, Sparks Center for Developmental and Learning Disorders, UAB, University Station, Birmingham, Alabama 35294.

RENITTA L. GOLDMAN, PhD, is associate professor of Special Education at the University of Alabama at Birmingham. Dr. Goldman has had 30 years of experience in working with students ranging from preschool age to graduate school. Although her professional focus mainly has been on helping meet the learning needs of special students and their parents and teachers, she has written and spoken extensively on the topic of abuse both nationally and internationally. Dr. Goldman's previous book on this subject is entitled *Silent Shame: The Sexual*

Abuse of Children and Youth. Dr. Goldman's mailing address is Department of Special Education, School of Education, University of Alabama at Birmingham, UAB Station, Birmingham, Alabama 35294.

MOLLY C. McGREGOR is a professional director of the Young Men's Christian Association (YMCA), currently serving as communications and marketing director and as executive director of the Five Points South YMCA Center for the Birmingham Metropolitan YMCA. With a B.S. degree in Social Services Administration from the University of Toledo, she has over 15 years of experience in community development utilizing a nonprofit corporate planning approach. Additionally, Mrs. McGregor has served as a trainer of organizational development and marketing issues for the U.S. YMCA office. Mrs. McGregor's mailing address is Five Points South Center, YMCA, 1911 10th Ave. South, Birmingham, Alabama 35203.

ROBERT P. McGREGOR is a graduate of the University of North Carolina and the University of Alabama School of Law. Mr. McGregor is currently serving as an assistant U.S. attorney. A former school teacher and swimming coach, he has spent most of his law career as a deputy district attorney in Shelby, Mobile, and Jefferson counties in Alabama. He has been recognized as one of Alabama's top prosecutors in the area of child abuse. His knowledge of child abuse, its perpetrators, and the steps to successful prosecution has won him acclaim. Mr. McGregor's mailing address is 1801 Napier Drive, Birmingham, Alabama 35226.

KRISTI M. MULCHAHEY, MD, is an assistant professor at the University of Alabama at Birmingham in the Departments of Obstetrics and Gynecology, and Pediatrics. As an adolescent and pediatric gynecologist, she is actively involved in the assessment of sexually abused children. In addition to being actively involved in community and educational activities related to sexual abuse, she also focuses on the diagnosis and treatment of sexually transmitted diseases in childhood. Dr. Mulchahey's mailing address is Department of Obstetrics and Gynecology, University of Alabama at Birmingham, UAB Station, Birmingham, Alabama 35294.

DEBBIE STEPHENS is currently completing requirements for a doctorate degree in child development. Ms. Stephens has a great deal of experience working with abused children both professionally and as a volunteer. Professionally she has worked as an educator with emotionally disturbed children in a residential treatment facility and has interned with a program designed to help sexually abused children through the legal system. Ms. Stephens has been a foster parent for five years and has had many sexually abused children living in her home.

Currently, she is very involved in advocating for children caught in the child welfare system and serves as president of a state-wide advocacy group. Ms. Stephen's mailing address is 542 Broadway, Birmingham, Alabama 35209.

LESLIE D. WEST, RN, MSN, is a doctoral student studying community/mental health nursing at the University of Alabama at Birmingham and an Instructor of Psychiatric Nursing at Columbia State Community College. Ms. West's clinical experience has involved work with victims of family violence, with an emphasis on sexual abuse. Ms. West's mailing address is Department of Nursing, Columbia State Community College, P.O. Box 1315, Columbia, TN 38401.